Old Age in the New Land

Old Age in the New Land

The American Experience since 1790

W. Andrew Achenbaum

THE JOHNS HOPKINS UNIVERSITY PRESS

Baltimore and London

Manufactured in the United States of America

The Johns Hopkins University Press, Baltimore, Maryland 21218
The Johns Hopkins Press Ltd., London

Library of Congress Catalog Card Number 77–28666
ISBN 0–8018–2107–x

Library of Congress Cataloging in Publication data
will be found on the last printed page of this book.

TO MARY

Grow old along with me!
The best is yet to be.

Contents

	Foreword	ix
	Acknowledgments	xi
	Introduction	1
Part I	**Changing Perceptions of the Aged's Roles in Nineteenth-Century America**	**7**
1	The Usefulness of Old Age	9
2	Variations on a Theme	27
3	The Obsolescence of Old Age	39
Part II	**The Demographic and Socioeconomic Dimensions of Old Age**	**55**
4	The Rhetoric and Realities of Growing Old Diverge in Nineteenth-Century America	57
5	Old Age Becomes "Modern" in Twentieth-Century America	89
Part III	**Contemporary Old Age in Historical Perspective**	**107**
6	Old Age Becomes a National Problem	109
7	Social Security: A Novel Solution for the Problem of America's Aged	127
8	Old Age in the United States since Social Security	143
	Conclusion	165
	Appendix	173
	Notes	185
	Selected Bibliography	219
	Index	229

Tables

4.1. Aged Population in the United States, 1830–1970   59
4.2. Percentage of Aged in the Population, 1830–1970   60
4.3. Percentage of the Very Old in the Population over 60 Years
     of Age, 1870–1970   61
4.4. Percentage of the Population over 65 Years of Age, by Region,
     1870–1970   63
4.5. Growth Rates of the Population over 65 Years of Age
     in the Northeast, 1870–1940   64
4.6. Selected Statistics on the Aged Population in Urban Areas,
     1855–1970   65
4.7. Percentage of the Population Gainfully Employed, 1890   67
4.8. Selected Occupations of Persons Gainfully Employed, 1890   70–71
4.9. Percentage of the Aged Population Gainfully Employed,
     by Region, 1890   73
4.10. Relationship of Native-born and German-born Subjects to Head of
      Household, Buffalo, New York, 1855   77
4.11. Relationship of Native-born and Foreign-born Subjects to Head
      of Household, Massachusetts, 1895   78–79
4.12. Selected Statistics on Almshouse Paupers, 1910   81
5.1. Percentage of the Population over 65 Years of Age, 1870–1970   91
5.2. Composition of the Aged Population, 1870–1970   92
5.3. Age-Specific Dependency Ratio, 1870–1970   94
5.4. Composition of the Population Gainfully Employed over 65 Years
     of Age, 1900 and 1970   97
5.5. Age-Specific Changes in the Percentage of Americans Working,
     1900–1970   99–101
5.6. Rate of Drop-Off from the Labor Force with Advancing Age,
     1890–1970   103

Foreword

This splendid study details the roles and status of the elderly in the United States since 1790. Its contribution to our understanding of the variations in our culture's attitudes is immeasurable. These attitudes are as varied as they are numerous, as evident in cultural artifacts as divergent as "wise, old Uncle Sam" and the "old witches of Salem." In analyzing the antecedents of our attitudes toward old age, we must consider intellectual, demographic, industrial, and attitudinal factors. In the same genre as Philippe Ariès's remarkable book, *Centuries of Childhood: A Social History of Family Life*, W. Andrew Achenbaum's *Old Age in the New Land* portrays old age as a period of life with its own perceptions, rhetoric, and realities. In so doing, Achenbaum provides scientists, scholars, policy makers, social workers, and health practitioners with an otherwise unavailable appreciation of the contemporary lot of older people.

The best of history, like the finest cultural anthropology, compares times, places, and cultures in order to identify universal truths, describe interesting events, and highlight exotic variations. In this book, Achenbaum illustrates that beneath the historical changes in the roles and status of the aged is an underlying and apparently universal ambiguity in people's attitudes toward aging. Understandably, there is both fear and distaste for the decline of the "self" with time. This fear is not easily overcome, even in a new land of plenty.

This volume is filled with interesting and useful historical information. It is intriguing, for example, to learn that at the beginnings of the republic, the patriot Thomas Paine proposed a nationally funded pension system to prevent indigency among the elderly. It is interesting, too, that in the hundred years between 1870 and 1970 the population of older people increased twentyfold, and that in the face of this growth neither unions nor business corporations developed policies to help the elderly substantially—even as an industrial economy replaced the agrarian economy, where older people thrived better.

Achenbaum's book suggests that many factors in our history have contributed to the poor status of old age. Thus, ageism, the cultural dread of aging and aversion to the old, did not simply result from the rapid increase in the population, nor did it spring solely from a stereotype of older people as obsolescent, poor, and dependent. Since World War II, however, the general public has been made more aware of the problems faced by the elderly. Attitudes toward the aged are once again in flux, and many sectors of our population have taken new interest in this large minority. New programs for older citizens, new centers for the elderly, apartment buildings specially designed to meet the needs of the aged—all these are indications of the impact the elderly have upon our society. What also seems clear, therefore, is that the situation can be improved: once society understands the genesis of its negative attitudes, it can begin to move toward meeting the needs of older people through legislative initiatives on income maintenance, health care, housing, and research.

In recognition of the major demographic changes of this century, Congress. created the National Institute on Aging in 1974 to conduct and support research and research training on the aging process and the special needs and problems of the aged in America. The ultimate goal of this research, like that of Achenbaum's work, is to increase our knowledge about aging, which in turn will allow us to take steps to improve the quality of life for the aged in America today, and for each and every one of us in the future.

ROBERT N. BUTLER
Director, National Institute on Aging

Acknowledgments

When I began this study in 1972, very few scholars had done any systematic research into the history of old age. Most of the work dealt with twentieth-century issues such as the development of the Social Security Act. Since then, studying old age has become fashionable among historians. To encourage research in this area, public and private agencies funded significant humanistic and social science symposia and proposals. Several articles and essays have appeared in scholarly journals and collected volumes, books and dissertations are becoming available, and many more studies are in progress. I consider myself fortunate to have entered this exciting field in its formative stages. I am very thankful to many kind people who helped me over the years: they made a fascinating project richly rewarding both professionally and personally.

I started my research in John Higham's seminar and have kept many of his original suggestions and hunches in mind as I expanded the scope of my work. In writing my dissertation, I found working individually and collectively with Robert F. Berkhofer, Jr., Wilbur J. Cohen, Kenneth A. Lockridge, and Maris A. Vinovskis an extraordinary experience. My mentors not only gave me complete freedom to design and execute my investigation as I saw fit but also made useful recommendations and judicious criticisms. Those who know them will well understand why I continue to ask their advice and enjoy their company.

Other scholars and friends offered gratifying encouragement and vital assistance. David D. Van Tassel invited me to join historians, philosophers, artists, and literary critics in his landmark "Human Values and Aging" project. Genevieve Berkhofer, John Demos, David Hackett Fischer, Raymond Grew, Jan Lewis Grimmelmann, Lilith Kunkel, and Daniel Scott Smith, as well as members of several University of Michigan research institutes, the Center for Psycho-Social Studies, and the Newberry Library Colloquium in Family and Community History, provided stimulating exchanges at various stages of my research. Erik Austin and John B. Sharpless saved me time and money at the computer center, and the staff of the University of Michigan Library System aided me in countless ways.

I also want to acknowledge those who helped me transform a two-volume dissertation into a publishable work. Peter N. Stearns, David Van Tassel, and an anonymous reader offered penetrating critiques of the thesis and invaluable recommendations for revisions. I also incorporated specific suggestions made by Robert Butler, Carole Haber, William Kelly, and students in seminars I taught during 1977 on the history of old age. Associates of the Institute of Gerontology at the University of Michigan, especially Harold R. Johnson, Peggy Kusnerz, and Eloise Snyder, helped me to rethink and restate my ideas more precisely and forcibly. Walter Sharrow, Joseph Bieron, James Valone, and Stephen Kruk, among others at Canisius, facilitated my endeavors immeasurably. Above all, I appreciate the efforts made by Henry Y. K. Tom and Wendy Harris of The Johns Hopkins University Press to improve the manuscript and to expedite its publication.

Finally, I would like to thank three wonderful people whose help far exceeds this present book. My longest-standing debt is to my parents, who have nurtured and encouraged me for decades. I owe the most to my wife, Mary Schieve: the things we share have given me the desire, strength, patience, and insights to grow as a scholar and as a human being.

Old Age in the New Land

The Universals of
Old Age in American History

Being old in America today is both remarkably similar to and incredibly different from conditions in past times. Old age clearly has assets and liabilities, and it arouses a mixture of feelings that transcend time and space. Contemporary Americans, however, do not share all of their predecessors' ideas about the functions and value of advanced age. While some of the elderly's current advantages and disadvantages resemble those that prevail in widely dissimilar societies or that existed in profoundly divergent temporal settings, other demographic, socioeconomic, and cultural features of old age today are truly novel. Many of the aged's present resources, problems, and opportunities, in fact, are distinctive products of the long-standing, complex, and cumulative interplay of historical events and personalities as well as ideational factors and structural forces. This history of old age in the United States begins, therefore, by distinguishing between what has remained constant and what has changed about growing old in the new land since 1790.

The first universal worth noting is that Americans have always perceived old age as a distinct phase of the life cycle. This point is more significant than it might initially appear. Scholars recently have been investigating the possibility that each stage of life has a history that is unique, or at least one that develops somewhat independently of continuities and permutations in the evolution of other stages.[1] For example, it seems likely that humans throughout much of recorded history did not consider "childhood" a special period of human development, and that the origins of the concept of "adolescence" lie in the nineteenth century. Far more research must be completed and evaluated, however, before we will fully understand the total picture. We are just beginning systematically to analyze variations in the lifetime experiences of generations who aged at different periods in American history. We cannot yet describe, much less explain, how the system of age relations in the United States was structured and operated in the past. But we can assert that people at the end of the life-cycle continuum have constantly been described as "old." Old age is an age-old phenomenon.

The chronological boundaries of old age, moreover, have remained relatively stable throughout American history. In part, this reflects the fact that many of the physiological and pathological processes and manifestations associated with aging occur in roughly the same way and according to an amazingly regular biological time clock. Most biogerontologists believe, in fact, that "the human life span" (or extreme limit of longevity) has not changed over the centuries. To be sure, there have been enormous long-term improvements in life expectancy at birth and notable ones at other points in the life cycle. In the United States during the past two hundred years, for instance, the *mean* life span was increased initially by preventing and controlling diseases that contributed to high infant and child mortality rates, and subsequently by reducing the incidence of death due to infectious diseases among people over the age of forty. But these gains do not necessarily prove that the human life span itself will or can be significantly extended beyond presently known limits. And at the moment, there is considerable justification for doubting such a possibility.[2] Thus, it has always been possibie for a baby to attain a visibly apparent and empirically verifiable "ripe old age" even though the likelihood of that event has increased tremendously since 1790.

And yet, biological and demographic realities are not the only criteria used in defining old age. Because prevailing social conditions and customs as well as an individual's personal notions and quirks also count, reasons for choosing one date or another as *the* decisive moment have varied. Indeed, there has never actually been a consensus about which birthday, if any, marks the beginning of old age. Earlier writers sometimes suggested that the "grand climacteric" at sixty-three signaled its onset; Social Security and other government policies as well as a variety of private retirement plans have made one's sixty-fifth birthday a crucial benchmark in recent decades. The ages of 55, 60, 62, 64, 67, 70, 72, and 75 are other perennial favorites, though there have always been those who claim that old age defies precise chronological definition. Furthermore, there has invariably been a considerable range in the lower and upper limits set. Some have contended that old age begins at fifty; others argued that no one is "old" before eighty. It should be noted, however, that such disparities in estimates existed in 1790 and have persisted to the present.[3] Consequently, Americans generally have defined old age chronologically in a broadly similar fashion.

Another universal of old age has been the marked variations within the aged population. Since people at extremely dissimilar ages have typically been designated as "old," it is not surprising that the elderly population has always been a heterogeneous group. Obvious differences in the aged's health status and physical condition aptly illustrate this point. Indeed, at

least two distinct phases of physiological "old age" have been recognized
throughout our history. Early Americans once distinguished between a
"green old age" (in which one experienced little, if any, physical restriction
in activities) and "decrepitude" or "second childhood" (where one's infirmities and debilities precluded working and, in many instances, being able
to remain independent). Today, health factors are among the criteria used to
differentiate between the "young-old" and "old-old."[4] Changes in physical
well-being are apparent in longitudinal as well as cross-sectional analyses of
the elderly population. Some older men and women maintain their health
and vigor until they die. Toward the end of their lives, others suffer
increasing infirmity and incapacity with each passing year. Still others have
been disabled or sickly since birth, or at least prior to their fiftieth birthday.
Hence, persons who might rightly be classified as "old" on the basis of their
chronological age diverge greatly in their physical attributes.

Needless to say, the diversity of the older population extends far beyond
matters of health. There also are, and certainly have been, enormous differences in older Americans' ability, willingness, and efforts to grow emo-
tionally, intellectually, and spiritually as well as to keep active and open to
new possibilities. At any given moment or during any specific period in our
history, there have been marked variations in older persons' actual
economic resources, marital status, household arrangements, and specific
needs and capabilities. Indeed, as the following analysis only begins to indicate, racial, ethnic, occupational, sex, and class distinctions often become
accentuated in later years. Subsequent investigations must determine (to a
greater degree than has been possible thus far) the precise ways and the
extent to which the perceptions about and experiences of various subsets
within the aged population might have departed from the overall patterns
delineated here and elsewhere.

In light of such diversity it is not surprising that a historian uncovers at
least one other universal of growing old: the existence and persistence of
ambiguous, ambivalent, and even conflicting, feelings about aging in general
and old age in particular. This plethora of opinions in part reflects the
eternally variegated assets and liabilities of the aged population as a group.
The perennially painful and positive varieties of experiences associated
with being old also affect feelings and beliefs expressed at any given point in
time. Furthermore, attitudes about other aspects of human existence color
perspectives on old age. Psychologists and anthropologists have demonstrated, for example, that the fluid relationships between parents and children in all types of cultural and temporal settings create differences in the
tenor and nature of intergenerational exchanges in both psychic and economic terms.[5] Those who are proud of their parents' accomplishments and
their lineage might lavish praise on their older kin, but they also may heap
abuse upon them because of overt or covert, longstanding or recent resent-

ments. Conversely, those who are ashamed of their parents or who wish to mask their roots either ignore their mothers and fathers or indulge them in attempts to expiate guilt. Divergent kin relationships undeniably motivate different perceptions of the elderly. Obviously, insights about old age are also shaped by many other things, including attitudes about death and dying, and one's expected or anticipated life satisfaction or discontent with living. Varied and inconsistent feelings about becoming old, in short, reflect the richness, contradictions, and paradoxes manifest in the human condition.

Such complexity, of course, is not just the hallmark of the current era. Life in past times was different from the present, but no less multifaceted in the realm of human emotions and situations. For that reason, philosophers, poets, and other writers for milennia have pondered the aged's strengths and weaknesses and alternately affirmed the potential and despaired the decline that comes with age. Few paeans to the experience, wisdom, and dignity of being old are as penetrating or moving as Cicero's *De Senectute*; few observers have surpassed Aristotle's brutal analysis of the elderly's disagreeable physical, mental, and psychological attributes. Relying on evidence from both high and popular culture since ancient times, one can trace comparably contrasting visions of old age. Americans have neither added to nor subtracted from the catalog of traits associated with being old. Novels, essays, poems, paintings, photographs, and prints among other sources consistently have expressed individual and collective hopes and fears about the last stage of life.[6]

Clearly, therefore, one must recognize that many important features of the meanings and realities of old age have remained unchanged amid the profound developments that characterize the making of American culture and society since the founding of the republic. Older Americans' current opportunities and predicaments are not wholly unprecedented, since many features of growing old are universal phenomena. Nevertheless, for all its timeless attributes, old age definitely has a dynamic history. There have been significant shifts in the ways Americans have described the aged as well as in the manner elderly Americans have lived since 1790. Reconstructing the history of old age is difficult, however, because much of the material needed to accomplish the task is biased, incomplete, or missing. Scholars endeavoring to trace the antecedents of older persons' contemporary circumstances, moreover, often handle data and interpret trends in wildly dissimilar ways and thus reach radically different conclusions. Hence it is essential that I briefly state at the outset where the following analysis concurs and how it departs from previous efforts.

I agree that there never was a "golden epoch" in the history of old age. The elderly once upon a time were *not* automatically granted positions of authority or invariable adoration in western civilization. The situation of aged men and women in early America, while different in some respects from other past (and present) preindustrial societies, was not exceptional in this regard.[7] I also contend that the perplexing and protracted process of "modernization" has affected the perceived and actual status of older Americans over time, but I sharply disagree with those who contend that significant changes and developments have neatly occurred in an inevitable and unidirectional manner. Frankly, the fundamental problem with many existing analyses is that they presume rather than elucidate relationships between the history of old age in American society and major forces that shaped our history. They rest on scanty, undigested evidence ripped out of its temporal context. I find neither sudden nor radical transformations in conceptions of old age or the elderly's condition during any specific decade(s) or period(s). Thus I seriously doubt that "from Thomas Jefferson's era to our own, the lines of change have been straight and stable."[8] The historical record, I intend to show, is far more complex and complicated.

Perceptions of elderly Americans' positions and functions since 1790 seem to have been related not only to definitions of old age's inherent assets and liabilities, but also to conditions and values prevailing in the United States at any given moment.[9] When it was commonly believed that older persons were qualified to perform certain vital tasks, writers emphasized the aged's useful and valuable social roles. Conversely, Americans generally played down the expertise of age if younger people or experts seemed better suited to do jobs once assigned to the old, or if the tasks the aged could accomplish were not deemed essential. In addition, assessments of the elderly's societal standing have depended upon the degree to which Americans believe that the disadvantages of growing older are an age-specific tragedy and that old age itself constitutes a social "problem."

New ideas about the elderly have evolved slowly, and old notions have persisted even when they no longer seemed valid. Significant longitudinal shifts in conceptions of older Americans' status, moreover, have not always been related to real changes in the aged's circumstances. Conversely, crucial alterations in elderly people's actual place in American society have not always coincided with key transformations in ideas about their circumstances. "Modernization," I believe, has affected prevailing perceptions and experiences of being old at different times and divergent ways, thereby causing periodic dysfunctions between the rhetoric and realities of growing old.

This work is not, and does not pretend to be, the last word on the history of old age. I have presented my argument in order to emphasize that over time the interplay of cultural trends and structural patterns has shaped the perceived meanings and actual experiences of being old in a subtle and surprising manner. Some rightly will suggest that there are other ways to interpret and organize the material. Others undoubtedly will prefer to pursue

other topics and employ alternate conceptual and methodological approaches. But I do hope that this book stirs—or at least provokes—
additional research and helps those who will build on my mistakes and
suggestions. (I have, accordingly, noted throughout the text places where I
think my interpretation is vulnerable and recommended areas where more
work needs to be done.) For I am convinced that historical perspectives in
gerontology are crucial. Studying the past can help us to understand the
predicament of older people in contemporary American society. Applying
the lessons of history might lead to better evaluations of current options and
to sounder preparations for future possibilities.

PART 1

Changing Perceptions of the Aged's Roles in Nineteenth-Century America

Portrait of an unidentified couple, c. 1850. Southworth and Hawes daguerrotype. (Courtesy of the International Museum of Photography, Rochester, N.Y.)

CHAPTER 1

The Usefulness of Old Age

Many images of old age that circulated in the United States from 1790 to 1860 resemble those that flourish today. Etchings, photographs, and prints of that period generally reveal the same gray hairs and deeply lined faces. They sometimes accentuate the economic and physical problems we still associate with being old. Graphics also confirm that the circumstances and experiences of pre–Civil War elderly Indians, blacks, and whites were no less diverse and that their various difficulties were no less acute than they are in the 1970s. Furthermore, the writings of the era—ranging from classic literature to popular almanacs and from poems to public documents— indicate that, like us, people faced the eternal advantages and hardships of growing old with a mixture of fear, dismay, and joy, acceptance, ambivalence, and reluctance. Visions of happiness and personal fulfillment as well as the specter of misery and despair were just as "real" then as they are now. And yet, for all these similarities, it becomes quickly apparent that some fundamental changes have taken place over time.

One of the most striking differences is in the way early Americans defined older people's place in society. Our predecessors would have been surprised to learn that the elderly as a group would be described one day as roleless and unproductive persons who inevitably and willingly disengage from active life. In sharp contrast, Americans between the Revolutionary and Civil wars believed that their infant republic depended upon the commitment and ability of men and women of all ages to work together in creating a new society. An orator elaborated on this idea during ground-breaking ceremonies for a new canal in Ohio on 4 July 1825. The state's ability to tap the resources of all its citizens, he remarked, provided it "at once, all the vigor and firmness of youth, the strength and firmness of manhood, and the wisdom of age. Great as is the undertaking, your powers are equal to its completion; be but united, firm and persevering, and if heaven smile on your labors, success is sure."[1] Americans claimed that the elderly, by complementing other age groups' assets, were indispensable in establishing a *novus ordo seclorum*—a new order of the ages—as the Great

Seal of the United States proudly declared. Indeed, ministers, scientists, essayists, and editors among others asserted in their writings that a lifetime of experience made older persons remarkable promoters of healthful longevity, ideal custodians of virtue, and seasoned veterans of productivity.

In large measure, the basic exigencies of nation building coupled with the articulated values and priorities prevailing before 1860 account for the (comparatively) favorable estimation of the aged's usefulness then expressed in this country. It is essential to remember that when the Constitution was ratified, America was an underdeveloped nation. The truly important political, economic, and social networks operated at the local, state, and regional levels. The federal government could barely muster the military force and diplomatic influence necessary to defend its national borders and maintain more than a low profile on the international scene. "Even after two centuries of struggling," Henry Adams observed long ago in his magisterial study of the Jeffersonian era, "the land was still untamed; forest covered every portion, except here and there a strip of cultivated soil; the minerals lay undisturbed in their rocky beds and more than two-thirds of the people clung to the seaboard within 50 miles of tidewater, where alone the wants of civilized life could be supplied."[2] Despite the striking economic and demographic growth and fundamental societal transformations that took place during the first half of the nineteenth century, the United States was still in the formative stages of its long-term development. By 1860, it had not yet achieved a well-integrated, functional, nationwide structure or assumed a role as a world power.

Commentators during the period were acutely aware of their country's perilous situation. From our perspective, especially with the bicentennial observances lingering in our minds, it is sometimes difficult to recognize and comprehend the sense of cautiousness and vulnerability that counterbalanced early Americans' avowed hopes and boasts of success in the proximate and indeterminate future. Yet the creators and heirs of the American Enlightenment, steeped in classical traditions and contemporary social theories, "had a keen sense of the precariousness of the felicity that they enjoyed, of the moral and social conditions which made its continuation possible, and of the ultimate likelihood of its dissipation."[3] And while the next generations clearly celebrated their apparently boundless resources as they envisioned and attained their seemingly "manifest destiny," they also were alarmed by the rampant individualism and other ominous trends unleashed by new forces in their midst.

Given the particular ways they defined "reality" and given their desire to establish those values, norms, and modes of behavior that would best serve their collective interests and private ambitions, writers prescribed and referred to a variety of methods to increase chances for national and personal success. In this context, Americans between 1790 and 1860 respected the wisdom of years and considered it appropriate to rely on the elderly's experiences and expertise, not because they were living in a bucolic elysium, but because they considered it sensible and worthwhile to do so. If this interpretation is correct, then there probably was *not* a fundamental alteration in age relations occurring immediately after the Revolution, which made old age seem increasingly worthless in young America. Rather, in the minds of their countrymen and in their own self-perceptions, the old should—and could—play useful roles in society. Thus under a specific set of historical circumstances, Americans judged the assets and liabilities of being old invaluable in shaping the cultural and social life of their new land.

To be sure, there were limits to such explicit esteem for the aged's worth. While the evidence strongly indicates that the elderly were ascribed important social roles because of their past accomplishments and presumed current utility, it does not necessarily follow that Americans exalted (or even preferred) old age more than any other stage of life, or that every older person found life rewarding. One can, after all, acknowledge the claims and achievements of age without invariably liking elderly people or even looking forward to growing old; material comforts and social responsibilities do not guarantee personal satisfaction in later years. Furthermore, no one suggested that *only* the aged were capable of performing essential tasks. "Youth" and "manhood," as the Ohio orator noted, also had important roles to play. Above all, the frequent references to the honor due age do not mean that the elderly *in fact* wielded vast power or held extraordinarily prestigious positions; I presently am analyzing *perceptions* of older persons' relative value, not reconstructing their actual social status. (It is conceivable that prevailing descriptions of the aged accurately elucidate most older people's true circumstances. But it is also possible that the ideas typically expressed by observers did not really carry over into the realm of behavior; precepts clearly were not always practiced. I will defer, however, my consideration of the possible relationships between the rhetoric and realities of being old in pre–Civil War America until Part Two.) For the moment, I shall explore in some detail the precise ways Americans defined the elderly's overall worth, and the reasons why they valued those who conformed to certain cultural norms and expectations and contributed to the well-being of their fellow citizens.

The Elderly Provide
Valuable Insights about Healthful Longevity

Americans before the Civil War regarded people who enjoyed a "ripe old age" with respect because they believed that living a long and fruitful life was a worthwhile achievement. Popular and scientific writers claimed that "longevity has always been highly estimated by man."[4] In a world in which sickness, injury, and death plagued all age groups, those who attained the biblically inspired "three-score-and-ten" seemed remarkable. In fact, the number of elderly people in the United States became a powerful ideological weapon to demonstrate that the New World environment was conducive to human existence and societal progress. During the early years of the republic, it was generally believed that the frequency of persons surviving to old age provided a valid measure of the impact of the civil and natural environment on human health. "Tables of longevity may be everywhere considered the touchstones of government," the Frenchman J. P. Brissot de Warville remarked in 1788, "the scale on which may be measured their excellencies and their defects, the perfection or degradation of the human species."[5]

Accordingly, scientists such as William Barton, a nephew of the astronomer David Rittenhouse, gathered bills of mortality and constructed elaborate tables to "prove" that life expectancy was greater in the United States than in Europe. In his *Observations on the Progress of Population and the Probabilities of the Duration of Human Life, in the United States of America* (1791), Barton recounted earlier studies and proceeded to "mention a few remarkable instances of longevity . . . to corroborate the truth of the position, that the people of this country are long lived."[6] (His "few" examples, fully documented from all sections of the country, fill six pages!) Comparing his data with European evidence, Barton deduced that the likelihood of a person living past eighty was greater here than abroad. Although few tried to replicate Barton's methodology, many reached the same sanguine conclusion. Almanacs featured items about Americans living to advanced ages because publishers deemed such information appropriate reading material.[7] Hezekiah Niles, editor of the most widely circulated and authoritative weekly magazine in the early nineteenth century, regularly reported the names and occupations of very old citizens. Finding it too overwhelming to print all of the cases of long life he received from correspondents, Niles decided in 1823 to limit his reporting to listing centenarians. He believed that even these figures confirmed American superiority over England in prolonging life, especially since the data seemed more conclusive with each passing year.[8]

Critics, geographers, and medical scientists among others contended that such empirical evidence justified their belief that America's environment promoted vigorous long life. One of the *Resources of the United States*, John Bristed argued in 1818, was that

> the aggregate salubrity of the United States surpasses that of Europe; the males are, generally, active, robust, muscular, and powerful, capable of great exertion and endurance; the females display a fine symmetry of person, lively and inter-

esting countenances, frank and engaging manners. . . . The Americans average a longer life than the people in Europe, where only *three* out of every thousand births reach the ages of eighty to ninety years; whereas, in the United States, the proportion is *five* to every thousand.[9]

Jeremy Belknap, in his *History of New Hampshire* (1813), credited the country's fresh air, moderate climate, and rich soil as part of the reason why the very elderly mainly succumbed only to "the gradual decay of nature."[10] Dr. Benjamin Rush, one of America's earliest and most famous students of old age, went a step farther and asserted that life in the new land actually may have enabled some to live longer than they had anticipated. In the course of his studies of people who lived past eighty, Rush "observed many instances of Europeans who have arrived in America in the decline of life who have acquired fresh vigour from the impression of our climate, and of new objects upon their bodies and minds, and whose lives in consequence thereof, appeared to have been prolonged for many years."[11] Americans extolled their seemingly greater likelihood for a long, healthy life as a source of national pride: it indicated to them that the new republic was beginning to reap its natural advantages.

Needless to say, interest in life expectancy—and people who lived long lives—extended beyond debates over the relative effects of political and natural environments on shortening or prolonging human existence. Questions about longevity per se attracted considerable attention. Three important treatises published by William Godwin, Antoine-Nicolas de Condorcet, and Thomas Robert Malthus during the 1790s stimulated decades of speculation about the possibility and desirability of prolonging life.[12] Regardless of whether they thought life expectancy could or should be increased, most Americans believed that trying to live a long, fruitful life was a significant personal goal. "The art of preserving life has become an important study,"Anthony F. Willich commented in his *Domestic Ency- clopedia* (1821), "and ought to form part of the education of every individual."[13] Determining why and how some people lived longer than others was considered a matter of utmost importance.

As they searched for ways to prolong life, Americans recognized that some factors affecting life expectancy were beyond human control. It was well established, for instance, that people who lived to very great ages often were descended from those who had themselves enjoyed a long life. Compilers such as William H. Hall noted, in *The New Encyclopedia* (1797), that "there is a great reason to believe that longevity is in great measure hereditary."[14] Investigators corroborated eighteenth-century be- liefs that a temperate climate, rural setting, and abundant food supply improved chances for a long life. Over time, in fact, commentators gave more and more prominence to variations in longevity. Examining the causes of death for people at all stages of the life cycle led observers like Dr. John

Bell, a member of the American Philosophical Society and professor at the College of Physicians and Surgeons in Philadelphia, to conclude that women's chances for long life were better than men's.[15] Racial differences in life expectancy also attracted increasing attention in antebellum America. While there seemed to be many reasons why blacks did not live as long as whites, investigators uncovered variations in life expectancy among blacks as well as whites. For example, Dr. Charles Caldwell, in *Thoughts on the Effects of Age on the Human Constitution* (1846), noted that there were more black than white centenarians in North Carolina. This statistic, Caldwell argued, appeared to contradict Benjamin Rush's observation that "none but men of very active minds attain to a high degree of longevity."[16] It did not challenge, however, the indisputable influence of heredity on life expectancy.

In addition, limitations in the then existing scientific thought and practice precluded applying ideas and means that would enable later generations to improve their overall life expectancy. Classifying, explaining, and treating diseases either in terms of a simple pathogenic condition, an imbalance of humors, or a loss of vital forces frustrated efforts to reduce the mortality rates associated with common contagious illnesses. A galaxy of partially valid but often contradictory theories about the external causes of diseases further limited the possibility of promoting longevity by improving public hygiene and preventing epidemics. Some concerned citizens gathered data and promoted sanitary reform measures, but no state established a public health department before the Civil War.[17]

Other obstacles kept scientists and doctors in the United States from embracing theories and techniques associated with the Paris School of Medicine, which were gaining vogue in Europe after 1820. Because most on this side of the Atlantic remained suspicious of the emerging concept of disease specificity and were indifferent to basic research, doctors' ideas about the best ways to promote a long and healthful life changed remarkably little between 1790 and 1860. Even those native-born doctors versed and skilled in the latest trends in European medicine lacked the opportunity and milieu necessary to influence and alter many of their colleagues' viewpoints and practices. For it is worth noting that scientists generally lacked the laboratory procedures, instruments, and facilities as well as the professional motivation and organizations essential for clinical studies. Furthermore, before orthodox practitioners would make real headway in improving health, they had to convince a skeptical and often disillusioned public that their education and therapies guaranteed better results than those offered by uneducated domestic doctors who dispensed patent medicines, by quacks who sold nostrums, and by sectarians such as the Grahamites, homeopaths, phrenologists, and mesmerists.[18] Indeed, to many patients before the Civil War, home remedies and herbs seemed just as effective (or illusory) in

curing illnesses and restoring health as treatments recommended by doctors with years of training.

While acknowledging that heredity, gender, and race affected life expectancy and admitting that no magic drugs or arcane medical techniques
guaranteed continuous vim and vigor, Americans before 1860 nonetheless
claimed that people could improve their own chances for a healthful long
life. Commentators agreed that one could increase the likelihood of
attaining a ripe old age by learning and adhering to certain "general
principles."[19] Encyclopedists invoked the example of Luigi Cornaro, a
sixteenth-century Venetian noble who claimed at eighty-five that virtuous
living was the *Sure and Certain Method of Attaining a Long and Healthful Life.* Contemporary newspapers, almanacs, and periodicals printed and
reprinted this time-tested piece of advice. Medical doctors also confirmed
the therapeutic advantages derived from observing elementary rules of
sensible living. Many of the maxims stressed the importance of fresh air,
regular exercise, cleanliness, a moderate diet, and sleeping only long enough
to restore strength to the body. Cultivating proper attitudes, including a
cheerful disposition and an ability to endure disappointments with courage
and resignation, was considered essential.

Precisely because most Americans believed that one's mental outlook
and personal habits affected chances for living a full life, older men and
women were ascribed an important function to perform: the aged, it was
said, demonstrated which lifestyles were more effective than others for
promoting healthful longevity. The elderly seemed to prove that following
certain rules could mean the difference between a short or long life and a
comparatively fit or disease-ridden existence. As Thomas Bailey pointed
out in *Records of Longevity* (1859),

> I mean—notwithstanding the instances which will be found in these records to the
> contrary—to establish the truth . . . that temperance, industry and exercise are
> the three great elements of longevity. A few slothful men have attained to
> extreme old age, and so have a few gluttons and drunkards, or at least, hard
> drinkers; but for the most part, and in an incomparably greater proportion, long
> livers have been distinguished for their sober and industrious habits.[20]

Scientists and popular commentators alike emphasized that the elderly
proved the efficacy of temperance, moderation, industry, and exercise in
prolonging life and promoting health. In so doing, they underscored the
value of the aged's example.

Believing that most older persons exemplified a desirable code of
behavior, Americans by and large attributed to the aged a second important
societal role. Moderation and industry, Dr. Charles Caldwell among other
pre–Civil War writers claimed, "do much more than merely contribute to
the preservation of health and the attainment of long life. They are the most

effectual *preventives of vice* and promoters of *virtue* and *good* conduct that nature affords."[21] Since it seemed clear to them that virtue was associated with longevity, Americans concluded that the elderly could teach others how to live morally and healthfully.

The Elderly Serve As Guardians of Virtue

Poets, essayists, scientists, and others writing between 1790 and 1860 claimed that, with few exceptions, the aged's moral faculties were highly developed. The presumption that virtue in old age was attained mainly through the cumulative effect of righteous living led to the conclusion that older people of all stations generally were paragons of virtuous behavior. Convinced that the elderly's advice was instructive, Americans prior to the Civil War considered it advantageous to rely on elderly men and women to help direct and safeguard the moral development of the young nation.

The stature gained from years of experience, it was generally agreed, made society's oldest members ideally qualified moral exemplars. Physical and moral well-being at advanced ages appeared to hinge in large part upon successfully avoiding the pitfalls and dangers at each stage of life. Abraham Shoemaker poetically declared in his 1797 *U.S. Almanack*, for instance, that

> as in the succession of seasons, each, by the invariable laws of nature, affects the productions of what is next in course; so, in human life, every period of our age, according as it is well or ill spent, influences the happiness of that which is to follow. Virtuous youth gradually brings forward accomplished and flourishing manhood; and such manhood passes of itself, without uneasiness, into respectable and tranquil old age. But when nature is turned out of its regular order, disorder takes place in the moral just as in the vegetable world . . . so if youth be trifled away without improvement, manhood will be contemptible, and old age miserable.[22]

According to the "invariable laws of nature," a respectable old age resulted from a life of virtue and benevolence. That nature was not false to itself was revealed in the fact that it endowed older men and women with the "nobleness of humanity."[23]

Not only did Americans believe that a long and upright life conditioned people's moral sensibility, but contemporary medical research indicated that the human capacity for virtue did not decline after a certain age. For instance, Dr. Benjamin Rush supported this proposition in his *Medical Inquiries on Diseases* (1812): "The moral faculties, when properly regulated and directed, never partake of the decay of the intellectual faculties in old age, even in persons of uncultivated minds."[24] Subsequent investigations conducted in both the north and south uniformly confirmed Rush's observation on this point even though they disagreed with one another on other matters. Scientific observation thus corroborated the widely held popular opinion that moral faculties could improve with age regardless of a person's prior education or current social standing.

Indeed, Americans described older persons as the most trustworthy counselors on moral matters because they believed that the unimpaired wisdom of age was essential to the well-being of the nation. We should not discount references to the elderly's desirable virtues and moral insights as mere propaganda designed to instill those values and instincts necessary to combat the decline in faith and increase in materialism and corruption many politicians, clergymen, and writers felt were perverting the ideals of Revolutionary America.[25] Some writers who characterized the older generation as custodians of virtue probably did hope that exhorting their fellow citizens to follow the aged's advice would have a stabilizing effect and a conservative influence on the young republic. And yet, just as people's fascination with the size of the elderly population went beyond its worth as evidence proving that human life did not invariably degenerate in the New World environment, so too recognition of and appreciation for the elderly's moral counsel and decorum were not based simply on their possible usefulness as an antidote to actual or imagined social ills.

In light of the special way they perceived "reality," most Americans before 1860 thought that the moral instruction offered by people who had lived long and upright lives was valuable because it had been proven successful. The presumption that people could attain virtue only through righteous living led to the conclusion that the elderly's opinions should be heeded. Hence, when "Senex" argued that properly educating young people was crucial because "the purity of *their* morals and the prudence of their conduct, the weal and permanence of this infant republic were essentially depending" upon it, readers assumed that they were hearing the sensible advice of a wise old man. The elderly could perform an important social role by actively engaging in the diffusion and enforcement of the "undoubted laws of virtue."[26]

The elderly's moral expertise, writers emphasized, was particularly valuable to youth. The Reverend Cortlandt Van Rensselaer elaborated on the significance of this function in a sermon on *Old Age* (1841):

> What a blessed influence the old exert in cherishing feelings of reverence, affection and subordination in families; in warning the young against the temptations and allurements of the world; in detailing the results of experience, in exposing the fallacies of worldly maxims; in rebuking the recklessness of indiscretion and the experiments of enthusiasm; in imparting judicious counsel in church and State and private life;—in short, how much good of every kind is accomplished by the tranquilizing, wise and conservative influences of age.[27]

Since older Americans were deemed well equipped to give sound advice on how to live in a respectable manner and to avoid or overcome worldly temptations, the beneficial relationship between age and youth was a favorite theme not just of ministers but also of social critics, novelists, and poets. "It was meant . . . that youth and age should exert upon each other a mutual benefit."[28] Aged men and women were thought to serve the rising generation by admonishing against levity, vanity, and idleness, and by instilling a sense of integrity, honesty, and responsibility. Youth repaid age by offering its companionship and sharing its joys. Mutual benefits, moreover, entailed reciprocal responsibilities. The elderly were obliged to set an appropriate model of decorum. The young, in turn, were expected to pay deference to the aged's virtue.[29]

Indeed, the belief that years of experience made older persons sagacious and exemplary was so widespread in pre–Civil War American culture that references to "venerable" old age were an unobtrusive part of everyday language. For example, in compiling *An American Dictionary of the English Language* (1828), Noah Webster illustrated his definition of the verb "to venerate" with the following examples: "We *venerate* an old faithful magistrate; we *venerate* parents and elders; we *venerate* men consecrated to sacred office; we *venerate* old age or gray hairs; we *venerate*, or ought to venerate, the gospel and its precepts."[30] Webster believed that Americans were ambivalent only in their veneration of Scripture. He assumed honor and respect for magistrates, ministers, parents, and older persons were prevailing cultural norms. Webster apparently was not alone in this judgment: the adjective "venerable" was often used in the writings of the era to identify relatively obscure aged men and women who were considered upright and respected members of their community. And white Americans did not think their value system was unique in this regard; other races in the United States were said "to venerate" their elders. Missionaries and hunters, for instance, duly noted "that respect for age and long experience, for which the Indians are remarkable."[31] Regardless of whether owners were kind or cruel to their aged slaves, considerable evidence from both white and black observers indicates that younger blacks generally endeavored to provide their "aunts" and "uncles" with emotional and physical security and treated them with dignity.[32] While far more research must be done before we can determine to what extent contemporaries actually contradicted and conformed to this prescribed "veneration" dictum, such honorific references to older people offer an important measure of the emphasis placed on the aged's role as wise and virtuous counselors.

This does not mean, however, that the elderly's usefulness was merely titular, confined to the comparatively passive tasks of dispensing recommendations on ways to live a healthful existence and/or offering advice concerning matters of morality. In the minds of their compatriots, older persons also had active roles to fulfill. Assuming that everyone shared a responsibility to serve his or her fellow citizens, writers entreated all age groups to work together harmoniously in building the new nation. Most Americans believed, in fact, that the practical knowledge and moral expertise accrued through years of experience enabled the aged to contribute to society in a variety of essential ways.

The Aged Actively Serve Others in Many Capacities

Like everyone else, the elderly were expected to remain economically and socially useful as long as they were physically able to work. Neither structural obstacles, such as mandatory retirement, nor social prejudice denied men and women because of their advanced age the right to engage in any trade, profession, or vocation (except for a few state judicial posts) before the Civil War. In fact, Americans considered it foolish for the elderly to quit their jobs merely on account of age: medical and popular writers noted that deterioration in later years less often resulted from natural decay than from disuse.[33] The prevailing notion that the old were seasoned veterans of productivity, whose advice and participation enhanced prospects for successfully accomplishing many tasks, justified ascribing to aged persons a variety of important societal tasks to perform.

For example, Americans between 1790 and 1860 fully appreciated older people's usefulness in farming. Evidence in almanacs and rural journals indicates that the aged's presumed importance in rural America was not merely a figment of genteel urban writers' imagination: those who worked in the fields claimed that the elderly's agricultural expertise made them living domestic encyclopedias.[34] The well-known *Farmers Almanac*, originally compiled by Robert B. Thomas, regularly featured suggestions by "Father Simkins" on shoeing horses, caring for farm implements, and keeping account books in order. Among "The Contents of an Old Man's Memorandum Book" in an edition of the *U.S. Almanack* was advice on naming sons and daughters, teaching children to be ambidextrous, traveling efficiently, exchanging ideas with friends, and selecting the best time to wind a watch. Writers indicated that the aged possessed helpful insights about nearly every aspect of farm life—a significant fact, since roughly sixty percent of all gainfully employed persons and a vast majority of all workers over sixty actually were farmers prior to the Civil War.[35]

Furthermore, the election and appointment of men to high public office in their later years attest to the favorable opinion of the elderly's value in government as well as on the farm. In the early years of the republic, septuagenarians were serving as chief warden of the ports of Philadelphia and Boston, and as administrators in Connecticut, Pennsylvania, and South Carolina; a number remained politically active at the city, state, and federal levels beyond the age of eighty.[36] Eleven of the twenty-one highest-ranking naval officers in 1839 were over sixty; seven others were fifty-nine years old.[37] Senior statesmen often held congressional seats. For example, two years after losing a reelection bid for the presidency, John Quincy Adams in 1830 won a seat at the age of sixty-four. Adams continuously represented his home district for the next seventeen years until he suffered a fatal stroke. "When persons of mature age and eminent for their experience, wisdom, and virtue" were elected to Congress, Hezekiah Niles, reflecting popular sentiment, editorialized, "it is a subject for gratitude and congratulation."[38] Americans believed that elderly candidates' political sagacity had been ripened by many years of service.

Voters clearly considered older men fit and even uniquely qualified for the presidency, as William Henry Harrison's 1840 bid aptly illustrates. After Ol' Tippecanoe was nominated to be the Whig standard bearer, opponents seized on his prior illnesses and age as campaign issues. Frank Blair's *Globe*, the Democratic party's most influential voice, declared that Harrison's "garrulity" could not be masked by appeals to log cabins and hard cider; one opposition bulletin blasted Harrison as a "superannuated and pitiable dotard."[39] Whigs tried to turn their candidate's "green old age" into a political asset by describing Harrison as a vigorous guardian of a simpler era's homespun virtues. When Democrats charged that he was an "old granny," Whigs countered that the voters wanted an "experienced and skilful 'granny' to deliver our young and beautiful mother of a nest of vipers, who are preying upon her vitals, and hurrying her to a premature grave."[40] Ol' Tippecanoe won 53.1 percent of the popular vote and 234 of the 294 electoral votes cast. And despite Harrison's untimely death a month after taking office, antebellum Americans continued to nominate and elect elderly men to the presidency. Old age often seemed to enhance rather than to reduce a candidate's attractiveness.[41]

In fact, prior to the Civil War, laws disqualified men from voting and holding hundreds of offices because they were too young, but there were only a few specific judicial posts throughout the land in which men over a certain age could not serve. Most places required men to be at least twenty-one to cast a ballot; no jurisdiction, however, disenfranchised any potential voter on account of advanced age. The Constitution established minimum ages for election to Congress and the White House, but there were no maximum age restrictions for any elected or appointed office at the federal level. States barred young but not elderly men from running for governor or the legislature. Unlike the federal constitution, however, a few states did impose definite limits on the number of years a person could serve as a justice. Some followed a 1780 Massachusetts constitutional precedent, and required that licenses to justices of the peace be renewed every seven years.[42] (Such restrictions, of course, were designed to guard against incompetency in general, not to discriminate against senior justices in particular.) In addition, seven states imposed upper age limits on holding judicial office. To avoid the problems experienced when a colonial chief justice became senile on the bench, New York state's 1777 Constitution prescribed that "the Chancellor, the judges of the supreme court, and the first judge of the country court of each county hold their offices during good behavior, or until they shall have respectively attained the age of sixty year." Revisions in the 1792 New Hampshire, 1819 Connecticut, and 1851 Maryland constitutions established seventy as the maximum age for judges and justices of the peace. Although none had imposed old-age restrictions in earlier constitutions, Alabama (1819), Missouri (1820), and Maine (1820) inserted maximum limits for judicial posts when they became states.[43] These are the *only* instances of discrimination against older men's rights to serve as justices before the Civil War. No other jurisdiction in the remaining twenty-six states making up the nation before the Civil War restricted elderly men from holding any other elected or appointed office.

Although prohibiting the aged from judicial office was an unusual custom between 1790 and 1860, even its limited practice aroused considerable opposition. John Adams found the removal of competent judges from office at seventy offensive: "To turn out such men to eat husks with the prodigal or grass with Nebuchadnezzer ought to be tormenting to the humanity of the Nation."[44] But it was the clause in the New York Constitution, which removed men from judicial office at sixty, that especially aroused waves of outcry. In 1788, Alexander Hamilton argued in Federal Paper 79 that the measure needlessly discriminated against able magistrates and denied elderly men the right to be useful and remain financially independent:

> when, in addition to this circumstance, we consider how few there are who outlive the season of intellectual vigor and how improbable it is that any considerable portion of the bench, whether more or less numerous, should be in such a situation at the same time, we shall be ready to conclude that limitations of this sort shall have little to recommend them.[45]

Chancellor James Kent's forced resignation on his sixtieth birthday in 1823 sparked another outburst. At a banquet in his honor at Harvard, Kent was toasted: "The James Kent—with better machinery, greater force, and greater safety than any other boat, yet constitutionally forbidden to take another trip." New York was criticized at the same time: "The Constitution of New York—we hear that it diverts the operations, but we see it neither abates the force nor obscures the splendor of intellectual light."[46] Both toasts proved to be accurate prophecies. Three years after his removal from office, Kent began publishing his famous *Commentaries on American Law* (1826–30), establishing him as the American Blackstone. He did not become infirm until a few months before his death at eighty-four, in 1847.

Kent's continued eminence and Chief Justice John Marshall's vigorous performance on the Supreme Court considerably beyond the age of sixty prompted periodic barbs at the New York age limitation. Finally, the state dropped the restriction when it revised its constitution in 1846.[47]

There was no comparable controversy in the private sector because mandatory retirement simply did not exist. No profession, industry, business, craft, or trade organization prior to 1860 required people to leave the labor force because they had reached a predetermined chronological age. Thus we must be careful not to attribute twentieth-century connotations to the ways that Americans of the period used the word "retirement": the idea that a person automatically stopped working at a prescribed age is absent from pre–Civil War definitions of the word. Men and women of all ages, not just the elderly, retired under different sets of circumstances. Farmers, according to almanacs, annually "retired" from winter's storms to their family circles. Noah Webster wrote in a 1790 essay "that the morals of young men, as well as their application to science, depend much on retirement."[48] In the first edition of *An American Dictionary* (1828), Webster defined retirement as "1. The act of withdrawing from company or from public notice or station. 2. The state of being withdrawn. 3. Private abode; habitation secluded from much society, or from public life. 4. Private way of life."[49] While the aged conceivably could be "retired" in any one of these uses of the word, no definition necessarily applied only to older people.

It is essential to note, however, that there were two limits to the pervasive cultural norm that the aged should play an active role in society. On the one hand, debilities and infirmities restricted some older persons' employment options. Declining health, for instance, reduced Daniel Boone and Natty Bumppo, perhaps the period's favorite symbols of energetic extreme old age, from hunters to trappers and guides. Indeed, Noah Webster's definition of the verb "superannuate" connotes the critical importance of health: "To impair or disqualify by old age and infirmity."[50] Increasing physical handicaps often prevented people from continuing in their jobs. On the other hand, the elderly had to assess honestly the strengths and liabilities of their years on all their activities. As Hugh Henry Brackenridge reminded readers in *Modern Chivalry* (1804), an old horse that trotted was respectable, but one that tried to speed would be contemptible. "The great secret of preserving respect is the cultivating and showing to the best advantage the powers that we possess, and the not going beyond them."[51] Older Americans were expected to know when it was time to let others assume more and more of their regular duties.

And yet, even those who curtailed previous occupations at advanced ages did not have to cease being useful. Antebellum Americans did not believe that people inevitably became obsolete as they grew older. Writers throughout the period echoed a theme Isaac Bickerstaff thoughtfully declared in the 1794 edition of his *New-England Almanack:*

> mankind is one vast republic, where every individual receives benefits from the labour of others, which, by labouring in his turn for others, he is obliged to repay; and that where the united efforts of all are not able to exempt all from misery, none have a right to withdraw from their task of vigilance, or be indulged in idle wisdom, and solitary pleasures.[52]

As long as evil and misery existed in the world, it was claimed, the aged had constructive roles to play.

Americans between 1790 and 1860 invariably extolled the elderly's contributions in the home. Widely circulated magazines and almanacs were frequently illustrated with essays, vignettes, etchings, and poems about the aged's value in performing domestic duties. For example, after leaving the bench, Judge Jeremiah Smith spent the next twenty-two years serving as a trustee of the local academy, reading, offering his seasoned advice to others, and sharing the pleasures and pains of his family circle. "We may even question," a reviewer in the *North American Review* observed, "whether he was ever more useful to his fellow-men than in this genial autumn of his days."[53] Artists working in all media capitalized on the theme. Stephen Foster sold about 130,000 copies of "Old Folks at Home" (1851) within three years; others profitably wrote imitations of the song. John Rogers created a statue of a family scene featuring the grandparents. Currier and Ives issued a large folio print of "Old Age" in 1868.[54] Such sentimental portraits not only enjoyed phenomenal financial success but they also reinforced in popular thought the value of special services older men and women fulfilled in the household. Among other things, observers pointed out that the elderly taught manners and served as models of behavior. Children and grandchildren also depended on their elders' recollections for biographical details about their ancestral roots.

But according to contemporary accounts, the aged's worth as oral historians usually extended beyond recounting family histories: to younger generations, the elderly seemed to be living monuments of the past. Those attaining old age between 1790 and 1830, in particular, provided their countrymen with a symbolic tie to the nation's revolutionary heritage. Magazine and newspaper editors occasionally reprinted the stories anonymous veterans told. The following incident appeared in the 1 October 1825 issue of *Niles Register:*

> "Here, boys, are the marks of war," said an old veteran the other day as he opened an old revolutionary vest, full of bullets and bayonet holes, and showed the scars on his breast. He was wounded, dreadfully wounded, *nine* times wounded, in the battle of Fort Griswold. His breast was literally torn open by

bayonets and musket-balls, so that the beating of his heart was distinctly seen. . . . The young soldier unexpectedly recovered and is now a venerable and respected inhabitant of this town. "Here, boys, are the marks of war," and his whole soul seemed beaming from his keen eye, as he exhibited his numerous wounds to a group of youths who had gathered around, and gazed with admiration on one, who in olden time, arose, as it were, from the dead.[55]

Americans believed that older people's first-hand accounts of heroic bravery and steadfast loyalty to the revolutionary cause were uplifting examples of patriotism for everyone to follow. Fourth of July festivities and ground-breaking ceremonies were not complete until audiences heard speeches by Revolutionary War veterans and acknowledged the presence of other survivors in the crowd.[56] The public activities of Charles Carroll of Carrolton, the last surviving signer of the Declaration of Independence, illustrates this ritualistic use of the elderly. Before he died in 1832 at the age of ninety-five, Carroll presided over the laying of the cornerstone of the Baltimore and Ohio railroad, served as president of the American Coloniza- tion Society, and rode a steamboat named in his honor. Carroll and his contemporaries thus served as a crucial link between America's past and present that inspired optimism about the future.

Nor did the elderly's role as repositories of the past diminish once the last Revolutionary War survivors died. Aged antebellum Americans remembered and retold the stirring episodes learned from those who had lived through the early years of the republic. During yarn-spinning sessions, in meeting houses and taverns, obscure inveterate storytellers dominated or attracted gatherings with their mixtures of fact and fiction.[57] Some people demanded that the elderly be accurate in recounting the past. John Greenleaf Whittier, for instance, relied upon his elders' memory of colonial folklore and incorporated experiences from their lives in his *Legends of New England*.[58] Writers of children's stories and other works, including Nathaniel Dodge, Nathaniel Hawthorne, and Hannah More, often made older men and women narrators in their books, since readers were accus- tomed to hearing the aged's sagas about the past. Essayists and poets recorded the visions their elders purportedly held of former days because they thought such materials were exciting, entertaining, or edifying.[59]

Because the elderly could synthesize and share vital lessons garnered from the past and present ages, Americans between 1790 and 1860 con- sidered it practical to heed an older person's counsel and to utilize his or her talents even in periods of rapid change. "By respecting the advice of an old man, we not only gratify the individual by making him feel that he is not living in vain, but we insure to ourselves a great chance of success in the matter at hand; for age advises us from experience, and not from untested theory.''[60] The experience and wisdom of years seemed indispensable in nurturing the well-being of the republic. For this reason, most people before the Civil War believed that the aged, except those whose unseemly behavior provoked contempt, made essential contributions to their contemporaries.

It should not be altogether surprising, therefore, that early Americans chose the image of a sinewy old man with long white hair and chin whiskers to symbolize their new land. Dressed in red and white striped pantaloons and a blue coat bespangled with stars, and sporting an unabashedly old-fashioned plug hat, "Uncle Sam" seemed to personify the honesty, self-reliance, and devotion to country so deeply cherished in the early decades of our national experience. Debate persists about whether the sobriquet and character were inspired by a certain Samuel Wilson of Troy, New York, who served as an inspector of provisions for the U.S. Army during the War of 1812. Yet there is little doubt that the nickname caught on before the Battle of New Orleans and that by the 1830s, "Uncle Sam" had joined the bald-headed eagle as one of this country's favorite symbols.[61] "Uncle Sam" not only epitomized the hopes of young America but he also seemed to demonstrate that the nation could be wise and experienced even in its formative years.

An 1849 engraving by James Smillie after a painting by Thomas Cole.
(Reproduced from the collection of the Library of Congress.)

CHAPTER 2

Variations on a Theme

I do not wish to leave the impression that there was a "golden" era before 1860 in which Americans discussed or emphasized only the sunny aspects of growing old and overlooked or dismissed its unpleasant features. Neither do I want to assert that perceptions of the elderly's worth remained static between the Revolutionary and Civil wars. On the contrary, the evidence indicates that there were significant twists and variations to the argument presented thus far.

Most antebellum observers, in describing the elderly's place in society, did not ignore or deny the problems associated with being old. Indeed, writers generally contended that the very infirmities and liabilities of old age increased aged people's societal value: the elderly could help their fellow citizens put the tragedies as well as the hopes of life into perspective. Because years of sorrow and joy gave older people valuable insights into the nature of the human condition, early Americans turned to them as sources of inspiration and consolation. Thus elderly men and women deserved respect, writers claimed, not simply because they exemplified healthful longevity, personified moral living, and possessed wisdom about a wide variety of practical matters. The aged were said to fulfill one other indispensable role: above all, they seemed to be essential keys to the ultimate meanings of life.

While this theme of regarding older persons favorably because they helped others deal with pain and suffering pervades pre–Civil War sermons, essays, and other literary artifacts, there was a subtle change over time in the presuppositions and rationale used to arrive at similar conclusions. One can identify distinctively "republican" and "romantic" modes of thought, which differ in emphasis rather than content. Americans writing prior to the 1830s generally endorsed a cardinal principle of the republican ideology dominating American thought after the Revolution. Although they recognized considerable disparities among people's appearances, traits, functions, and behavior, they esteemed most highly that which was common to all men and women. Those writing in the middle decades of the nineteenth century, on the other hand, acknowledged but usually did not stress

27

the principle of uniformity in Nature that earlier commentators had extolled. Instead, they reflected a romantic sensibility by focusing on the variations in human nature and emphasizing the potential social usefulness of such multiformity.

Insofar as their appreciation of diversity colored their beliefs, romantic writers described the functions and worth of old age differently from republican observers. Implicit in the earlier respect for old age had been the idea that old people were more similar to other age groups than they were different. In the romantic period, it was the dissimilarities in the assets and liabilities of every stage of life that made each age group seem important. Believing that certain characteristics of old age made the elderly special, such writers emphasized the ways in which the old contrasted with other people and idealized them because of their distinctiveness. The shift from republican to romantic justifications for the elderly's physical and economic woes ultimately had a profound impact on perceptions of the aged's worth because it made the liabilities of age subject to a less rosy interpretation later in the century.

The Problems of Aging

Most Americans between 1790 and 1860 were keenly aware of the difficulties that accompanied growing old. There were exceptions of course. Some images of old age created in the period—such as the sentimental lithographs of elderly men and women sold by Currier and Ives—exaggerated the advantages and overlooked or understated the liabilities of aging. By and large, however, observers described the aged's woes as well as their pleasures.

For instance, contemporary medical research corroborated the prevailing popular view that the chronic ailments and acute diseases that ravaged the elderly were the inevitable effects of Nature.[1] With the passage of years, scientists observed, cellular tissue became less elastic, muscles decreased in bulk, cartilage ossified, brain membranes thickened, sensory organs dulled, male reproductive organs shrank in size, and the capacity of blood vessels changed. Doctors reported that age not only modified the structural conditions of various parts of the body but also affected their chemical properties and functional capabilities: phosphates and other earthy salts accumulated, the heart beat more slowly and often irregularly, the circulatory and nervous systems became more sluggish, muscle strength weakened, and all other organs performed more imperfectly. Palsy, apoplexy, pneumonia, deafness, and poor vision were common at advanced ages. Several mental faculties also declined over time. Medical observers reported frequent cases of speech defects, loss of memory, and garrulity among extremely old men and women.[2] The actual extent of physical and mental incapacity among the elderly before the Civil War is unknown, but it undoubtedly was widespread. Even in the 1960s, fourteen to twenty-four percent of all people over sixty-five in three industrial countries suffered a major disability; the probability of incapacity increased over the age of eighty.[3] Since medical advances during the twentieth century have made significant progress in reducing the incidence and severity of disability in old age, it is reasonable to hypothesize that comparable health status statistics would indicate that a greater proportion of old people a century or more ago suffered from diseases and debilities than today.

Furthermore, economic problems often increased when chronic illnesses and physical disabilities prevented older persons from continuing on the job. Since formal retirement pension plans and government-sponsored old-age insurance schemes did not yet exist, superannuated workers had to rely on savings, assets, profits from the sale of their business or practice, and other means of support to maintain their economic independence. For example, to reduce the risk of poverty, aged farmers occasionally sold part of their land or made special arrangements with tenants. Laborers were sometimes able to secure part-time or less physically demanding jobs. Prudent parents carefully stipulated in legal deeds all provisions and obligations due them or their spouses in their declining years when they turned over their holdings to the rising generation.[4] Despite such practices, however, many remained or became poor in old age. According to recent estimates, more than a quarter of all elderly men around the Civil War had estates worth less than $100. The incidence of indigency among women, especially those who were widowed, never married, or lived alone, was possibly higher. Blacks endured poverty to an extent probably exceeding their white counterparts. If the law did not forbid it, some slaveowners "emancipated" superannuated blacks, thereby "freeing" themselves of caring for elderly slaves. Others heartlessly banished their worn-out slaves like old horses to eke out an existence on their own.[5] Not even former presidents were exempt from economic hardships at the end of their long lives. Thomas Jefferson brushed against bankruptcy several times: repeated crop and bank failures, debts, forfeited notes, fluctuations in land prices, his own fiscal mismanagement, and preoccupation with civic causes put Jefferson in such desperate straits by 1826 that it appeared he might lose Monticello. James Monroe was reduced to poverty a few years after leaving the White House and had to sell his family estate in Albemarle, Virginia, to pay his creditors.[6] Thus, escaping financial ruin in later years was no easy task in pre–Civil War America. The threat of old-age dependency and the specter of the almshouse hovered over many who had only marginal resources at their disposal.

The physical debilities and economic hardships of age, popular and scientific commentators agreed, often nurtured unpleasant traits. Older men and women seemed to complain incessantly about their ailments. Fear of want sometimes made them greedy. Feeling useless and neglected was said to exacerbate their indifference about their appearances and surroundings. Mounting difficulties, in turn, often caused the aged to lose all desire to be congenial companions and reduced their tolerance for others' foibles. As L. Maria Child pointed out in *The Mother's Book* (1844), "The aged, from loneliness of their situation, the want of active employment, and an enfeebled state of health, are apt to look upon the world with a gloomy eye; and sometimes their gloom is not unmixed with bitterness; hence arises the complaint of their harshness and asperity towards the follies of youth."[7] Yet such feelings, however justifiable, merely compounded the elderly's woes. Preferring to indulge in self-pity, some withdrew from social contacts. Others carped so much that they repelled those who might have comforted them.

Older people's attitudes not only magnified their sense of rejection but often caused them social opprobrium. Although linguistic experts and other evidence indicate that "fogy" did not become an epithet Americans applied exclusively to old people until after the Civil War, a few writers before 1860 did use the disrespectful term to describe those elders who seemed to hold old-fashioned ideas.[8] Some even suggested that the elderly could forfeit the respect due age if their current beliefs were deemed unacceptable. John Greenleaf Whittier expressed the disappointment of antislavery advocates at Daniel Webster's decision to support the Compromise of 1850 by writing "Ichabod" (Hebrew for "inglorious"). Whittier urged his readers not to scorn the sixty-eight-year-old Webster, since he was already suffering the consequences of his action: "When faith is lost, when honor dies/ The man is dead!"[9]

Indeed, death loomed as the ultimate source of grief in old age. Neither physical health nor economic security offered any assurance of well-being at the close of life, especially if one's last years were spent burying friends and kin.[10] One of the bitter ironies of surviving to an advanced age was that it entailed losing through death the very love and support of those who had made a long life worth living. Even elderly persons who faced their own death with resignation or relief admitted moments of doubt and dread. And while Americans reacted differently to deaths of the young, the middle-aged, and the old, the fact that someone died at an advanced age did not necessarily mitigate the sense of loss. Indeed, the passing of aged loved ones reminded antebellum Americans of the certainty of death: "Gray hairs and feeble limbs teach us our mortality more impressively and certainly than the passing hearse and funeral bell."[11]

Needless to say, Americans between 1790 and 1860 were not the first people to describe and experience the woes of aging; debility, dependency, deprivation, and death in old age are universal occurrences. And yet, although such phenomena transcend time and space, the ways that commentators in disparate periods and places philosophize about pain and suffering vary considerably. Subtle differences appear, for instance, in materials written in the United States between the Revolutionary and Civil wars. Americans generally agreed that physical, economic, psychological, and existential difficulties enhanced rather than diminished the elderly's social usefulness, but over time they altered the definitions and justifications for the afflictions of age.

The Aged Corroborate the Republican Theodicy

In keeping with the prevailing republican ideology, which emphasized the perennial aspects of the human condition, Americans between 1790 and 1830 stressed that tragedy touched *all* age groups, not just the elderly. Because pain, hardship, grief, and sorrow could strike people at any moment, republican writers did not consider the problems encountered in old age unique. Everybody had to face life's tribulations.

For example, republican writers never specifically associated physical decay solely with the elderly. "In estimating the infirmity peculiar to age . . . we must not place to separate account of old age what is common to every period of life."[12] It was difficult to identify and treat diseases in old age, scientists observed, because certain chronic illnesses and acute diseases manifested themselves differently among various age groups. There was, in fact, no generally accepted word at the time to define the state of infirmity in old age. Noah Webster included the noun "senility" in the 1828 edition of his dictionary, but most medical dictionaries did not. The word, as Webster noted, was "not much used."[13] Furthermore, doctors believed that old people were protected against certain maladies: madness, Dr. Benjamin Rush among others claimed, tended to attack mainly between the ages of twenty and fifty.[14] Thus, when scientists and writers referred to "predisposing debility" in describing the ailments of age, they were well aware that debility was "prevalent, even in the bloom of life, and among those who ought to form the most vigorous and robust part of a nation."[15] All age groups were susceptible to diseases and incapacity of some sort.

Indeed, every disadvantage associated with being old threatened the young and middle-aged as well. Besides physiological pain and decay, everyone risked economic dependency and miserable destitution, the loss of family and friends, and death sooner or later. Because no stage of life was spared sorrow, Americans between 1790 and 1830 considered old people's problems merely aspects of the tragic nature of the human condition.

Believing that suffering was always a part of living, ministers, poets, philosophers, and others who wrote consolatory literature tried to help readers of all ages understand and cope with their current afflictions. It is wrong to entertain hopes of perfect happiness at any point in this transitory life, they claimed, since such aspirations only lead to disappointment. Instead, they encouraged their contemporaries to deal with their problems in a manner aptly summarized by Philip Freneau: "When fortune quits, or our strength decays,/ Pain is our lot, and Patience is our praise."[16]

While they did not advocate that people exult in their pain, writers between 1790 and 1830 nevertheless contended that tragedy nurtured emotions that should be an essential component of everyone's mental outlook. As an essayist in the *North American Review* explained, "The melancholy feelings, when called up by their proper and natural causes and confined to their proper limits, are the parents of almost all of our virtues. The temperament of unbroken cheerfulness is the temperament of insensibility."[17] According to the republican conception of the "happy temperament," melancholy served not only to balance cheerful exuberance but also to make the heart better by promoting compassion for others. A mixture of melancholy, cheer, patience, sympathy, fortitude, hope, and resignation, writers noted, comforted all people in time of need.

The religious teachings of the era complemented and reinforced this stoic attitude toward pain. "The Gospel has opened purer sources of Consolation than are to be found in Polytheism and heathen philosophy."[18] To early nineteenth-century Americans steeped in Protestant theology, the Bible and various homiletic tracts provided both a convincing explanation for afflictions in this world and a hopeful vision of happiness in the hereafter. Religion provided an intellectual, emotional, and social milieu in which to understand how and why grief developed the soul.

In this context, the aged had an important social role to play: by following the advice set forth in consolatory literature, the elderly helped to demonstrate the efficacy of such advice. Although I cannot determine whether most old people actually did adopt "correct" responses to tragedy, it is suggestive that John Adams, a candid and perceptive student of human nature, confirmed at the age of eighty-one the need to face tragedy as a stoic Christian.

Did you ever see a portrait, or a statue of a great man, without perceiving strong traits of pain and anxiety? . . . And who were these sad men? They were aged men, who had been tossed and buffeted in the vicissitudes of life—forced upon profound reflection by grief and disappointment—and taught to command their passions and prejudices. . . . Grief drives men into habits of serious reflection, sharpens the understanding, and softens the heart; it compels them to arouse their reason, to assert its empire over their passions, propensities and prejudices; to elevate them to a superiority over all human events; to give them the *felicis animi immota tranquilitatum*; in short, to make them stoics and Christians. . . . Though stoical apathy is impossible, yet patience, and resignation, and tranquility may be acquired by consideration, in a great degree, very much for the happiness of life.[19]

The means by which John Adams tried to come to grips with grief in his own "sad" last years—resignation, patience, and tranquillity—were the very sources of strength and consolation that republican writers believed would foster charity and virtue in everyone.

The aged helped others put life's ultimate meanings into perspective, therefore, by confirming and exemplifying the perennial principles of the republican theodicy. Having endured hardships throughout their lives, old people were considered ideally suited to affirm the painful limits of human happiness. As they dealt with problems plaguing their declining years, the aged proved the continual importance of patience and faith in coping with adversity throughout life. Precisely because the elderly had years of experience in handling afflictions common to all people, their insights were inspirational and applicable to all ages.

The Romantic Path to Immortality

New intellectual perspectives, blossoming in America during the second quarter of the nineteenth century, gradually modified some of the basic tenets of this republican outlook on the human condition and changed the reasons why old people deserved respect for helping others cope with tragedy. It was less important for people to recognize the common bonds of joy and sorrow linking them with other members of society, according to writers reflecting a romantic sensibility, than it was for each person to grapple with the meaning of his or her own life. For that reason, interpretations written after 1830 of the role older Americans performed in explaining life's challenges and crises resembled, but ultimately went beyond, previous judgments. Commentators played down the previous era's assumption that the good and evil encountered at each stage of life were manifestations of universal phenomena impinging on everybody's life. Instead, more and more commentators sensed that each encounter with pleasure and pain was a unique occurrence in an individual's striving toward immortality.

Although they still acknowledged that every season of life had its problems, writers after 1830 stressed that people faced "*peculiar* sorrows" in old age. For example, antebellum medical scientists generally continued to subscribe to nosologies and etiologies that had prevailed in the United States between 1790 and 1830, but their descriptions of the aged's health diverged in tone and emphasis from earlier analyses. Physicians made a point of stressing the material differences in the health of youth and the health of age in cataloguing the physiological decline and predisposition to disease associated with natural decay. Their schema for classifying the diseases and characteristics of the aged organism seem more elaborate than their predecessors'.[20] Similarly, while noting that poverty among the "righteous" was always unfortunate, essayists observed that it was

especially tragic when a person managed to stay independent throughout life
and then had to spend his or her last years in want. Furthermore, only those
who had experienced a loss of interest in surroundings and new ideas as well
as increasing feelings of uselessness, rejection by youth, and a lifetime of
grieving over the deaths of family members and friends, it was said, could
understand the bitterness of living too long.[21] Since they considered the
problems of growing old intrinsically different from those encountered at
other periods of life, Americans before the Civil War believed that existing
explanations for suffering in old age were inadequate.

In formulating a new rationale for the consolations of age, writers in the
romantic period incorporated many earlier presuppositions. Understanding
the meaning of suffering remained the foremost comfort of age. Like their
predecessors, observers claimed that disabilities gave the aged a certain
elevation above passion and action and enhanced their character. Ministers,
scientists, and essayists continued to urge the elderly to reconcile themselves to their tribulations with a mixture of stoicism and Christianity. And
yet, the "peculiar sorrows" of age were not just phenomena that required
consolation. Americans in the middle decades of the century perceived a
potential social value in the ways older people coped with their dilemmas
that went far beyond earlier notions that the elderly's meekness of spirit,
delight in prayer and the Bible, piety, and resignation to God's will clearly
established them as moral exemplars. Writers between 1830 and 1860
claimed that the old were the only age group truly in the position to grasp
fully the meaning of life and death.

Indeed, to an even greater degree than "republican" writers, "romantic"
commentators emphasized the distinctiveness of the aged's function as a
key to the ultimate truths of the human condition. In so doing, they underscored the excited moralistic spirit of the antebellum era. For while preserving public virtue and instilling proper decorum had always been national
priorities, concern for the perfectibility of the soul and moral self-
improvement was becoming a nationwide obsession by the 1830s. Revivals,
abolitionism, utopian experiments, and the temperance movement among
other things attest to the intense and multifaceted efforts to promote
goodness in a world beset with tragedy and mired in sin.[22] Older people, to
be sure, were not America's only moral watchdogs and crusaders: as historians amply have demonstrated, women, ministers, and others also were
perceived as vital in this capacity. But aged persons were the only members
of the population who could rely on long years of experience in teaching
others how to realize their blessings and to deal with the miseries of mortal
existence.[23] Precisely because longevity was considered a socially beneficial goal obtained only through righteous living, writers in the middle third of
the nineteenth century embellished previous arguments about the inherent
worth of old age. They proclaimed that the old were in the enviable position

of being able to carry out the lessons of benevolence and morality for the greatest good of the greatest number during the longest period of time. The wisdom elderly Americans had accrued through a lifetime of pleasure and pain has shown them how to live and suffer properly. That experience, in turn, enabled them to prepare to die correctly.

Those imbued with the romantic sensibility described old age as *the* transitional stage of development that moderated between life and death. More than anything else, in fact, the elderly's proximity to the supernatural enhanced their special value: having experienced all there was to experience on earth, the aged stood at the ultimate vantage point from which to perceive that which lay beyond.[24] Thus, writers before the Civil War urged all people to observe carefully the aged's reactions and preparations for death and eternal life. "There is a manner of meeting death which is appropriate to a man's manner of life, to the principles which he had held, and which have been the guide of his conduct, . . . which will be a proper *completion* or *rounding out* of the character as a man leaves the world."[25] To die the natural death of an old person who had been upright and successful in surmounting all moral dilemmas in life was a noble goal.

Indeed, tracing the course of life was a profoundly important theme for artists, philosophers, poets, and essayists during the antebellum period. One of the most popular treatments of the subject was the allegorical *Voyage of Life* conceived by Thomas R. Cole, the most famous artist of the Hudson River school. Cole painted four pictures of the voyager on the stream of life: Childhood, Youth, Manhood, and Old Age. For my present purposes, Cole's conception of "old age" merits special attention. The scenery is barren and dull, symbolizing that the world no longer interests the traveler. The voyager, once an infant, has grown old. Storms have battered his boat. An opening in the clouds and a host of angels beckoning the ancient mariner puncture the overall gloom pervading the painting. In the artist's words,

> The chains of corporeal existence are falling away, and already the mind has glimpses of Immortal Life. The angelic Being of whose presence until now the voyager has been unconscious, is revealed to him, and with a countenance beaming with joy, shows to his wondering gaze such as the eye of mortal man has never yet seen.[26]

Old age was the ultimate stage of life in Cole's description of human existence. Considered as a whole, his paintings captured the dynamism, contrarieties, and ambiguities inherent in the process of "becoming." A sense that life is a progressive course of personal, moral, and mental improvement permeates Cole's work as it did other interpretations in the romantic period.[27]

Americans just before the Civil War, in short, did not merely acknowledge the elderly's past accomplishments and present usefulness. Believing that the progress of human life was never direct but moved in ascending circles, like a spiral, ever growing in understanding and self-awareness, many observers proclaimed that old age marked the ultimate stage in the process of self-formation: "An aged Christian is not an old man only; he is of all ages. . . . All that is best in our nature is strong in him."[28] Since old age was considered the stage in which virtue, piety, and all other ennobling characteristics of human nature arrived at their highest perfection, people idealized the attainments of the aged in the United States between 1830 and 1860.

In 1862, at the age of fifty-nine, Ralph Waldo Emerson pulled together more than twenty years of notes jotted in his journals and published an essay on "Old Age" in *The Atlantic Monthly*. The piece is a fitting apostrophe for the pre–Civil War era. Like so many of his contemporaries, Emerson sought inspiration from Cicero's famous treatment of the subject in *De Senectute*. Just as Cicero had defended old age against four alleged liabilities, Emerson pointed to four benefits associated with old age that made it uniquely advantageous over all other stages of life.[29] First, old people had weathered the physical, emotional, and moral dangers of youth and middle age. Second, they rightly understood the relative insignificance of social "success." Since what a person could and could not do had already been determined, an old person was free of the anxieties motivated by a relentless grasp for achieving success. Third, the aged possessed a serenity of thought and behavior that youth lacked. Finally, only the elderly could set their affairs in order in a reasonable manner.

In the middle of his paean to old age, however, Emerson interjected a discordant note as he compared youth and age.

> Youth is everywhere in place. Age, like woman, requires fit surroundings. Age is comely in coaches, in churches, in chambers of State and ceremony, in council-chambers, in courts of justice, and historical societies. . . . But in the rush and uproar of Broadway . . . [f]ew envy the consideration enjoyed by the oldest inhabitant. We do not count a man's years, until he has nothing else to count. . . . In short, the creed of the street is, Old Age is not disgraceful, but immensely disadvantageous.[30]

Emerson dismissed the disadvantages of age by claiming that years of experience assured the elderly an important place in society. "Universal convictions" that justified a favorable status for old people, he asserted, "are not to be shaken by the whimseys of overfed butchers and firemen, or by the sentimental fears of girls who would keep the infantile bloom on their cheeks."[31]

Emerson's essay might be taken as a turning point in the history of ideas about the aged's status in nineteenth-century America. Emerson recognized that at least some people believed that being old was disadvantageous and that not all of age's liabilities could be rationalized convincingly. He did not anticipate, however, that the so-called "creed of the street" would permeate and eventually spoil the favorable estimates, much less the idealizations, of the elderly's role in society then in vogue.

In retrospect, there was no reason for Emerson to have foreseen the imminent assault on existing attitudes about older people's worth. A lifetime of astute observations had convinced him that longevity was a distinctive achievement and that the assets of old age outweighed its defects. He rightly perceived that his contemporaries shared his opinion that the elderly's moral advice was valuable and that their contributions in other endeavors were special. He reflected the dominant opinion of his era when he claimed that the aged generally possessed the insight necessary to put the whole meaning of life into perspective. Finally, Emerson voiced popular sentiment when he claimed that the elderly should enjoy an exclusive social position precisely because old age differed from other stages of life: old people's unique access to life's experiences made them paragons of practical, moral, and spiritual insight, thereby ensuring them respect and wisdom.

And yet, by emphasizing how different old age was from other stages, writers in the romantic period unintentionally made their ideas about the aged's status vulnerable to future attack. As they dwelt on the peculiar disadvantages of age in order to glorify the usefulness of the elderly in interpreting life, essayists before the Civil War accentuated the unpleasant features of growing old more than their immediate predecessors. Asserting that the favorable status of the aged rested on the belief that old age's assets were special and its sorrows distinctive, they conceptually segregated the old people's position from other groups in American society and unwittingly helped to undermine their own exultation of the elderly's usefulness.

Because of the way they perceived reality, there was no reason for Emerson or his contemporaries to suspect that a different set of presuppositions or circumstances might turn every argument for supporting old people's worth to society into a damning indictment. New theories about societal and individual progress, however, emerged in the United States during the latter half of the nineteenth century; industrialization, bureaucratization, and urbanization continued to transform the structure of American society. Reflecting upon and applying these novel notions in an effort to understand the forces reshaping their world, later generations would look from a different perspective at the categories of problems associated with old age that Americans in the romantic era had differentiated through explicit description and idealization.

"Death's Slumber," an undated engraving by E. Heinemann. (Reproduced from the collection of the Smithsonian Institution.)

CHAPTER 3

The Obsolescence of Old Age

During the last third of the nineteenth century, no dramatic event or theory suddenly transformed prevailing perceptions of the elderly's position in society. Many Americans continued to acknowledge the aged's worth and to idealize their usefulness.[1] Some writers, in fact, sought to demonstrate that novel ideas inspired and popularized by Charles Darwin's monumental *Origin of Species* (1859) warranted assigning the aged a favorable place in society. Inferring that Darwinism lent support to the romantic claim that old age represented the culmination of life, Americans sometimes blended a mixture of antebellum notions and current scientific belief about evolution, and argued that the elderly deserved respect because their contributions were unique and their achievements distinctive.[2] Hence, once again we find the resilience of positive opinions about old people's presumed value despite the ceaseless reworking of the normative and intellectual foundations of American culture at large.

Nevertheless, with growing frequency after the Civil War, Americans began to challenge nearly every favorable belief about the usefulness and merits of age that had been set forth by republican and romantic writers and that still appeared in contemporary literature. Instead of depicting the elderly as stately and healthy, more and more observers described them as ugly and disease-ridden. Instead of extolling the aged's moral wisdom and practical sagacity, popular and scientific commentators increasingly concluded that old people were incapable of contributing anything to society. By the outbreak of World War I, if not before, most Americans were affirming the obsolescence of old age.

The period roughly between 1865 and 1914, therefore, constitutes an important transition in the history of ideas about growing old. (More precise dating is impossible because the flowering of predominantly unfavorable perceptions about old people's worth occurred in medical and business

An earlier version of this chapter appeared in *Journal of Social History* 8 (Fall 1974): 48–62, but it has been substantially altered.

circles, among other groups, at different moments and developed at dissimilar rates.) It is not the first time that definitions of the aged's usefulness altered; there had been subtle continuities and changes since at least the 1790s. Nor did scientists or essayists discover any liability or disadvantage associated with old age that earlier observers had not already catalogued. But the era does mark a watershed in which the overall estimation of old people's worth clearly changed.

How, then, do we account for this significant change in perceptions? Why did Americans after the Civil War conceptually strip the aged of roles once described as essential and assign them no new functions to compensate for the loss? It is tempting to say that the answer lies in the shift from romanticism to realism. That is, the evanescence of the romantic sensibility, especially its emphasis on subjective experience, its pious overtones, and its idealistic world view, was eventually displaced by a more objective, secular, and dispassionate perspective.[3] However, this shift taking place in high culture is too diffuse and its timing is too imprecise to explain satisfactorily how and when new ideas arose in the specific sphere of defining older people's roles and places in American life. And while negative opinions about the elderly's worth were consonant with the pessimistic version of Social Darwinism articulated during the latter decades of the nineteenth century, they were neither solely dependent upon nor derived from it.

The obsolescence of old age cannot be fully understood by referring to broad cultural tendencies alone. Rather, it is necessary to delineate and explain the interplay of a particular set of attitudes and circumstances, which vitiated the generally complimentary concepts of older people's status and caused new ones to emerge. As I shall show, the unprecedented disesteem for the elderly reflected and resulted from the impact of new scientific, bureaucratic, and popular ideas converging with innovations in medical practice, the economic structure, and American society itself.

"It's Not Old Age, But Length of Life, Which All Men Desire."

One of the reasons why antebellum America had considered elderly men and women useful was because they exemplified the rules of conduct then considered the surest way of enjoying a ripe old age. Although the aged remained living proof that adhering to prescribed modes of behavior enhanced the possibility of a long life, writers after 1865 gradually became less willing to claim that the elderly possessed the most efficacious means of promoting longevity. Specialized scientific knowledge seemed to promise even greater success than enlightened common sense in increasing life expectancy and preventing disease.

Efforts to improve public health and to promote hygiene received tremendous support after the Civil War. States began creating and authorizing boards of health to establish and regulate more sanitary living standards and to investigate the causes and prevent the spread of contagious diseases. The discovery of different bacteria and the reformulation of the germ theory in the latter half of the nineteenth century, moreover, provided a sounder rationale for combating disease than had been available to earlier sanitary reformers. In addition, observers asserted that reductions in infant and child mortality and increases in life expectancy could be attributed to better infant care and improvement in nutrition at early ages as well as to advances in caring for the sick and infirm.[4] Success in applying new ideas and techniques led Americans to believe not only that people were living longer than ever before but also that more gains could be expected in the future. Improved life expectancy, writers increasingly concluded, "depends on no mysterious law of development. . . . It is the necessary result of agencies so obvious and so powerful in our civilization that we need statistics not so much to prove their existence but to measure their results."[5]

Physicians, biologists, and sanitary engineers, therefore, assumed a greater and highly technical role in studying and advancing the principles conducive to increasing longevity and improving hygiene. Americans after the Civil War still acknowledged the importance of moral and sensible deportment, but they steadily preferred to rely on the advice of experts rather than the insights of experience.[6] As more and more Americans deferred to the collective wisdom of professionals, the value of older men and women as promoters of healthful living decreased.

And yet, through the articles and ideas they contributed to magazines like *Harper's* and *Popular Science Monthly* as well as their own professional journals, scientists and doctors did more than displace the elderly from their long-standing societal function as examples of healthful lifestyles. Advances in American medical theory and practice during the last third of the nineteenth century also legitimized the invidious distinction people were making between desiring a long life and wanting to grow old. The practical question was "not whether we can push the natural age of man to ninety or one hundred years, but whether we can keep our bodies so pure and active, and so preserve the integrity of our mental powers, that between fifty and ninety, our place will not be in seclusion, but in some degree, at least, in the full tide of world's activities."[7] In contrast to earlier medical opinions, scientists gradually concluded that the debilities of age were not simply the result of natural decay, but stemmed from more deplorable causes.

It is important to note that the first important changes in medical ideas about old age occurred across the ocean, especially in France and Germany. Many researchers designed their investigations on the principle, circulating in Europe since the second quarter of the nineteenth century, that it was important to correlate localized pathological lesions with symptoms in identifying particular diseases. Such studies received added impetus after 1858, when Rudolph Virchow demonstrated that one could actually observe pathological lesions in cells under a microscope. Virchow not only improved the possibility of refining localized pathology but also endeavored to synthesize the prevailing concept of pathology with an older and more holistic theory of pathology by stressing the need to observe the total bodily reaction to specific, localized diseases.[8]

The most influential work on old age published in Europe during the 1860s and 1870s was Jean-Martin Charcot's *Leçons cliniques sur les maladies des vieillards et les maladies chroniques* (1867), a systematic study of the relationship between old age and disease among inmates at a large public hospital for women in Paris. Charcot's major finding was that there were some diseases that arose from the general physiological modifications of an aging body, a second group of diseases that existed at other periods of life but presented special characteristics and dangers in old age, and a third class of diseases from which old people seemed to be immune.[9] His clinical work indicated that the degeneration and weakening of the cells of specific organs and vessels during the latter stages of life caused specific diseases. Hence, Charcot documented both the importance of identifying localized structural lesions and recognizing that the bodily reactions associated with diseases at other ages did not always manifest themselves in old age: "In old age, the organs seem, as it were, to become independent of one another; they suffer separately, and the various lesions to which they may become subject are scarcely echoed by the anatomy as a whole."[10]

Charcot's work was not a radical departure from existing ideas about diseases in old age; Charcot acknowledged, for example, that scientists had been studying the pathological manifestations of old age for more than a century. Nor was he the first to gather together in a systematic manner evidence indicating that specific diseases existed in old age.[11] At the time of its publication, however, Charcot's work was considered the most extensively researched exposition based on the belief that one could understand diseases in old age only by clinically investigating localized structural lesions. Charcot's publication was not only accepted as the standard monograph on the subject but also was well circulated; a second edition was published in 1874. It is significant for my purposes that Charcot's study of the diseases of old age was the only European work of its kind to be translated into English.[12] In 1881, William Tuke translated Charcot's lectures for the New Sydenham Society in London, and two New York doctors published an American edition the same year. For the majority of doctors in the United States who were not bilingual, the English translations of

Charcot's lectures provided their first full-length contact with current European ideas about the pathological aspects of growing old.

The timing of the translations themselves, moreover, gave Charcot's
work an importance as a model for future research in the United States far
beyond its actual merits. By 1881, American medical theory and practice
had advanced sufficiently to permit doctors to engage in research using the
same theoretical framework and clinical techniques on which Charcot had
based his inquiry.[13] An increasing number of physicians during the post–
Civil War period were familiar with the concepts, methodology, and instruments necessary to study structural pathology. Doctors and scientists interested in doing research received professional encouragement and rewards
for their work and could associate with medical faculties and hospitals
willing to support pure research. Medical schools at Harvard, Pennsylvania, Columbia, Johns Hopkins, and Michigan and hospitals in metropoli-
tan centers and elsewhere began to receive greater financial support from
the private sector to underwrite research. Thus, when the first English
editions of Charcot's work appeared, the American medical profession was
predisposed to accept and then develop its premises and findings.

This does not mean, of course, that American doctors after the Civil War
suddenly embraced all new medical ideas or rushed into laboratories to look
at lesions under microscopes. Most doctors, in fact, were more inclined to
continue the antebellum practice of recommending ways to postpone the
effects of old age than they were to devote years to investigating its causes.
Articles on old age in popular and scientific journals as well as in family
medical guides typically offered practical advice on personal habits, diet,
and exercise.[14] Prescribed medications further demonstrate the persistence
of traditional practices: homeopaths and other sectarian physicians still
offered recipes for home remedies to cope with minor ailments; some
orthodox doctors continued to recommend opium as an analgesic for the
elderly.[15]

Nevertheless, new ways of conceptualizing, researching, and treating
diseases in old age began to circulate with increasing frequency and
significance in the United States during the last decades of the nineteenth
century. For example, once American doctors began to accept new European ideas about senile pathology, they needed precise, not general, terms
to define its manifestations. "Senility," which was once simply a synonym
for "old age" as a stage of life, now referred specifically to the "weakness
and decrepitude characteristic of old age." The word gradually gained
pathological connotations; it is suggestive that the American biologist
Charles Sedgwick Minot noted in his definition of "senility" for the
Reference Handbook of Medical Science (1885) that he chose to "follow
Charcot closely." Doctors also enlarged their lexicon to describe diseases
peculiar to old age.[16] These new definitions underlined the growing interest

in defining the pathological aspects of old age as unique and localized entities. In addition, more and more American investigators following in the direction elucidated by Charcot began to research and operate on the ailments and diseases of old age.[17] Case studies of senile gangrene, senile bronchitis, senile pneumonia, and senile chorea among other disorders appeared in medical journals. Refined clinical observations of localized lesions also facilitated surgeons' efforts to relieve the suffering of their aged patients.

Some research proved to be controversial and unsuccessful. For example, Dr. Charles E. Brown-Séquard, a French-American scientist chiefly known for his research on the nervous system and adrenal glands, attributed senility to "diminishing action of the spermatic glands," and reasoned that injecting semen into the blood stream of old men might restore lost vigor. In 1889, at the age of seventy-two, Brown-Séquard injected himself with a mixture of water, semen, and testicular fluids and claimed, "I regained at least all the strength I possessed a good many years ago."[18] The effect lasted four weeks. Brown-Séquard's formula appeared on the market within months as "Pohl's Spermine Preparations." Despite the enthusiasm greeting the initial findings, general interest waned after high expectations were not met. The seminal experiment was not rejuvenating: the drug's effect wore off quickly and did not restore complete physical strength. It also was not totally effective: Dr. Brown-Séquard died five years later even though he injected himself regularly with his mixture. Brown-Séquard had not discovered the elixir of life; by studying an aspect of senile pathology, he only had devised a way to excite the nervous system. But his failure neither deterred other scientists from pursuing new lines of inquiry nor discouraged them from publishing revolutionary ideas about the nature of disease in old age.

Indeed, around the turn of the century, Elie Metchnikoff, a bacteriologist working in Paris, believed that he had discovered the cause of old age: poisonous microbes accumulating in the intestines produced toxic reactions that, he claimed, caused the human organism to degenerate and eventually to die. He recommended as an antidote that people drink sour milk, because the lactic acid in it prevented putrefaction in the intestinal tract. Metchnikoff noted that sour milk was a staple in the diet of Bulgarians, who were thought to be Europe's healthiest and longest-lived people. Popular confidence in this panacea was somewhat shaken by the scientist's death at seventy-one. Subsequent research, moreoever, invalidated Metchnikoff's hypothesis that a pathologic phagocytosis caused senescence.[19]

Elie Metchnikoff's significance in the history of medical ideas about old age, however, transcends both his particular theory and his specific therapy for degeneration in old age. Metchnikoff built his theory on Charcot's work, but differed from his predecessor on one essential point: "The senile degeneration of our organism is entirely similar to the lesions induced by certain maladies of a microbiotic origin. Old age, then, is an infectious, chronic disease which is manifested by a degeneration, or an enfeebling of the noble elements, and by the excessive activity of the microphages."[20] Whereas Charcot verified the existence of a senile pathology, Metchnikoff characterized old age as an atrophy *sui generis*.

Metchnikoff's assertion that old age itself was a chronic, infectious disease was well publicized and had a significant, and sometimes paradoxical, impact on medical research and popular thinking at the beginning of the twentieth century. Some researchers, sharing Metchnikoff's opinion that old age was a curable disease, hoped to eradicate toxic disturbances located in various parts of the body. Sir Victor Hursley, for example, concentrated on the degeneration of the thyroid gland; Dr. Arnold Lorand stressed the simultaneous deterioration of several ductless glands.[21] However, many doctors doubted that scientists could ever cure old age precisely because they agreed with Metchnikoff that it *was* a progressive disease. Nihilism flourished among those believing that "the ravages of years remain as irreparable in the twentieth century as they were in the time of Solomon."[22] The general public, meanwhile, kept informed of debates and developments in the medical sciences by reading articles on old age in encyclopedias and popular journals. Regardless of their optimism or pessimism about the advances made or anticipated in aging research, all these articles confirmed that experts had not yet succeeded in making old age more healthy and attractive, and thus they provided a scientific basis for dreading the coming of age: "If there is any disease in the world it is this. No one looks forward to it with eager anticipation. Nobody welcomes it, nobody enjoys it. . . . It is a disease, that is to say it is essentially a pathological condition. . . . But for it there exists no therapy, no cure."[23] Contrary to previous judgments, attaining old age no longer seemed either a remarkable or a desirable achievement.

By the first decade of the twentieth century, therefore, specialists had not only superseded the elderly as experts in health matters but had also convinced the general public that old people suffered incurable pathological disorders. The ultimate result of living a long life, medical evidence confirmed, was often more deleterious than useful. Consequently, new scientific theories and data forced people to reevaluate their opinions about the elderly's value in other capacities.

"Not All of the Centenarians Are Paragons of All the Virtues."

Scientists, almanac compilers, philosophers, and other commentators increasingly challenged the antebellum assumption that surviving to old age proved a person's inherent goodness and sagacity. "Survival was a precondition of progress, but it did not insure progress or define its essence. . . . Survival was a brute fact, not a moral victory."[24] Thus people became less inclined to claim that wisdom necessarily improved with age. In fact, they claimed to have data confirming that old age was a dreadful stage of life ravaged by diseases and debilities that eventually destroyed all cerebral powers.

Research published after the Civil War seemed to demonstrate, contrary to earlier opinions, that people's intellectual faculties declined with age. Sir Francis Galton, an English biologist and statistician, and an American named George M. Beard conducted research in the 1860s and 1870s indicating that people's mental capabilities were greatest between the ages of thirty and forty-five. Significantly, they attributed the decline in intellectual accomplishments after sixty to pathological disorders common to old people.[25] Subsequent studies corroborated their findings. According to W. A. Newman Dorland's *The Age of Mental Virility* (1908), for example, man's creative power developed steadily to the age of sixty and then fell off. "While in the vast majority of cases [of people over sixty] declining physical and mental ability progressed *pari passu* to the cessation of life, there loom up, amid the general wreck of bodily and cerebral powers some striking instances of remarkable vitality and virility, standing out, like beacon lights of hope, far beyond the period of normal decay."[26] Writers cited such evidence, which was consistent with current theories about senile pathology, to substantiate the idea that old age corroded the mental capacities of most men and women.

Many observers claimed, moreover, that old people often compounded their difficulties by making themselves inaccessible to new ideas or alternate ways of doing things. In *Principles of Psychology* (1890), for instance, William James argued that people became more and more enslaved to familiar conceptions and established ways of assimilating ideas as they grew old: "Old-fogyism, in short, is the inevitable terminus to which life sweeps us on."[27] James's reference to "old fogyism" is suggestive. Although the word "fogy" was occasionally used before the Civil War, it did not yet refer exclusively to old people. According to the lexicographers of Webster's dictionary, who cited it for the first time in the 1880 edition, a "fogy" was a "dull old fellow; a person behind the times, over-conservative, or slow:— usually preceded by *old*."[28] By the latter decades of the nineteenth century there was a special term to describe old people who would not, or could not, keep up with the times.

The very factors that accounted for old people's declining mental capacities and decreasing ability to absorb new information seemed to explain their unpleasant personality traits. As George Beard explained, "The querulousness of age, the irritability, the avarice are the resultants partly of habit and partly of organic and functional changes in the brain."[29]

They also provided plausible reasons for questioning an earlier assumption that people invariably gained in moral stature as they aged. "Not all of the centenarians," one commentator pointedly observed, "are paragons of all the virtues."[30]

Old people's unwillingness to conform to cultural conventions, in turn, confirmed the evolving contention that their behavior was not always exemplary. Physicians recommended, for example, that men over fifty and women over forty-five curtail their sex lives. They justified abstention with medical evidence couched in moral tones. Dr. John Harvey Kellogg contended that seminal fluid deteriorated in old age: "Even at its best, its component elements could only represent decrepitude and infirmity, degeneration and senility."[31] The children of old men, he claimed, were feeble and died prematurely. Women, on the other hand, should recognize that menopause signaled the end of sexual activity.[32] Older people who defied the dictates of nature could expect to suffer the consequences. "When the passions have been indulged and their diminishing vigor stimulated, a horrid disease, *satyriasis*, not infrequently seizes upon the imprudent individual, and drives him to the perpetration of the most loathsome crimes and excesses."[33] Others claimed that emotional numbness, loneliness, physical pain, mental anguish, and economic difficulties often drove the elderly to desperate measures. Dr. Elie Metchnikoff, for example, reported that elderly men committed suicide more frequently than young men and that the aged poor were more likely to take their lives than those who were financially secure.[34]

Contemporary medical research and everyday observations, therefore, persuaded Americans to reject the antebellum notion that being old intrinsically bestowed better judgment or guaranteed moral behavior. "Years do not make sages;" the *New England Almanac for 1872* informed readers, "they make only old men."[35] Reaching this verdict, however, did not automatically lead to the deduction that old people were physically, mentally, or morally incapable of contributing to society. The conviction that old age was a period of economic obsolescence arose primarily in the minds of observers and participants in big business.

"The Superannuated Man"

The rise of large-scale business and organizations is one of the major factors affecting life in late nineteenth-century America. Although the slow transition from an agrarian to an industrial-based economy had already begun, the big business corporation as well as a variety of other economic institutions and government offices did not grow in size and scope until after the Civil War. These new structures had a profound effect: "Corporate structures gradually altered the meaning of property, the circumstances and motivations of economic activity, and the careers and expectations of most citizens."[36] Accompanying the evolution of these organizations was the emerging idea that bureaucratic principles should be employed to ensure that workers performed tasks competently and punctually and to establish channels of authority and responsibility. Efficiency had become the *sine qua non* of any successful enterprise by the turn of the century. Consequently, impersonality symbolized a bureaucratic order in which functions and procedures, not particular men, were indispensable.[37]

Precisely because the rise of large corporate structures and the formulation of bureaucratic principles were incremental processes, Americans did not instantly or completely overturn favorable assessments of the aged's worth in the marketplace. Some writers as late as 1900 still affirmed that old people had vital roles to play. Even if the elderly were not actively directing operations, their experience assured them a place as consultants; at the very least, they could perform ancillary tasks.[38] And yet, observers of the emerging industrial order did become more articulate over time in describing how new conditions and ideas were reducing Americans' dependence on older workers' seasoned experience to ensure economic success.

> In the search for increased efficiency, begotten in modern time by the practically universal worship of the dollar . . . gray hair has come to be recognized as an unforgivable witness of industrial imbecility, and experience the invariable companion of advancing years, instead of being valued as common sense would require it to be, has become a handicap so great as to make the employment of its possessor, in the performance of tasks and duties for which his life work has fitted him, practically impossible.[39]

An unmistakable shift was occurring in perceptions of the elderly's value in the labor force.

A new trend in discharging employees after they had attained a certain age provides one of the clearest indications that ideas about old people's usefulness were changing. The practice had precedents: some states had set retirement ages for judges in the antebellum period. And yet, infirmity, debility, or an employer's displeasure were the only reasons why older workers had normally been forced to quit their jobs; age per se had not been a decisive factor in leaving the labor force before the Civil War. Then, between 1861 and 1915, the federal government and especially private industry began to design and implement policies that discharged workers because they were considered too old to stay on the job.

The first federal retirement measure became law in December 1861, when Congress passed an act requiring any naval officer below the rank of vice admiral who was at least sixty-two to resign his commission; the retirement age for naval officers was raised to sixty-four in 1916.[40] The earliest policy applying to sailors entitled them to retire, because of age or infirmity, on half pay after twenty years of service. There was no fixed age for retirement for sailors until 1899, however, when a minimum age (fifty), not a maximum limit, was imposed.[41] A measure passed in 1869 permitted, but did not require, a federal judge to retire after serving ten years and reaching the age of seventy on a pension equal to his salary at the time of retirement.[42] "An Act to promote the efficiency of the Revenue-Cutter service" (1902) required all incapacitated officers to be dropped from service by the president; all officers were required to retire at sixty-four. Because these were the only retirement policies instituted at the federal level by World War I, it is fair to conclude that the practice of retiring government officials was still in the embryonic stages and affected only a limited number. Nor were there any uniform standards in the measures established: specific acts set different retirement ages for each group; receiving a pension was not always contingent on having served a certain number of years.

Retirement policies in the private sector also were in the formative stages. Transportation companies inaugurated the earliest pension programs. In 1875, the American Express Company permitted workers past sixty to receive some compensation upon retirement. The Baltimore and Ohio Railroad retirement policy (1884), which stipulated minimum age (sixty-five) and service (ten years) requirements, has been called the "pioneer in this country in the movement to pension its employees."[43] There was considerable variation in the pension programs instituted. For example, although most corporations did not require workers to contribute to pension funds, contributory programs did exist. The age of retirement and the number of years of service required for an employee to be eligible for a pension also differed from company to company. Nevertheless, it is apparent that an increasing number of firms appreciated the need to establish some sort of policy to remove older workers from the labor force. Although only eight companies instituted programs between 1874 and 1900, twenty-three others began policies between 1901 and 1905, and twenty-nine more offered employee retirement pensions between 1906 and 1910. Ninety-nine additional corporations initiated policies between 1911 and 1915.[44] The idea of requiring people to retire or offering them the option to do so because they had attained a particular age was gaining acceptance in the private sector.

Disesteem for older employees' worth clearly motivated a company's decision to exact mandatory retirement. As F. Spencer Baldwin, an economics professor at Boston University, explained:

> It is well understood nowadays that the practice of retaining on the pay-roll aged workers who can no longer render a fair equivalent for their wages is wasteful and demoralizing. The loss is twofold. In the first place, payment of full wages to

workers who are no longer reasonably efficient, and in the second place, there is
the direct loss entailed by the slow pace by the presence of worn-out veterans, and
the consequent general demoralization of the service.[45]

From management's viewpoint, retirement systems improved efficiency
and morale by removing expendable workers. From a larger perspective, it
was claimed that corporations that offered job security, merit promotions,
and adequate compensation in old age "inevitably attract the highest grade
of men and women, and obtain from them the most efficient work."[46]

The meanings of "retirement" and "superannuation" changed to embrace the policies implemented by large-scale organizations. The primary
sense of "retire" in 1828—to withdraw from public notice—had become
obsolete according to the lexicographers of the 1880 edition of Webster's
American Dictionary. Instead, they attributed a new meaning to the verb:
"retire" among other things meant "to cause to retire; specifically to desig-
nate as no longer qualified for active service; as to *retire* a military or naval
officer." An additional definition was added to the verb "superannuate":
"To give pension to, on account of old age, or other infirmity."[47] Note the
derogatory attitude toward old age displayed in both definitions. Retirement now meant that people reached a stage of their careers at which they
were *no longer qualified* for gainful employment because of age. Reaching
old age entitled a person to a pension just as other disabilities qualified
workers for special considerations.

The unprecedented devaluation of older workers' usefulness was felt
even more deeply and pervasively in the marketplace than was signified by
new retirement policies and dictionary definitions. Many writers commented on "the tendency—visibly increasing in this country—of relegating
the older and middle-aged men to the oblivion of an 'innocuous desuetude.' "[48] Laborers and craftsmen over forty-five who were worn out or
displaced by machines found reemployment opportunities limited. Taking
an inferior job was not always a satisfactory solution, writers warned, since
workers rarely regained steps taken backward.[49] If employment prospects
were poor for those in their fifties, they were even worse for people in their
sixties. "The things that most promote the welfare of the wage-earning class
militate most against old age employment. . . . The old man today . . . slow,
hesitating, frequently half-blind and deaf, is sadly misplaced amid the death
dealing machinery of a modern factory."[50] The evidence reveals similarly
negative sentiments about older workers outside the factory gates. Civil
Service employees over sixty were said to retain only "partial efficiency"
despite years of service; older clergymen, lawyers, or doctors, it was said,
were rarely offered new opportunities for service or advancement.[51] While
recognizing that men often ceased working more abruptly than women,
commentators noted that society often made both sexes feel superfluous.
"We soothe our souls and say to ourselves, 'Grandmother is comfortable
and content.' We rarely ask if grandmother is useful and happy." [52] Writers

described their contemporaries as treating older women as if they were baubles with only negligible jobs to fulfill.

Thus by the turn of the century, even those who asserted that the elderly *could* contribute something to society admitted that they no longer reflected the opinions of most Americans.[53] Changing circumstances and new priorities seemed to have diminished the aged's worth as veterans of productivity and enhanced the purported value of youth. "Not all the sandwich men in our large cities or the sitters in our public parks are victims of intemperance or shiftlessness; they are, in many cases, the product of an industrial and economic system that thrives only on young blood."[54] This observation was not confined to the economic sphere. Modern conditions, people increasingly believed, required youth, not age, to assume the roles of advancing society and putting life into perspective.

"Old Age, Like Death, Is Merely Incidental."

Although Americans after the Civil War generally considered it axiomatic that the human condition improved as society progressed, this did not mean that the human life cycle necessarily followed the same pattern of development. "The dominant aspect of evolution was to be not the genesis of species, but the progress of Civilization."[55] Progress had a dual nature. Blessed with infinite possibilities, civilization was ultimately evolving to its most perfect culmination. Human development, on the other hand, was finite. The retrogression and eventual demise of man was viewed as a necessary and inevitable law of nature that insured the continual unfolding of mankind's destiny.[56]

This concept of evolutionary progress had ominous implications for the aged. New scientific theories and economic realities convinced Americans that individuals declined in old age as human existence marched on. Because they perceived the elderly to be afflicted with pathological disorders and no longer able to keep up with the pace, it is not surprising that writers claimed old people had lost their grasp on the meaning and nature of societal development. Presuming it to be a law of nature that an individual's connection with societal progress relaxed with the coming of age, Americans gradually discounted the value of old people's insights and claimed that young people were in the best position to understand the meaning of life.

Old men cherish a fond delusion that there is something mystically valuable in the mere quantity of experience. Now the fact is, of course, that it is the young people who have all the really valuable experience. It is they who have constantly to face new aspects of life, who are getting the whole beauty and terror and cruelty of the world in all its fresh and undiluted purity. . . . Old age lives in the delusion that it has improved and rationalized its youthful ideas by experience and stored-up wisdom, when all it has done is to damage them more or less—usually more.[57]

More and more people came to the conclusion that digesting a lifetime of experience in old age served little purpose. Circumstances seemed to be changing too rapidly to warrant copying the practices of the past; the elderly often imitated or reiterated earlier insights anyway.[58] Youth's enthusiasm, versatility, self-confidence, and pluck, it was said, more than compensated for the lack of seasoned experience. Psychologist G. Stanley Hall captured the heightened sense of importance attached to "youth" as a vital social asset in his monumental work, *Adolescence* (1905): "Despite our lessening fecundity, our over-schooling, 'city-fication,' and spoiling, the affectations we instill and the repressions we practice, [youths] are still the light and hope of the world."[59] Historians point to the economic, educational, and religious changes occurring in the latter quarter of the nineteenth century as factors leading to the tremendous value placed on youth. Because of young people's ambiguous relationship to a society that simultaneously abhorred and participated in the quest for power and order affecting every aspect of existence, radicals and conservatives alike could agree on the appropriateness of that stage of life as a symbol of regenerative power.[60]

Consequently, Americans after the Civil War increasingly challenged the antebellum notion that youth should heed the wisdom of age, and proposed instead that youth was the most exalted stage of life. "As a rule the energy which moves the world in the right direction is that of young men, and correspondingly and naturally the only deference and respect worth having or that can bring satisfaction and happiness to the recipient go to them."[61] This is not the first time in American history, of course, that people celebrated young men and women's zest and potential. Furthermore, pages of advertisements for hair dyes or "physical culture rejuvenation" programs and advice columns recommending that older women wear brighter clothes or stop knitting in the far corner of the parlor represent variations on an age-old phenomenon: many Americans have been trying to look and act younger than their years ever since Ponce de Leon first searched for the fountain of youth.[62] And yet, while it would be incorrect to claim that the cult of youth instigated or even necessitated the depreciation of age, it is clear that the changes in the social as well as economic structure of society, coupled with new ideas about the meaning of progress and experience, forced Americans to reevaluate the relative merits of both age groups and to reach a new verdict. "The whole world is charged with youth," most were concluding by the turn of the century. "Old age, like death, is merely incidental."[63]

The association of death with age as well as the implication that both were incidental to the twentieth-century world of the young is tantalizing. Before we can accept such an observation as representative of the period, far more research must be done on the history of attitudes toward death per se. Nevertheless, primary resources and recent scholarship do suggest that new attitudes toward death may have exaggerated Americans' exultation of youth and denigration of age. Advances in science and technology did not mitigate youth's fear of death, but they apparently lessened the risk of dying young: actuarial statistics computed at the time indicated that the death rate was declining after the Civil War for all age groups under fifty. Improvements in sanitation and public health promised more favorable mortality rates for all but the elderly.[64] Writers reasoned, moreover, that the potential problems of overcrowding and cultural stagnation in a world "over-shadowed by too many hoary Methuselahs" made the elderly's demise societally beneficial. In addition, there was an acceptable biological explanation for death among the aged: life was finite because wornout tissues became increasingly vulnerable to pathological disorders and decay.[65] There was even psychological evidence suggesting that the old, unlike the young, were reconciled to dying. According to a study conducted in 1896 on the relationship between old age and death, a majority of old people thought life was most enjoyable in youth, but would not care to live life over and longed for death.[66]

Hence, theories propounded and evidence presented by biologists, statisticians, public health experts, and psychologists among others confirmed that old people were in the best position to understand the meaning of death. Had the republican and romantic assumptions about the need for all people to come to grips with their own mortality continued to prevail, Americans might still have recognized that old people's perceptions on dying were a valuable asset. But unlike their predecessors, people tended to ignore the potential usefulness of old people's proximity to death. Perhaps they had no other choice, given their belief that youth had a monopoly on all valuable experiences. As William James noted in *The Varieties of Religious Experience* (1901), the reality of death poignantly reminded people that "old age has the last word: the purely naturalistic look at life, however enthusiastically it may begin, is sure to end in sadness."[67] Because the aged had the last word about the inevitability of death, they were excluded from a world awed by the vitality of youth, a world that increasingly chose to deny the existence of death. "Slowly and with difficulty the septuagenarians climb the steep hill leading to the great temple of youth. . . . They beat at the doors, and alas! these do not open. They crave only admittance, and a stool in a quiet corner, but the ruthless revellers turn a deaf ear."[68] The young refused the old admission into their world. Youths no longer considered it vital to acknowledge the wisdom and talents of age; they discounted its worth, feared its association with death and excluded it from their midst.

Because of changes after the Civil War in societal patterns and cultural trends, Americans by the outbreak of World War I no longer claimed that the elderly exclusively fulfilled roles that would guarantee them respect. As efforts to increase life expectancy and improve hygiene became more technical and successful, specialists gradually replaced the aged as promoters of healthful longevity. New ideas about pathological disorders weakening the intellectual capacities and moral faculties at advanced stages of life, which the elderly's own seemingly aberrant behavior confirmed, undermined older people's functions as guardians of virtue. Science alone, however, did not condemn the elderly to uselessness. Americans increasingly perceived that the rise of large-scale organizations and the implementation of new bureaucratic principles not only reduced the need to tap the aged's assets but also accentuated their handicaps. In fact, the growing belief that society was changing at a progressively quicker rate further reduced the estimated value of the elderly's cumulative experience; "youth" was thought to be most attuned to modern conditions and most capable of ensuring continued progress. Thus, the stage of life once characterized as the culmination of human existence had become obsolescent.

The unprecedented devaluation of old people's worth is fraught with irony. For it was the lingering romantic notion that every stage of life was unique that encouraged writers, faced with different circumstances and armed with new ideas, to revise the value system implicit in earlier conceptions of the stages of life. Observers between 1865 and 1914 increasingly explained that the heightened worth of youth arose in response to, and as a product of, a new realistic era. Yet writers justified youth's importance by appropriating the assets previously ascribed to the old. Hence, they increasingly contended that the elderly lacked the very experience, wisdom, and power that earlier generations had once claimed made it sensible for youth to honor, or at least heed, age. Perhaps even more ironically, this new, objective, tough, vigorous realism was premised in part on the denial of death. Death had not lost its sting, of course, but new ideas and conditions prevailing in society did enable contemporaries to reach the conclusion that the reduced probability of dying young was a clear indication of the march of progress in the United States. Hence, more and more Americans in the last decades of the nineteenth century overcame death by ignoring it in youth and associating it with age.

PART II

The Demographic and Socioeconomic Dimensions of Old Age in American History

Photo by C. H. Gilbert, c. 1910. (Reproduced from the collection of the Library of Congress.)

CHAPTER 4

The Rhetoric and Realities
of Growing Old Diverge
in Nineteenth-Century America

Thus far I have confined my attention to *perceptions* of the value and functions of the elderly in American society between 1790 and 1914; very little has been said about their *actual* demographic, occupational, and economic positions. The distinction is critical. Comments by contemporary writers do not necessarily convey an accurate, "objective" description of the way elderly men and women lived in the past. Fortunately, published census volumes, among other sources, provide much of the information needed to ascertain the size and composition of the aged population, the percentage of older workers in the labor force, and the types of jobs they held, as well as the nature and extent of old age dependency before World War I. One can also determine, after reconstructing a demographic and socioeconomic history of old age, how uniformities and variations in popular ideas about older Americans may have been related to long-term alterations in the elderly's situation. Indeed, knowing that overall estimations of old people's value first began to change markedly during the latter third of the nineteenth century, I shall investigate whether changes in old people's actual condition caused new ideas about the elderly to emerge.

Three relationships between "rhetoric" and "reality" are possible. First, marked alterations in the aged's circumstances could have precipitated unfavorable evaluations concerning their usefulness. This hypothesis posits that there were subtle but significant increases in the number of older people in the population, reductions in their employment opportunities, and/or changes in the plight of aged dependents before the Civil War. Because antebellum writers did not recognize the importance of these developments at first, they continued to affirm and even idealize the elderly's relatively favorable social position. As the continuing deterioration of older people's position in society became more and more apparent, however, Americans began to revise their opinions about growing old and to denigrate the elderly.

A second possibility is that changes in conceptions of old people's status and in the aged's actual place in society occurred simultaneously. If so, one would argue that notions about the older Americans' overall worth remained unchanged before the Civil War partly because the elderly's actual conditions were fairly stable throughout the era. Then, increasingly after 1865, the proportion of persons over sixty-five grew, the percentage of gainfully employed elderly men and women declined, and the incidence of old-age pauperism swelled. Discernible discontinuities in older people's circumstances, coupled with the contemporaneous transformation of the structural and cultural bases of American society, therefore, necessitated a redefinition of the elderly's functions and value.

A third relationship is conceivable. The truly profound changes in the elderly's demographic and socioeconomic status may have taken place after World War I, not before. If so, it would appear that Americans already considered older people obsolete burdens before the aged's actual situation, statistically speaking, warranted such a verdict. According to this interpretation, it would remain accurate to argue that new ideas and developments in society at large had an enormous impact on prevailing assessments of the aged. However, it would be erroneous to claim that these same forces simultaneously wrought the most important changes that ever occurred in the elderly's observed status.

It must now be determined which of the three models most accurately describes the interplay between evolving ideas about older Americans and unfolding patterns in the elderly's actual situation prior to 1914. The obvious prediction at the outset is that changes in the aged's circumstances presaged and/or corroborated negative judgments about their value. But tracing older people's demographic and socioeconomic trends over the longest possible time frame may reveal an unanticipated divergence between the rhetoric and the reality of growing old in nineteenth-century America.

Demographic Patterns

The absolute number of old people living in the United States has been increasing since at least 1830, the first year in which the federal census office published such information (see table 4.1). The 1830 census reported that 420,840 white men and women were at least sixty years old. Nearly 960,000 Americans were over sixty in 1850. There were more than twice as many old people in 1870, four times as many in 1890, eight times as many in 1920, and nineteen times as many in 1950; there were thirty times as many elderly in 1970 as in 1850. The same trend obtains for the population over sixty-five. The 1870 census reported that 1,153,649 Americans were sixty-

Table 4.1—Aged Population in the United States, 1830–1970 (in thousands)

Year	Age	
	Over 60	Over 65
1830*	421	...
1840*	559	...
1850	959	...
1860	1,351	...
1870	1,937	1,154
1880	2,822	1,723
1890	3,887	2,417
1900	4,860	3,080
1910	6,225	3,950
1920	7,925	4,933
1930	10,358	6,633
1940	13,694	9,019
1950	18,328	12,270
1960	23,772	16,679
1970	28,682	20,177

SOURCE: Calculated from U.S. Bureau of the Census data

*whites only

five years old or older. By 1900, slightly more than three million people were at least sixty-five; the figure surpassed nine million in 1940 and soared past twenty million in 1970. The number of older Americans has grown tremendously, especially in the twentieth century.

The relative number of all Americans considered "old" has also been growing over time. Men and women over sixty constituted anywhere from 1.7% to 6.4% of the population listed in scattered eighteenth-century state and town records.[1] Assuming that at least 1.7% of the total population was over sixty by the Revolution, it is very unlikely that the proportion of *all* older Americans nationwide increased any more than 1% between 1790 and 1830. The evidence in table 4.2 indicates, in fact, that the most profound increases in the proportion of old people in the United States have occurred during the twentieth century. The percentage of the population over sixty grew rather gradually until 1920, and then more rapidly within the past fifty years. A comparable and even more striking change occurred in the proportion of the population over sixty-five. There was a 59% rise in the relative number of people at least sixty-five years old between 1870 and 1920, and an incredible 115% increase between 1920 and 1970.

The growth of the aged population has been steady but not uniform; the greatest increases have taken place since World War I. This strongly suggests that negative perceptions of the aged's role in society probably had emerged before older people constituted a noticeably larger share of the total population. And yet, before accepting this conclusion, other demographic patterns should be explored. It is possible that the statistics examined so far mask gradual but crucial changes in the composition of the older population. For example, if more and more aged men and women

Table 4.2—Percentage of Aged in the Population, 1830–1970

	Age	
Year	Over 60	Over 65
1830*	4.0%	...
1840*	4.4	...
1850	4.1	...
1860	4.3	...
1870	5.0	2.9%
1880	5.6	3.4
1890	6.2	3.8
1900	6.4	4.0
1910	6.8	4.3
1920	7.5	4.6
1930	8.4	5.4
1940	10.4	6.8
1950	12.1	8.1
1960	13.1	9.2
1970	14.1	9.9

SOURCE: Calculated from U.S. Bureau of the Census data

*whites only

actually were perceived to be infirm and/or incapacitated, this could explain why opinions about the elderly's usefulness began to change. It might not simply have been an increasing proportion of people over sixty or sixty-five years old, but rather a growing percentage of much older people in their late seventies, eighties, or nineties that prompted Americans to devalue the aged's worth. After all, current health statistics clearly demonstrate that people over seventy-five were more likely than those not so old to suffer the chronic disabilities and debilities associated with advanced years.

Evidence in published federal censuses however, severely undermines the hypothesis that unfavorable opinions about the elderly emerged before World War I because Americans saw more very aged and possible debilitated people in their midst. The proportion of the population over sixty that has attained eighty years remained almost constant between 1870 and 1920. The subset of "old" old people then rose sharply thereafter. A similar pattern prevails for the proportion of the elderly population older than seventy-five. In 1870, 17% of all Americans over sixty were also over seventy-five; the relative size of this age group increased only 1.6% during the next fifty years. The proportion of older Americans over seventy-five then swelled from 19.2% to 26.6% between 1940 and 1970 (see table 4.3). Hence the subset of very old people in the population actually did not gain a significantly larger proportional share of the elderly sector until after 1940.

Efforts to describe fully the longitudinal changes in other components of the aged population are hampered because the federal census did not begin reporting people over sixty-five by sex, race, and place of birth until 1870. This means that there is no hard evidence to reject the hypothesis that demographic shifts *within* the aged population before 1870 caused subsequent

Table 4.3—Percentage of the Very Old in the Population over 60 Years of Age, 1870–1970

Year	Age	
	Over 75	Over 80
1870	17.0%	8.0%
1880	17.8	7.8
1890	18.2	8.2
1900	18.3	7.7
1910	18.6	7.9
1920	18.6	7.7
1930	18.4	...
1940	19.2	...
1950	21.0	9.3
1960	22.5	10.0
1970	26.6	13.2

SOURCE: Calculated from U.S. Bureau of the Census data

observers to discard antebellum conceptions of the elderly's worth and functions. Nevertheless, it is doubtful that there was any radical change in the relative number of any of the subsets of the elderly population before the Civil War, because the aggregate proportion of old people increased very little between 1830 and 1870. Furthermore, the available data indicate that the most striking rise in the percentage of any subgroup of the aged population and the most significant changes in the composition of the elderly population as a whole have occurred since 1920.

It seems unlikely, for instance, that either the slowly widening difference in the total proportions of men and women who were old or the fluctuations in the male-female ratios of the elderly population before World War I prompted new ideas about growing old.[2] The proportions of all men and women over sixty-five were identical during the latter part of the nineteenth century. In 1900, 4.0% of all men were over sixty-five, compared to 4.1% of all women; by 1920, the figures were 4.6% and 4.7% respectively. Probably few people noticed that a somewhat greater proportion of women than men were over sixty-five. Variations in the sexual distribution of the aged population also seem inconsequential before 1920. A slight majority of all older people throughout the period were males: 50.3% of all Americans over sixty-five were men in 1870, compared to 50.4% in 1920. As I shall discuss in greater detail in the next chapter, the truly remarkable changes occurred after World War I, thus *after* negative conceptions about old people's worth had become predominant.

Analyzing the trends of the elderly black and white populations over time reveals different patterns, but leads essentially to the same conclusion. About 2.5% of all blacks were over sixty-five years old in 1870, compared to 3.1% of all whites; the figures in 1920 were 3.2% and 4.8% respectively.[3] Since the difference in the proportions of older whites and blacks widened over time, it is doubtful that emerging negative attitudes about old people were covertly racist. Such a conjecture is further undermined upon noticing that the percentage of all Americans over sixty-five who were black actually *declined* steadily during the period. Hence alternations in the racial composition of the elderly population probably did not have any connection with new ideas about the elderly's worth.

Although on the basis of existing evidence one cannot entirely rule out the possibility that shifts in the absolute and relative numbers of aged immigrants fomented unfavorable opinions about older Americans' social value, far more convincing data are necessary before such a hypothesis could be accepted. Nativist sentiments conceivably might have reinforced the growing disesteem for the elderly between 1870 and 1910, since the proportion of immigrants in the older population was greatest during that period.[4] (In 1900, 30.1% of all people over sixty-five were foreign-born; the percentage has never been higher.) And yet, other facts and figures erode the argument's plausibility. Contemporary writers who disparaged aged immigrants, for instance, typically were discussing an aspect of the "immigrant problem," not the plight of old people per se.[5] The demographic history of aged immigrants, moreover, conforms to the long-range patterns of every other elderly subgroup in at least one major respect: the most dramatic increases in the proportion of foreign-born Americans who were old occurred after World War I.

Indeed, the growth rate of the elderly foreign-born group, like that of all other components of the older population, was least impressive precisely during the decades in which new estimates of the worth of the aged were arising.[6] The rate of growth for every group slowed down in the latter part of the nineteenth century, reaching its nadir sometime between 1890 and 1920. Each component's growth rate then began to increase after 1920. Because this pattern is pervasive, it tends to contradict hypotheses suggesting that conceptions of older people's value declined because the number of elderly men and women—blacks or whites, native or foreign-born—was growing at a perceptibly greater rate between the Civil War and World War I.

Nor does it seem very probable that data aggregated at the national level hide any regional peculiarities that might indicate a direct relationship between shifting attitudes toward the aged and demographic changes in the elderly population before 1914 (see table 4.4). Regional patterns actually are consistent with national trends in three important ways. First, although the percentage of old people has always been increasing, the most dramatic increases have occurred after World War I. Second, the proportion of aged men and women as well as native-born and foreign-born whites became more pronounced after 1920.[7] Third, the aged population's rates of growth at the regional level (particularly in the Northeast, where much of the evidence about older people was written) conform to the national model: every subgroup in New England and the Mid-Atlantic states grew more slowly during the decades between 1880 and 1920 than between 1870 and 1880;

Table 4.4—Percentage of the Population over 65 Years of Age, by Region, 1870–1970

Year	Region			
	Northeast	North Central	South	West
1870	4.2%	2.4%	2.6%	1.2%
1890	4.8	3.8	3.0	2.5
1910	5.1	4.0	3.3	3.8
1930	5.7	6.3	4.3	5.8
1950	8.7	8.9	6.9	7.9
1970	10.6	10.1	9.6	8.9

SOURCE: Calculated from U.S. Bureau of the Census data

each component of the aged population then grew more rapidly after 1920 (see table 4.5).[8] Reconstructing the demographic history of old age at the regional level, in short, corroborates the credibility of previous findings.

Finally, it is possible that conceptions about the elderly's worth changed as more and more Americans (particularly older ones) lived in an urban environment, a setting often described as a mecca for the young and a wasteland for the aged. For that reason, the proportions of older Americans residing in rural areas, small cities, and large urban centers over time should be determined. I am especially interested in the northeast section of the United States, since so many of the publishers and writers of literary evidence were located there and because so many states in that region became predominantly urban between 1860 and 1920.

Unfortunately, the inadequacy of statistics gathered by the federal census bureau impedes my study. (No nationwide age-specific statistics exist for urban populations before 1890; the way the 1900 and 1910 data are tabulated precludes their usage for my purposes.) Consequently, I must rely on state-level data to give some sense of the rural-urban shift in the nineteenth century. I have selected the urban populations of three states— Rhode Island, New York, and Michigan—not only for the availability and quality of their census records, but also because they represent different patterns of urbanization.[9] Rhode Island has always been the nation's most urban state: 88.5% of all Rhode Islanders and more than three-quarters of its citizens over sixty lived in an urban environment by 1865. Hence, the state's aged population already was overwhelmingly urban before the era in which ideas about old age were changing nationally. New York, on the other hand, became predominantly urban after 1865; a majority of the state's elderly lived in urban areas by 1910. Michigan's population also became more than 50% urban, albeit at a later date, during the period in which Americans were reevaluating old people's worth. Most people in Michigan did not live in urban areas until the 1910s, when the auto industry mushroomed; 51.9% of the population over sixty still lived in rural areas in 1920. Thus, all three states became urbanized before the nation at large: a majority of all Americans were not reported as residing in urban areas until the 1920 census, and most older persons dwelled in rural locations until an even later date (see table 4.6).

Table 4.5—Growth Rates of the Population over 65 Years of Age in the Northeast, 1870-1940

Subject	Years						
	1870–80	1880–90	1890–1900	1900–1910	1910–20	1920–30	1930–40
*New England states**							
Male	.027	.017	.007	.017	.012	.012	.036
Female	.024	.016	.011	.015	.012	.022	.030
Black	...	...	...	.018	.019	.028	.044
White	.026	.016	.009	.016	.012	.017	.033
Foreign-born white	.061	.057	.020	.030	.017	.039	.029
Native-born white	.020	.006	.006	.011	.011	.024	.035
*Mid-Atlantic states**							
Male	.033	.028	.014	.021	.017	.030	.032
Female	.036	.026	.019	.022	.018	.029	.032
Black	...	...	...	.021	.021	.036	.068
White	.034	.026	.017	.021	.017	.029	.031
Foreign-born white	.049	.038	.026	.019	.010	.029	.033
Native-born white	.028	.022	.013	.023	.021	.030	.030

SOURCE: Calculated from U.S. Bureau of the Census data

NOTE: The following formula was used to calculate the growth rate: $\frac{P_2}{P_1} = e^{rn}$

where "P_1" represents the population at the initial date, "P_2" represents the population at a later date, "r" represents the annual rate of growth, "e" represents the natural logarithm, and "n" represents the exact number of years between P_1 and P_2.

* I used the regional schema devised by the Inter-University Consortium for Political and Social Research (ICPSR). New England states include Connecticut, Maine, Massachusetts, New Hampshire, Rhode Island, and Vermont. Mid-Atlantic states include Delaware, the District of Columbia, New Jersey, New York, and Pennsylvania.

Table 4.6—Selected Statistics on the Aged Population in Urban Areas, 1855–1970

Case Study Area	Population in Urban Setting
Rhode Island Cities over 10,000	
1865	
Total population	50.9%
Members of population over 60	42.6
1895	
Total population	73.4
Members of population over 60	64.1
New York cities over 100,000	
1855	
Total population	24.1
Members of the population over 60	13.8
1875	
Total population	35.3
Members of population over 60	21.4
1920	
Total population	65.6
Members of population over 60	41.7
Michigan cities over 10,000	
1895	
Total population	26.3
Members of population over 60	21.9
United States urban areas over 2,500	
1910	
Total population	45.6
Members of population over 65	42.9
1920	
Total population	51.2
Members of population over 65	47.4
1930	
Total population	56.1
Members of population over 65	53.1
1940	
Total population	56.5
Members of population over 65	56.2
*1960**	
Total population	69.9
Members of population over 65	69.0
*1970**	
Total population	73.5
Members of population over 65	72.9

SOURCE: Calculated from U.S. Bureau of the Census data and pertinent state census data

*definitions used in 1960 and 1970

The extent of urbanization in Rhode Island, New York, and Michigan suggests that an increase in the proportion of old people in an urban setting could have influenced new ideas about the elderly. It is worth noting, however, that even in states that became extensively urban before the country as a whole, the process of urbanization appears to have directly affected older people to a lesser degree than it did the general population. Old people in the three case studies were less likely than any other age group to live in cities, especially the largest ones. The aged were more often found

in rural locations than the average citizen. Thus, insofar as the sheer pervasiveness of urbanization shapes cultural norms and conditions, it is conceivable that an urban milieu has had a greater impact on ideas about the
aged as well as their actual circumstances in the twentieth century, when
most older Americans live in urban areas, than in the nineteenth century,
when only a minority did.

This suggests that the relationship between the number of urban dwellers
over sixty and negative conceptions of old age might best be understood in
economic rather than demographic terms. Perhaps the decisive factor has
not been whether elderly persons dwelled in an urban or rural environment,
but whether they were able to support themselves where they lived.
Suppose, for instance, that there was relatively little difference in work
participation rates among older men in primarily agrarian and basically
urban areas of the country in the nineteenth century. One could then argue
that urbanization in its initial stages fostered unfavorable ideas about old
people's usefulness before it adversely affected the elderly's opportunities
to support themselves and to contribute to the support of others. Therefore, I
shall move from discussing the aged as a demographic subset of the population to examining changes in proportions of older men and women working
in the United States.

Occupational Trends

The earliest reliable nationwide age-specific data on the proportion of
Americans gainfully employed appeared in the 1890 federal census.[10]
Although it obviously would be preferable to have statistics from earlier in
the century, the 1890 data are sufficiently detailed to permit descriptions of
the types of remunerative tasks older persons performed and estimates of
their work force participation rates before that date (see table 4.7). Other
information can also be used in conjunction with census material to assess
the probable impact of industrialization on the elderly's job opportunities
prior to World War I.

Three striking facts, derived from the data summarized in table 4.7,
provide key parameters for examining the occupational trends of men and
women over sixty-five. First, women of any age generally were not gainfully employed, although at some stage(s) of their lives they may have
worked outside of the home. Few females earned money in old age: women
constituted 48.8% of the total population over sixty-five in 1890, but only
9.7% of all older people classified in the census as gainfully employed were
women. Because it is extremely probable that most older people earning
money throughout the nineteenth century were males, I shall pay particular
attention to the labor experiences of elderly men.

Table 4.7—Percentage of the Population Gainfully Employed, 1890

	Age		
Subject	15–44	45–64	Over 65
Males			
Agriculture, fishing, or mining	36.7%	45.4%	44.5%
Professional service	2.8	3.9	2.9
Domestic or personal service	13.2	12.3	7.3
Trade or transportation	15.8	13.2	6.0
Manufacturing or mechanics	19.5	20.4	12.7
All occupations	88.1%	95.0%	73.2%
Females			
Agriculture, fishing, or mining	2.7%	4.1%	3.4%
Professional service	2.0	0.5	0.2
Domestic or personal service	9.2	5.5	3.5
Trade or transportation	1.4	0.4	0.2
Manufacturing or mechanics	6.2	2.1	1.0
All occupations	21.5%	12.5%	8.3%
Both sexes			
Agriculture, fishing, or mining	20.1%	25.5%	24.2%
Professional service	2.4	2.3	1.6
Domestic or personal service	11.3	9.2	5.6
Trade or transportation	8.8	7.1	3.3
Manufacturing or mechanics	13.0	11.6	7.0
All occupations	55.7%	55.5%	41.4%

SOURCE: Calculated from U.S. Bureau of the Census data

NOTE: Due to the rounding off of percentages, the sum of subtotals does not exactly equal the proportion of an age group gainfully employed in *all* occupations.

Second, the likelihood that a person would be gainfully employed decreased with the coming of age. The percentage of the total population over sixty-five that was gainfully employed in 1890 was smaller than those for both younger age groups. This pattern exists for both sexes. A man over sixty-five was only 77.1% as likely to be gainfully employed as a man between the ages of forty-five and sixty-four. The drop-off rate for older women was even greater: a woman over sixty-five was only 66.7% as likely to be gainfully employed as a middle-aged female in 1890. These data are indicative of the fact that health was a major factor limiting a person's opportunity to work in the nineteenth century. (And this remains true today. In 1970, 16.4% of all people over sixty-five were physically unable to work or keep house, and another 20.7% had a chronic condition that seriously limited their activities.)[11] Given the incidence of incapacity among the elderly, therefore, it would not make sense to predict that 90–100% of all men over sixty-five could have been gainfully employed at *any* point in the nineteenth century; 70–80% is a more reasonable ceiling for the maximum percentage of older men in the labor force.

Finally, the distribution of persons over sixty-five years old in the 1890 occupational structure differed from the patterns of younger workers. Approximately 60% of all gainfully employed men over sixty-five were farmers, fishermen, or miners, whereas only 47.8% of all men between forty-five and sixty-four, and 41.7% of all men between fifteen and forty-five, were so engaged. Conversely, older men were somewhat less likely to be employed in manufacturing or mechanical industries and far less generally found engaged in trade or transportation than any other age group. Not only were there age-specific variations across the five major occupational categories in 1890, but there were also marked differences in the types of jobs *within* each occupational category that older and younger men held (see table 4.8). For example, less than 6% of all professional males were clergymen, but 25% of all professional men over sixty-five were ministers. (A quarter of all clergymen, in fact, were at least sixty-five in 1890!) Comparable age differences exist in the sorts of tasks women performed for pay. Like older men, a greater proportion of women over sixty-five were engaged in agricultural pursuits than younger working women. And while roughly 42% of all young, middle-aged, and elderly gainfully employed women provided domestic or personal services, older women tended to be more often listed in the census as board- and lodging-house keepers and less frequently than younger women as servants.

Indeed, older workers were far more likely to be engaged in traditional jobs and crafts than in functions vital to the emerging industrial order. The proportion of men over sixty-five engaged in transportation as agents or collectors and in trade as merchants or hucksters was twice as great as the proportion of all men performing these jobs. A greater percentage of younger men than older men employed in transportation worked as locomotive engineers or railroad employees; among tradesmen they were more frequently salesmen, bookkeepers, clerks, and copyists. Younger women, moreover, were more likely than older ones to work as sales clerks in department stores or as typists and telephone operators in large businesses.

Such differences were particularly striking in manufacturing and mechanical industries. For instance, the percentage of elderly men who were carpenters and masons, boot or shoemen, coopers, and blacksmiths—all occupations that had flourished in the United States since preindustrial times—exceeded the average for all men in these jobs. It is worth mentioning that none of these fields, except the boot and shoe industries, was transformed by the introduction of new equipment or innovative manufacturing techniques between 1860 and 1893.[12] The situation was very different in occupations that had been revolutionized under the impact of industrialization. The percentage of all males over ten who were iron or steel workers, machinists, saw or planing mill employees, plumbers, steamfitters, and printing operatives exceeded the percentage of elderly men employed in these fields. A similar pattern appears in the census data for women engaged in manufacturing and mechanical industries. Women of all ages employed in this sector of the economy tended to be seamstresses, tailors, milliners, and dressmakers. But women over sixty-five apparently had fewer alternatives. They less frequently were employed in cotton, wool, and silk mills, in the shoe, boot, hosiery, and knitting industries, or in the production and processing of tobacco. Compared to younger females, older women were less likely to be found working in jobs revamped by new machines and methods.

Because older workers in 1890 tended to be clustered in traditional industries and handicrafts, it is tempting to hypothesize that those economic forces that were transforming the American landscape also adversely affected the aged's opportunities for gainful employment over time. Overall changes in the occupational structure, after all, reflect the broad shift from an agrarian- to an industrial-based economy in the United States during the nineteenth century. In 1820, the earliest date for which such statistics are available, 71.9% of all workers were engaged in agricultural pursuits; by 1890, the percentage had declined to 41.9%. The proportion of people gainfully employed in manufacturing and mechanical pursuits during the same period rose from 12.2% to 25.6%. The percentage occupied in trade or transportation grew from 2.5% to 15.7% between 1820 and 1890.[13] As opportunities in heavy industry and new business concerns expanded, and as advances in agricultural science and technology reduced the need for a large percentage of workers to be farmers, older people unable to adapt to changing conditions may have been squeezed out of the labor market. If so, the actual trends in the occupations of the aged certainly could have instigated or confirmed the popular notion emerging after the Civil War that workers became obsolescent in old age.

There is very little evidence, however, to support the hypothesis that new ideas about the aged's economic worthlessness were triggered by percep-tions of a marked decline in the actual proportion of older workers before 1890. Assuming that my estimates are valid, the percentage of elderly white persons who were working declined only slightly, if at all, between 1840 and 1890. In 1840, the earliest year for which such figures can be estimated, 38.1% of all white people over sixty-five were gainfully employed; 37.2% of all aged whites in 1890 were working.[14] More importantly, there was minimal change in work force participation rates of elderly males in the nineteenth century. Probably no less than 61.6% and no more than 76.1% of all white males over sixty-five were gainfully employed in 1840; the most reasonable estimate is 70.1%. According to the federal census, 72.4% of all white males over sixty-five in 1890 were gainfully employed. John D. Durand, using figures adjusted to be comparable to 1940 census data, calculated that 68.4% of all native white males over sixty-five were in the labor force.[15] These estimates strongly indicate that any effect the aged's actual occupational trends may have had on popular ideas about the elderly's worth occurred *after* 1890.

Table 4.8—Selected Occupations of Persons Gainfully Employed, 1890

Occupational Category	Male Workers over 10 Years of Age	Male Workers over 65 Years of Age	Female Workers over 10 Years of Age	Female Workers over 65 Years of Age
Agriculture, fishing, or mining				
Farmer, planter, overseer	60.7%	85.9%	33.3%	83.4%
Agricultural laborer	30.7	9.7	65.8	15.4
Gardener, florist, nurseryman	0.8	1.7	0.4	0.8
Fisherman	0.7	0.5		
Miner	4.2	1.2		
Professional service				
Clergyman	5.9	25.0		
Physician, surgeon	15.9	24.4	1.5	14.9
Lawyer	14.1	17.3		
Government official	11.8	11.0	1.6	7.8
Engineer	6.8	3.9		
Teacher, professor	16.0	7.4	78.7	52.4
Musician, music teacher			11.1	7.7
Artist, art teacher			3.5	5.3
Actor			1.3	0.5
Domestic or personal service				
Laborer (not specialized)	69.0	77.7		
Watchman	2.8	3.0		
Servant	8.8	4.0	73.0	49.8
Engineer, fireman (not locomotive)	5.2	2.8		
Janitor	0.7	1.7		
Barber	3.1	0.8		
Hotel keeper	1.4	2.9		
Bartender, saloon keeper	4.6	1.8		
Housekeeper			5.2	16.4
Board and lodge keeper			2.0	4.5
Laundress			13.0	16.8
Nurse			2.5	6.2
Trade or transportation				
Merchant	19.1	38.5	10.9	60.6
Agent, collector	5.5	10.7	2.1	6.8
Drayman, hackman, teamster	11.9	8.9		
Clerk, copyist	15.9	6.4	28.1	5.7
Steam railroad employee	12.3	5.4		

Occupation				
Banker	1.0	4.0	1.0	11.4
Huckster, peddlar	1.8	3.5	12.2	1.5
Bookkeeper, accountant	4.2	2.7	25.6	4.4
Sales	6.6	2.7		
Locomotive engineer	2.6	0.5		
Stenographer, typist			9.3	
Telegram and telephone operator			3.7	0.4
Manufacturing or mechanics				
Carpenter	15.0	22.7		
Boot or shoe maker	4.4	9.2	3.3	0.8
Tailor	3.0	5.1	6.2	11.7
Seamstress			14.2	32.0
Dressmaker			28.1	20.1
Milliner			5.8	7.4
Blacksmith	5.1	7.3		
Iron or steel worker	3.5	1.5		
Mason	3.9	6.0		
Painter, varnisher	5.4	3.2		
Manufacturing officer	2.5	3.7		
Cooper	1.2	2.3		
Miller	1.3	2.4		
Apprentice	1.8			
Butcher	2.6	1.5		
Baker, confectioner	1.9	1.2		
Machinist	4.4	2.6		
Plumber, steamfitter	1.4	0.2		
Printer, print operative	2.1	0.7		
Saw-planing mill employee	3.3	1.0		
Mill operative			4.1	6.5
Cotton mill operative			9.0	2.3
Woolen mill operative			3.6	1.1
Silk mill operative			2.0	0.2
Carpet maker			1.0	5.8
Hosiery knitter			2.0	1.5
Tobacco processor			2.7	1.0

SOURCE: Calculated from U.S. Bureau of the Census data

NOTE: Due to rounding off and omitted occupations, the figures within each category do not add up to 100%.

Nationwide trends do not obscure the patterns at the regional level that might have revealed that the proportion of older men gainfully employed in 1890 was higher than the national average in predominantly agrarian areas of the country and substantially lower in heavily industrialized sections. Although most older workers were farmers, there is no clear-cut relationship between the percentage of aged men or women working in agriculture and the total percentage of elderly people gainfully employed at the regional level (see table 4.9). To be sure, the South, which had far more older Americans engaged in farming than any other region, also led the nation in its percentage of gainfully employed older workers. And yet, the proportions of all older men gainfully employed in New England (72.4%) and the Mid-Atlantic states (69.8%), which had the largest concentrations of men over sixty-five engaged in manufacturing and mechanical industries, were not appreciably below the national average (73.2%). In fact, the smallest proportion of elderly workers in the nation was found in the East North Central states, which actually had a far larger proportion of older people employed as farmers than the Northeast. Even the Mountain and Pacific states (where a relatively large proportion of aged men and women were engaged in trade, transportation, manufacturing, and mechanics) surpassed the extensively agricultural North Central states in their proportions of aged workers. Regional statistics, therefore, challenge the plausibility of arguing that the shift from an agrarian- to an industrial-based economy significantly reduced the aged's employment opportunities before 1890.

Examining the employment status of elderly men in Massachusetts in 1840 and 1885 further erodes the hypothesis. New industrial techniques and mechanization had a tremendous impact on the state's occupational structure during the nineteenth century: Massachusetts still had basically an agrarian economy in 1840 but was predominantly industrial by 1885.[16] Yet if my estimates are correct, no more than 88.9% and no less than 58.5% of all men over sixty were working in 1840; the most reasonable estimate is 74.6%. In 1885, 71.1% of all older men were gainfully employed. The percentage of workers over sixty declined very little, it appears, in the midst of a profound alteration in the Bay State's economy. Although all age groups over time increasingly had to secure employment off the farm, nevertheless considerable opportunities remained for older men in farming at the end of the century. In addition, many jobs existed for the aged in the industrial sector of the economy even though there undoubtedly were skilled laborers who had to take on menial or temporary jobs with the coming of age.[17] Thus, while the process of industrialization caused many changes in nineteenth-century Massachusetts, it neither immediately nor dramatically affected the elderly's ability to remain in the work force.

Needless to say, rejecting the hypothesis that shifts in the aged's occupational trends caused conceptions to change before 1890 does not rule

Table 4.9—Percentage of the Aged Population Gainfully Employed, by Region, 1890

Region	Occupation					
	Agriculture, Fishing, or Mining	Professional Service	Domestic or Personal Service	Trade or Transportation	Manufacturing or Mechanics	All Occupations
Males over 65						
New England	35.0%	2.8%	7.5%	8.0%	19.1%	72.4%*
Mid-Atlantic	30.1	3.1	10.1	8.5	18.1	69.8
South Atlantic	58.1	2.9	6.9	4.5	9.9	82.4
East North Central	42.0	2.8	7.1	5.4	11.6	68.9
West North Central	50.5	3.0	5.0	4.7	8.9	72.0
East South Central	65.9	3.0	5.3	3.5	7.2	84.9
West South Central	60.9	3.8	7.3	4.9	7.2	83.9
Mountain	45.1	3.6	11.2	6.4	14.0	80.4
Pacific	39.5	4.9	8.9	9.6	13.2	76.1
Females over 65						
New England	0.9	0.2	3.3	0.1	1.2	5.7
Mid-Atlantic	1.3	0.1	3.1	0.3	1.1	5.9
South Atlantic	6.6	0.2	6.8	0.3	1.0	14.9
East North Central	3.0	0.1	1.7	0.2	0.8	5.7
West North Central	3.9	0.1	1.8	0.1	0.6	6.5
East South Central	8.6	0.1	6.3	0.1	0.7	15.8
West South Central	6.7	0.2	7.3	0.4	0.7	15.3
Mountain	2.4	0.3	3.1	0.2	1.3	7.3
Pacific	2.5	0.4	3.1	0.3	0.9	7.2

SOURCE: Calculated from U.S. Bureau of the Census data

NOTE: states included in regional coding: *New England:* Maine, Vermont, New Hampshire, Massachusetts, Connecticut, Rhode Island; *Mid-Atlantic:* New York, Pennsylvania, New Jersey; *South Atlantic:* Delaware, Maryland, West Virginia, Virginia, North Carolina, South Carolina, Georgia, Florida; *East North Central:* Wisconsin, Michigan, Illinois, Indiana, Ohio; *West North Central:* North Dakota, South Dakota, Nebraska, Kansas, Missouri, Iowa, Minnesota; *East South Central:* Kentucky, Tennessee, Mississippi, Alabama; *West South Central:* Oklahoma, Arkansas, Texas, Louisiana; *Mountain:* Montana, Idaho, Wyoming, Nevada, Utah, Colorado, Arizona, New Mexico; *Pacific:* Washington, Oregon, California. A different regional schema is adopted here from that in table 4.5; I changed schema because it was easier and faster to use data aggregated at the regional level as defined by the census bureau. This technical change, however, does not affect the interpretation.

*Due to the rounding off of percentages, the sum of the occupational categories does not exactly equal the total gainfully employed in *all* occupations.

out a relationship shortly after that date. The census reports that the percentage of all gainfully employed men over sixty-five years old dropped from 73.2% in 1890 to 68.7% in 1900 to 59.9% in 1920. (Data are not available for 1910 because the census lists all men over forty-five in one category.) This decline in older men at work may have fueled negative opinions about the aged's usefulness that emerged between 1865 and 1914.

Other evidence, however, tends to deflate the overall persuasiveness of such an argument. While the proportion of working men over sixty-five was falling, most elderly males were gainfully employed as late as 1920. The most pronounced withdrawal of older males from the marketplace has actually occurred during the last fifty years: less than 23.9% are in the labor force today. This suggests that age discrimination in the marketplace significantly increased *after* negative notions about the aged were already commonplace. And yet, it is important to note that the exodus of older men from the employment ranks is not simply a function of diminished opportunities in an industrial system that disdained old age. During the past century, the number of unemployed older people has grown in part because retirement plans and alternative sources of income have made it possible for many to afford to quit working. This suggests that changes in the social structure at large and marketplace in particular did not always work to the disadvantage of aging workers.

New developments in business and professional groups, in fact, may have enhanced to some degree the elderly's social position during the very era in which people thought it was diminishing. Although some were lucky enough to be born leaders or to marry into prominence, most nineteenth-century Americans attained power and fortune through a series of promotions during their careers. This pattern became more elaborate and complicated after the Civil War as organizations created and/or expanded levels of authority in the corporate chain of command. While these bureaucratic procedures were designed to make operations more efficient and rational, they also extended the time it took people to reach the top. Hence, it is not surprising that many important figures in American society around World War I were at least sixty years old.[18] B. C. Forbes published a study in 1917 indicating that the median age of the country's foremost businessmen was sixty-five. According to another contemporary study, 56% of the "Men Who Control America" were over sixty. So were 48% of the people earning $1,000,000 annual incomes between 1915 and 1919. A majority of the men serving as bishops in the Episcopal and Methodist churches or as presidents of other Protestant groups were over sixty around the turn of the century.

Indeed, the most telling illustration of the divergence in the realities and rhetoric about old people's worth after the Civil War was the growth of the seniority system in the U.S. House of Representatives. Between 1880 and

1910, several innovations gradually reduced the Speaker's flexibility in designating committee chairmen, requiring him to appoint those who had served the longest. Congress inaugurated the seniority system to curb the Speaker's prerogatives and to routinize operations, not to honor its aged members. Yet as a consequence of this new practice, the House leadership was filled by comparatively older men who gained in power the longer they stayed in office.[19] Thus despite all contemporary evidence "proving" that judgment steadily declined with age, negative ideas about the aged's worth neither curtailed the development of the seniority system nor prevented congressmen from wielding more power with each passing term. Conversely, the rising median age of congressmen did not prompt Americans to question the validity of unfavorable perceptions of older people's roles in society. Ideas about the aged and the politics of aging at the time seem to have operated in separate spheres.

There is one final reason for questioning whether shifts in the elderly's occupational trends caused negative ideas about the aged's value to flower. Initial declines in older people's labor participation rates apparently did not cause any radical change in the manner in which Americans before World War I perceived or treated those unable to support themselves financially in old age, through work or other means. To determine why this is so, I shall turn now to the history of old-age dependency in the United States between 1790 and 1914.

Old-Age Dependency before World War I

One of the universal facts of growing old is that some men and women become incapacitated, others become impoverished, and still others become physically and economically helpless with the coming of age. Old-age dependency is an age-old phenomenon. Nevertheless, there have been important differences over time in the ways Americans defined the plight of needy old people and sought to assist them. Between 1790 and 1914, for instance, several new methods of dealing with old-age dependency were developed. But such innovations arose in a piecemeal manner and at first had a negligible effect. Traditional agents of relief—kith and kin, the poorhouse, old-age homes, and, in some cases, veterans' benefits—remained the chief means of support for the elderly, if and when support was needed. For this reason, it is highly unlikely that any developments in the history of old-age dependency before 1914 caused the dramatic reevaluation in ideas about the elderly's status prior to World War I.

In keeping with earlier customs, the family was the aged's primary source of consolation and assistance between 1790 and 1914. Writers throughout the period, reflecting longstanding cultural norms, stressed in poems, essays, and sermons that, as far as possible, the "declining years and increasing infirmities of old age [should] be cheered by frequent contact and buoyant cheerfulness of children, and the kindly deference and sympathy of all in the family and social circle."[20] Statutes, modeled in part upon the Elizabethan poor law of 1601 and a 1692 act passed in the Massachusetts Bay Province, made family members legally as well as morally responsible for their poor and infirm kin, including old folks. By 1860, eighteen of the nation's thirty-three states had enacted laws designed to cope with dependency among family members of all ages; thirty-two states had passed such measures before 1914. No state made special provisions for aged relatives, however, until litigation forced courts and legislators to define the precise responsibilities adult children owed their parents.[21] These actions in turn magnified differences already existing from state to state in family members' duties. An Indiana court ruled after the Civil War, for example, that because the state's statutes imposed no familial responsibility for poor relatives, a son could not be charged for necessities furnished his aged parents. Colorado, Ohio, and Kentucky, on the other hand, in the early twentieth century made adults who refused to care for their aged parents liable for criminal charges.[22] Over time, some jurisdictions began to distinguish between old-age dependency in particular and poverty in general in laws affecting family relationships.

Did children really help their aged parents? It is impossible to respond definitively to this question. Extensive research must be done to determine how much older people's actual reliance on kin for support varied nationwide by age, race, sex, and ethnicity. It cannot yet be determined whether states enacted legislation in order to preclude a possible failure of the family to care for its own poor or whether they were responding to actual changes in relatives' ability or willingness to assume such responsibility. For the moment, however, census data on the aged's household status in Buffalo (1855), rural Indiana (1880), and Massachusetts (1885 and 1895) enable one to formulate tentative answers (see tables 4.10 and 4.11).[23] Obvious ecological and temporal variations notwithstanding, the following residency patterns existed in all locations. More than three-quarters of all foreign-born and native-born men over sixty were heads of household. With advancing age, the proportion of men who continued in this capacity declined, and the proportion of men who resided with a child, in-law, or sibling increased. Surprisingly few did not or could not turn to kin for help; it is significant that only 9.8% of all native-born and 13.4% of all foreign-born men over eighty years old in Massachusetts in 1895 lived with strangers or in institutions. Older women's behavior differed from elderly men's in two respects. First, although the proportion of women who headed households increased as the proportion listed as wives decreased, no more than a third were ever designated as household heads. Second, a greater proportion of women at a

Table 4.10—Relationship of Native-born and German-born subjects to Head of Household, Buffalo, New York, 1855

Subject	Age 41–60 (Native)	Age 41–60 (German)	Age 60–70 (Native)	Age 60–70 (German)	Age Over 70 (Native)	Age Over 70 (German)
Male						
Son	0.4%	0.4%	2.0%	0.4%		
Relative	1.9	0.8	4.6	4.9	5.7%	17.5%
Servant	0.4	0.9				
Boarder	6.9	2.9	6.0	2.2	5.7	4.6
Father	0.9	1.1	9.9	9.0	28.6	18.5
Head	88.3	93.5	76.2	80.7	54.3	55.6
Other	1.2	0.4	1.3	2.8	5.7	3.8
Number surveyed	1,125	1,548	151	223	35	63
Female						
Daughter	0.9%	0.8%	1.5%	1.9%	5.7%	···
Relative	9.8	5.0	17.9	16.0	17.1	20.6
Servant	1.2	0.9	0.1	0.8	2.9	1.6
Boarder	5.8	0.5	0.4	1.1	4.3	3.2
Mother	6.3	2.8	31.1	21.8	28.6	46.0
Wife	62.5	78.3	27.0	44.1	24.3	8.6
Head	13.1	11.6	16.8	14.1	8.6	14.3
Other	0.4	0.1	5.1	2.9	8.5	5.7
Number surveyed	915	1,310	196	170	63	70

SOURCE: Calculated from data in Laurence A. Glasco, "Ethnicity and Social Structure" (Ph.D. diss., State University of New York at Buffalo, 1973).

NOTE: roman type indicates native-born; italic type indicates German-born

Table 4.11—Relationship of Native-born and Foreign-born Subjects to Head of Household, Massachusetts, 1895

Subject	Age							
	50–59		Over 60		60–79		Over 80	
Male								
Head	83.4%	85.1%	79.5%	76.4%	81.3%	77.9%	62.4%	48.3%
Husband						0.1		
Father	0.5	0.7	4.4	5.6	3.5	4.9	13.2	19.3
Father-in-law	0.6	1.0	4.0	5.7	3.4	5.1	10.6	15.1
Stepfather			0.1	0.1	0.1	0.1	0.2	0.4
Grandfather			0.1	0.1	0.1	0.1	0.8	1.1
Brother	1.5	0.9	1.3	0.7	1.3	0.7	1.0	0.5
Brother-in-law	0.8	0.5	0.7	0.5	0.8	0.5	0.4	0.3
Son	1.5	0.2	0.2		0.2			
Son-in-law	0.5	0.1	0.1		0.1			
Uncle	0.2	0.1	0.6	0.4	0.5	0.4	1.5	1.2
Nephew	0.1							
Cousin	0.1	0.1	0.1	0.1	0.1	0.1	0.1	0.4
Boarder	3.5	4.6	3.2	3.1	3.1	3.1	4.5	3.6
Lodger	4.5	3.4	2.8	2.5	2.9	2.6	1.5	1.8
Hotel guest	0.4	0.1	0.3	0.1	0.3	0.1	0.1	
Inmate/patient	1.4	2.2	1.8	3.9	1.7	3.7	3.1	7.7
Servant	0.2	0.2	0.1	0.1	0.1	0.1		0.1
Hired man	0.5	0.5	0.4	0.4	0.4	0.4	0.2	
Other	0.3	0.3	0.3	0.2	0.1	0.1	0.4	0.2
Number surveyed	53,031	41,201	59,409	35,542	53,831	30,837	5,578	1,705

Female

Head	18.7%	*26.5%*	28.7%	*31.3%*	28.3%	*31.8%*	31.2%	*22.4%*
Wife	57.2	*54.8*	32.9	*30.1*	36.4	*31.7*	7.4	*4.9*
Mother	2.1	*2.8*	10.5	*12.0*	9.0	*11.1*	21.6	*26.7*
Mother-in-law	2.6	*3.5*	10.4	*12.2*	9.4	*11.5*	18.3	*23.5*
Stepmother		*0.1*	0.2	*0.2*	0.2	*0.1*	0.5	*0.3*
Grandmother			0.5	*0.4*	0.3	*0.3*	2.1	
Sister	4.1	*1.8*	4.1	*1.7*	4.3	*1.7*	2.9	*1.9*
Sister-in-law	1.9	*0.9*	1.6	*0.9*	1.7	*0.9*	1.0	*1.3*
Daughter	3.2	*0.3*	0.4	*0.1*	0.4	*0.1*		*0.7*
Daughter-in-law	0.1							
Aunt	0.4	*0.4*	1.8	*1.2*	1.4	*1.1*	4.3	*2.6*
Niece	0.3		0.1		0.1			
Cousin	0.3	*0.1*	0.3	*0.2*	0.3	*0.2*	0.3	*0.2*
Boarder	1.8	*1.2*	3.2	*2.1*	2.8	*1.9*	5.6	*4.5*
Lodger	2.8	*1.5*	1.6	*1.4*	1.7	*1.4*	1.0	*1.4*
Hotel guest	0.2		0.1		0.1		0.2	
Inmate/patient	0.8	*1.5*	1.6	*3.6*	1.4	*3.2*	3.1	*8.8*
Servant	1.4	*3.3*	0.8	*1.8*	0.9	*1.9*	0.1	*0.2*
Housekeeper	1.2	*0.9*	0.9	*0.7*	0.9	*0.8*	0.2	*0.2*
Other	0.9	*0.4*	0.3	*0.1*	0.4	*0.3*	0.2	*0.4*
Number surveyed	59,695	*45,584*	72,808	*40,045*	64,006	*37,620*	8,802	*2,425*

SOURCE: Calculated from data in the Massachusetts state census for 1895

NOTE: roman type indicates native-born; italic type indicates foreign-born given age were residing with a child, grandchild, or in-law than obtained for their male counterparts. Insofar as these living arrangements are comparable to those existing elsewhere, they suggest that most older people placed a premium on maintaining an independent residence. When that no longer was feasible, the aged often could rely on kin for assistance.

The local community generally assumed responsibility for relieving the needy, but only those who were legally residents of the jurisdiction, if family members did not reside in the area or defaulted on their obligations. Sometimes the poor received provisions at home or were boarded out at town expense to the person submitting the lowest bid. They also could take shelter in public almshouses, which had existed since colonial times to support and maintain "a certain number of poor, aged, or infirm persons during their lives."[24] Existing evidence reveals that the percent of people over sixty years old in a given poorhouse before the Civil War ranged from 16% to 25%. Some inmates had grown old within the institution; others entered in old age. And while officials and commentators frequently claimed that most aged residents should not be treated like those who drank, gambled, or wilfully reduced themselves into straitened circumstances, the elderly did not always receive special consideration. Several contemporary reports noted that the odor of sickness, decay, and death pervading the halls added to the aged's discomfort.[25]

The almshouse clientele changed during the nineteenth century, but the institution itself remained a place where unfortunate, feeble old people could go to die. Although local and state legislatures raised funds to erect an extraordinary number of asylums and buildings for particular groups of their society's criminal, dependent, or incapacitated population, they neither requested nor allocated money to establish any public facilities expressly to care for the aged. As a result, the proportion of old people within almshouses rose sharply. By 1910, roughly 45% of all native-born and 70% of all foreign-born inmates were at least sixty years old (see table 4.12). A few who worked in such institutions altered their programs to reflect new realities. The commissioner of public charities in New York City, for instance, converted a public facility intended for the general relief of paupers into the Home for Aged and Infirm in 1903.[26] But it is worth noting that these developments did not foster any new images of old-age dependency that might have changed overall conceptions about the elderly. While an increasing proportion of almshouse inmates were old, less than 2% of the entire population over sixty actually lived in poorhouses at any moment; this figure remained relatively constant. And despite the publication of heartrending poems (such as "Over the Hill to the Poorhouse" in 1871) and shocking exposés (such as an 1883 New Jersey Bureau of Labor report), people continued to regard the almshouse as a generally dreadful but necessary "last resort."[27]

Table 4.12—Selected Statistics on Almshouse Paupers, 1910

Age	Native-born Whites		Foreign-born Whites		Blacks, Indians, Orientals	
	Male	Female	Male	Female	Male	Female
Age at Admission to the Almshouse in 1910						
20–30	8.7%	15.3%	8.8%	13.4%	19.9%	23.5%
30–40	12.5	12.7	10.4	11.6	15.1	13.9
40–50	16.5	9.9	14.5	11.1	12.4	8.6
50–60	21.5	10.0	19.4	13.6	12.7	6.6
60–70	16.1	10.3	25.3	21.2	11.9	9.1
70–80	9.3	8.4	15.2	17.2	9.1	8.2
Over 80	3.2	3.8	3.5	6.7	4.9	5.9
30–60	50.5	32.6	44.3	36.3	40.2	29.1
Over 60	28.6	22.5	44.0	45.1	25.9	23.3
Total number admitted	34,617	11,821	26,683	6,670	4,612	2,195
Proportion of the Entire Population in Almshouses on 1 January 1910						
All ages	0.1%	...	0.3%	0.1%	0.1%	0.1%
Over 60	1.5	1.6%	1.8	0.7	0.7	0.5
Over 80	1.6	1.9	3.3	1.6	2.1	1.2
Proportion of All Almshouse Paupers over 50 Enumerated on 1 January 1910						
50–60	23.4%	16.4%	16.6%	14.0%	14.7%	11.2%
60–70	21.7	18.0	32.0	28.1	17.8	17.3
70–80	16.0	16.4	27.5	29.2	16.3	15.1
Over 80	7.6	9.2	10.0	14.1	12.3	13.6
Over 60	45.3	43.6	69.5	71.4	46.4	46.0
Total	28,321	15,933	24,605	8,520	3,900	2,564

SOURCE: Calculated from U.S. Bureau of the Census data

Fortunately, an increasing number of alternatives to the poorhouse did appear over time. Philanthropists, for example, had recognized the need for private old-age homes since colonial times. Yet compared to the number of groups devoted to caring for the blind, the deaf, the mentally ill, and the orphan, there were relatively few benevolent societies directly assisting the aged; even the largest and best-endowed organizations rarely helped more than a hundred people per annum. Hence, charitable agencies actually did not relieve very many elderly men and women before 1860.[28] The number and variety of private institutions for the aged, however, exploded after the Civil War: nearly two-thirds of the 1,200 benevolent homes operating in 1939 were founded between 1875 and 1919. Institutions catering exclusively to elderly members of particular denominations or nationalities flourished. During the same period, old-age homes began to systematize admissions standards and procedures.[29] Thus the years between 1865 and 1914 mark the period in which the building and managing of private asylums specifically for the old became fully developed.

Not only did Americans after the Civil War maintain and expand existing means of assisting the elderly, but they also inaugurated new ways of relieving some of the financial worries of growing old. As noted in Chapter 3, the first retirement pension programs in industrial, mercantile, and financial establishments went into effect. Large insurance corporations, as well as local, fraternal, and mutual benefit societies, began selling old-age annuities. Several states permitted savings banks to write life insurance and annuity contracts.[30] The new rich provided money for special groups. The Carnegie Foundation for Advancement of Teaching set aside ten million dollars in 1905 for college instructors in the United States and Canada who retired from active duty at sixty-five. Benjamin Rose, a Cleveland philanthropist, left three million dollars in 1911 for "respectable and deserving" older people who lived at home and needed help.[31] Unions and fraternal orders and lodges offered other kinds of relief. Some organizations took up special collections or periodically authorized appropriations for aged and incapacitated fellows. A few built old-age homes and/or sponsored pensions. One union permitted superannuated members to receive money by commuting their death benefits.[32]

While big business and union interest in old-age programs represents an important development in the history of old-age dependency, it is essential to recognize that the private sector's attempts before World War I were extremely circumscribed, both in scope and in the number of old people who actually benefited. In 1910, for instance, only about sixty of the several hundred thousand corporations in the United States offered employee retirement plans. Furthermore, the absence of any legal guarantee that pensions would be paid even if all eligibility requirements were satisfied left those who might have benefited with only "the shadow of provision for old age and not the substance."[33] Annuity plans attracted minimal interest, moreover, because they offered paltry returns and most workers could not afford to save even small amounts of money on a regular basis.[34] Union-sponsored programs benefited very few people. Only 7% of all American workers were in unions in 1904. Most of those belonged to the American Federation of Labor, which voted down the earliest resolution for old-age pensions in 1903 and whose leadership would reject subsequent resolutions for decades. [35] In sum, less than 1% of all workers on the eve of World War I could rely on assistance in old age from their employer or union; the rest ensured their financial independence by staying in the labor force as long as possible or by relying on savings and gifts.

The potential significance but limited impact of all developments in the history of old-age dependency before World War I is underscored by the legislative records at the state and federal levels between 1790 and 1914. Besides their efforts to enforce family obligations to aged relatives, state governments occasionally implemented measures to assist certain segments of the elderly population. Roughly twenty states authorized disability and old-age pensions for school teachers, primarily in urban areas, based on service and age; some permitted cities to give pensions to superannuated police and firemen. Otherwise, state aid to the aged was limited to those who qualified for veterans' benefits.[36] Pioneer efforts to provide more extensive coverage generally proved disastrous. For instance, the California legislature repealed an 1883 act, which defrayed part of the cost of caring for the aged in private institutions, after courts declared some provisions invalid and when cases of fraud were uncovered. Furthermore, the earliest calls for statewide old-age welfare assistance, which began in Massachusetts in 1903, fared poorly. Efforts in the Bay State were stymied in part by a series of reports issued by the Commission on Old Age Pensions, Annuities, and Insurance, appointed by the legislature to study the issue. Investigators discovered that conditions in 1910 for the noninstitutionalized aged poor were "comparatively good," and concluded that pensions would be expensive, destroy thriftiness, disintegrate the family, and lower wages, and that they might also be unconstitutional. So instead of authorizing public relief for the aged, the Commonwealth in 1915 made it a criminal offense not to care for destitute parents. In fact, Arizona was the only state to pass an old-age assistance law before 1914, but even its act was quickly ruled unconstitutional by the state supreme court.[37]

The federal government paradoxically was less responsive and more generous than state governments in helping older people in need. In the early years of the republic, writers such as Thomas Paine and Alexander Everett proposed nationally-funded pensions to prevent indigency among the elderly, but their suggestions attracted negligible attention.[38] Some old people, however, did qualify for federal assistance through veterans programs. Disability pensions were provided in 1789 for Revolutionary War veterans. In 1818, Congress granted pensions to U.S. citizens who had served in the Revolution for at least nine months, were "in need of assistance," and relinquished "claim to every pension heretofore allowed." In addition, funds were appropriated to build a U.S. Naval Home (1833) and a U.S. Soldiers Home (1851).[39] It is necessary to point out that before the Civil War, the federal government provided such pensions and benefits to impoverished and/or incapacitated veterans (and, in some instances, their wives and dependents) as gratuities for prior military services; it did not assist poor, helpless people simply because they were old. To minimize costs, moreover, Congress deliberately restricted the scope and provision of pensions to limit eligibility to as few veterans and dependents as possible: in 1840, for example, only 3.7% of all Americans over sixty years old were recipients of federal military pensions.[40]

As time passed, however, the federal veterans program grew enormously, and old age itself sometimes became an eligibility criterion for benefits. Additional wars, the inauguration of military retirement policies for selected career officers and enlisted personnel, and various other administrative decisions caused a tremendous increase in recipients and a staggering rise in costs: the number of pensioners jumped from 126,772 in 1886 to 921,083 in 1910; disbursements swelled from 60.4 million dollars in 1883 to nearly 160 million in 1910. The National Home for Disabled Volunteer Soldiers officially became an institution for aged and infirm soldiers and sailors. In 1912, Congress liberalized existing laws by granting benefits to any Union soldier over the age of sixty-two who had served at least ninety days in the Civil War; this act signalled that the federal government·was willing to recognize being old as a disability under certain specific circumstances. The new measure increased not only the number of people eligible for assistance but also the benefits of many already receiving pensions.[41] The cost of all military pensions in the fiscal year 1913 soared to 174.2 million dollars—a figure representing 18% of the year's total federal expenditures.

Despite its munificence to a select group of older people, the federal government evinced little interest in old-age pensions for the population at large. Suggestions that the United States emulate Germany, New Zealand, and Denmark, among others, and enact old-age assistance legislation initially met considerable resistance: most dismissed such measures as impractical, unnecessary, socialistic vagaries of exotic, far-off lands. Even after Great Britain inaugurated a pension program in 1908, Congress rejected bills introduced in 1909, 1911, and 1913 to accept responsibility for the welfare of the entire elderly population. The 1911 measure is particularly noteworthy because its sponsor contended that "the work of the soldier of industry is infinitely more necessary than the bloody work of the soldier. . . . The aged working men and women have therefore a claim on society that is even better than the claims of the soldier."[42] The analogy between federal military and industrial pensions was clearly astute but apparently unpersuasive.

Why were there no dramatic departures from the status quo before World War I in any sphere of society? A major reason is that professional opinions about old-age dependency were not significantly altered by late-nineteenth-century theories, organizations, and legislation reshaping the ways Americans perceived "poverty" in general. Grasping that urbanization and industrialization adversely affected various impoverished groups in society, philanthropists and activists relied on facts, rhetoric, lobbying, and sheer persistence to ensure the passage of legislation providing more stringent public health standards, better housing, stricter labor legislation to protect women and children, public school reform, and closer regulation of the liquor trade, among other measures.[43] Progressive reformers and "professional altruists," however, minimized the impact of new labor and living conditions on the aged. On the basis of their case studies, most analysts concluded that instances of old-age dependency resulted mainly from physical debility, mental incapacity, a spouse's death, or loss of property—circumstances that always had threatened the old—rather than industrialization per se.

> The tendency of modern industry is to discard from its ranks younger and younger men. If chance throws them out of employment, men who have passed sixty almost invariably resort to casual labor. . . . The men of these latter ages who find themselves obliged to apply for charity solely for this reason are, of course, very few in number compared to those who have passed sixty and who find the infirmities of a real and not of arbitrarily fixed old age complicating their problems of employment.[44]

Most commentators on poverty, in fact, argued that old-age dependency had not yet become a serious dilemma in the United States. They contended that a smaller proportion of older people sought relief in American cities than in European cities, and they considered old age a less significant source of dependency than unemployment, physical disabilities, overcrowding, desertions, or character defects. As a distinguished encyclopedist of social reforms observed, "In the United States, the old-age problem is not yet so serious."[45]

Since even reformers minimized both the extent of old-age dependency and the degree to which industrial as well as urban forces exacerbated the plight of the elderly, it is not surprising that few advocated any radical alternative to existing means of relieving needy older men and women, or that their proposals aroused little enthusiasm even at the height of political progressivism. Indeed, Lee Welling Squier's *Old Age Dependency in the*

United States, the earliest full-length monograph on the subject written by an American, did not appear until 1912, nearly two decades after muckrakers and scholars had begun advocating their new diagnosis of the social causes of pauperism. It is doubtful, therefore, that such relatively scattered and rare efforts to propose and implement new ways of viewing and coping with old-age dependency caused Americans to reformulate their ideas about the elderly in general before World War I.

At the beginning of the chapter, I proposed that changes in popular conceptions of the elderly's status in the United States between 1790 and 1914 were probably related to observable shifts in older Americans' actual places in society. Surprisingly, this prediction has not been confirmed by the evidence. Insofar as demographic factors have influenced ideas about the elderly, their effect has undoubtedly been greatest during the past fifty years, when the most significant changes in the composition, distribution, and growth of the aged population have taken place. Similarly, it is unlikely that variations in the aged's labor force participation rates fostered disesteem for the usefulness of older workers. The proportion of older men in the marketplace declined rather slightly compared to subsequent trends. And while intellectual currents and developments in the late nineteenth and early twentieth centuries foreshadowed some of the ways Americans eventually would define the nature and extent of old-age dependency and seek to deal with it, one should not mistake scattered precedents for prevailing tendencies. It is unlikely that any new ideas or solutions for the problems of incapacity and indigency in old age caused unfavorable conceptions of the elderly in general to emerge.

The fundamental lesson to be drawn from this analysis, therefore, is that the intellectual history of old age in the United States prior to World War I is not identical to the social history of the aged. Continuities and changes in the way Americans thought about elderly men and women before 1914 did not simply reflect shifts in the relative number of people over sixty in society, variations in the proportion of older workers in the labor force, or alterations in the perception and treatment of the aged poor. Ideas about the worth and functions of the elderly have a life of their own: the unprecedented denigration of older Americans arose independently of the most important observable changes in their actual status. The interplay of broad intellectual trends and pervasive structural changes in society at large between 1790 and 1914 profoundly affected prevailing notions about the elderly without having either an immediate or a dramatic impact on the aged's demographic and socioeconomic situation, or vice versa.

SOME ANTIQUES HAVE A MARKET VALUE; OTHERS HAVEN'T.

Cartoon by Rollin Kirby, *The World*, 1 September 1929.

CHAPTER 5

Old Age Becomes "Modern" in Twentieth-Century America

Although the United States has been "modernizing" since at least the last part of the eighteenth century, the actual place of older Americans in society did not really become "modernized" until the twentieth century. Net declines in fertility rates, steady gains in life expectancy at birth, and sharp fluctuations in domestic and international migration patterns profoundly influenced the shape and composition of the American population structure. Before 1914, however, these demographic factors did not substantially increase the relative size of the elderly population nor significantly add to the life expectancy of those past the age of sixty. Moreover, the spread of an urban network and the maturation of an industrial economy transformed the nation throughout the nineteenth century without causing fundamental changes in the behavior of the aged as a group. Even in the most extensively and intensively developed regions of the country, old people preserved a stake in the economy and maintained their financial independence by engaging in agricultural pursuits and traditional crafts. If and when relief was necessary, they continued to rely primarily on family members and institutions in the local community. The societal position of the elderly was not radically altered overnight or even within a generation.

Nevertheless, older men and women were eventually engulfed by the long-term and large-scale forces reshaping American society. The distinctively "modern" trends associated with aging societies in western civilization—a rise in the absolute and relative size of the aged population, a decreasing percentage of elderly workers, and an increasing reliance on pensions and other means of income maintenance in old age—have become more and more pronounced in the United States during the past fifty years. And, as I shall indicate in greater detail in Part 3, the aged themselves, to a degree unprecedented before the twentieth century, became prime targets and agents of social and cultural changes transforming the United States. For the first time in American history, the aged as a group became the focus of national attention; some of the woes of being old were perceived as "social problems" demanding comprehensive remedies. Indeed, the elderly in this context made an increasingly concerted, collective effort to articulate and to improve their own economic, physical, and social well-being. But I am getting ahead of the story. For the moment, I shall continue to examine patterns in the elderly's demographic and socioeconomic history, because such an analysis confirms that modernization, in its more recent stages no less than its initial ones, is a complex and protracted process. It affects various groups within society in different ways and at varying times. Its impact on America's elderly population has been greatest in the relatively recent past.

The Aging of America

Ever changing fertility, mortality, and migration rates have made older Americans more visible in the twentieth century than ever before. Increases in the total number of live births, gains in life expectancy due to lower death rates among younger people, and the heavy volume of immigrants have all contributed to a rise in the absolute number of persons who are at least sixty-five years old. Declining birth rates, which have been falling with few exceptions (notably the post–World War II "baby boom") from 1790 to the present, largely explain the growth in the relative size of the elderly population. [1] Although a net decline in fertility always results in a gain in the aged's share of the total population, this relationship was partly offset by other demographic factors throughout much of the nineteenth century. For instance, declines in mortality rates actually helped to produce a somewhat more "youthful" population in the past, since improvements in life expectancy generally were confined to the youngest age groups. Yet once substantial reductions in infant and child mortality rates were realized, the degree to which subsequent improvements in mortality rates rejuvenate the population structure correspondingly has diminished. The effect of migration patterns in determining the size of the elderly population also has changed over time. Twentieth-century legislation has significantly limited the number of middle-age and younger people who legally enter this country. Consequently, the older population has become proportionately "larger" than it would have been if late-nineteenth-century immigration patterns had persisted.

Gerontologists and demographers forecast that the proportion of older people in the population will continue to grow in the near future. In 1900, 4.0% of the population was at least sixty-five; the figure rose to 9.9% by 1970, and it will probably reach 11% within the next twenty years. Whether the marked increase in the proportion of old people persists beyond that date depends mainly on future fertility trends. [2] Under certain circumstances, the proportion of men and women over sixty-five might remain the same as it is today, or even drop slightly. Older people may constitute as much as 16% of the total population, however, should Americans attain and maintain a replacement fertility level. (See table 5.1.)

As the proportion of elderly people in the total population has risen, the older population itself has been aging, and it is expected to continue to do so. Although prior to World War I there had been only negligible increases in life expectancy past the age of sixty, important gains have been recorded since then. The average life expectancy of white men at age sixty has increased from 14.35 years in 1900 to 16.2 years in 1973. Women's gains are even more remarkable. The average life expectancy of a sixty-year-old white woman in 1900 was 15.23 years; by 1973 it had soared to 21.1 years.[3] As a result, the proportion of very aged people in the older population has grown steadily during the past forty years. In 1900 and 1930, 29% of all Americans over sixty-five were at least seventy-five years old. The percentage then rose to 31.5% in 1950 and 38.2% in 1970; census officials project that 43.2% of all older Americans in the year 2000 will be over seventy-five.[4] Thus, the age structure within the aged population has undergone a potentially significant transformation in recent decades.

Other important changes in the composition of the aged population, especially since World War I, merit scrutiny. For instance, differences in the relative numbers of older men and women have become more noticeable during the course of this century. Table 5.1 reveals that between 1900 and 1930, only a slightly greater proportion of all women than men were over sixty-five years old. By 1970, however, 8.5% of all men, compared to 11.2% of all women, were at least sixty-five. Table 5.2 indicates that although males over sixty-five maintained a slight numerical majority until 1930, there were more older females than males by 1940. This new sex ratio

Table 5.1—Percentage of the Population over 65 Years of Age, 1870–1970

Year	Male	Female	Black	White	Foreign-born White	Native-born White
			Subject			
1870	3.0%	3.0%	2.5%*	3.1%	4.0%	2.9%
1880	3.4	3.4	2.7*	3.6	6.2	3.1
1890	3.8	3.8	2.9	3.9	7.7	3.3
1900	4.0	4.1	3.0	4.1	9.3	3.3
1910	4.2	4.4	3.0	4.1	8.9	3.6
1920	4.6	4.7	3.2	4.8	9.7	4.0
1930	5.4	5.5	3.1	5.6	11.9	4.7
1940	6.7	7.0	4.8	7.1	18.0	5.9
1950	7.7	8.6	5.8	8.4	26.7	7.0
1960	8.3	9.8	6.2	9.4	33.5	7.9
1970	8.5	11.2	6.9	10.3	...	...

SOURCE: Calculated from U.S. Bureau of the Census data

*statistics include Orientals and Indians as well as blacks

Table 5.2—Composition of the Aged Population, 1870–1970

Year	Male	Female	Black	White	Foreign-born White	Native-born White
			Subject			
1870	50.3%	49.7%	10.7%*	89.3%	19.0%	81.0%
1880	50.9	49.1	7.2*	92.8	16.1	83.9
1890	51.2	48.8	11.3	88.7	29.0	71.0
1900	50.5	49.5	8.5	91.5	30.1	69.9
1910	50.4	49.6	7.4	92.6	29.9	70.1
1920	50.4	49.6	6.7	93.3	26.9	73.1
1930	50.1	49.9	5.6	94.4	25.1	74.9
1940	49.0	51.0	6.8	93.2	22.8	77.2
1950	46.8	53.2	7.0	93.0	22.0	78.0
1960	45.3	54.7	7.2	92.8	19.2	80.8
1970	41.9	58.1	7.8	92.2	...	...

SOURCE: Calculated from U.S. Bureau of the Census data

*statistics include Orientals and Indians as well as blacks

has become a familiar characteristic of the aged population in the contemporary era. In 1970, there were one hundred women over sixty-five for every seventy-two men. Experts predict that there will be only sixty-eight men for every hundred older women by 1990, even though boys outnumber girls at birth.[5] Furthermore, the progressive effect of higher death rates for men than for women at each stage of life has widened the disparity in the proportional sizes of the elderly male and female subsets.

Differential fertility, mortality, and migration rates also account for important variations over time in the racial composition of the elderly population.[6] Black fertility rates, which had been higher at the outset anyway, have declined more slowly than white rates since the Reconstruction. Mortality rates for blacks persistently have been, and remain, higher than those for whites. Foreign migration to the United States, moreover, affected the black and white populations differently: the upper bounds of the white age structure increased as immigrants aged; black immigration, which has been minimal since the early nineteenth century, had no discernible effect on the black age structure. As a result, there has always been a smaller proportion of all blacks than all whites past the age of sixty-five. The disparity actually has widened since 1920. In addition, the percentage of blacks in the elderly population has been markedly smaller than the national average of blacks in the total population throughout the century.

The most striking recent alteration in the foreign-born component of the elderly population, on the other hand, was caused by the long-term effect of laws passed since the 1920s that have reduced and attempted to regulate the influx of foreign-born persons into the United States. According to data in tables 5.1 and 5.2, there has been a slight reduction over time in the proportion of all old people who are foreign-born, although the percentage actually had been falling since 1900. Far more significant has been the enormous rise in the proprotion of all immigrants who are old. In 1920, 9.7% of all foreign-born whites were over sixty-five. The figure soared to 33.5% during the next forty years. This illustrates an earlier observation: developments (such as new immigration legislation) that immediately affect trends in the population at large sometimes do not significantly affect patterns in the elderly subset until a later point in time.

The cumulative effect of demographic trends and historical events, in fact, transforms not only the composition but also the geographic distribution of successive cohorts of older Americans. Not surprisingly, the elderly have tended to be most numerous in states with the largest populations. Differences in regions' shares of the aged population, however, have been mainly a function of variations in regional fertility rates and internal migration patterns.[7] The proportion of people over sixty-five years old in the northeast section of the country, for instance, has always been greater than the national average because the region has long been an area with comparatively low fertility and high out-migration rates. In fact, the percentage of all old people living in the region has always exceeded the percentage of the total population living in the Northeast. The percentage of all southerners who were old, on the other hand, has always been less than the national average; the region's share of the total population surpasses its portion of the elderly population. Persistently high fertility rates, which have rejuvenated the area's age structure, explain the region's relatively youthful population. (Florida, it is worth noting, differs from other southern states. Because a growing number of older Americans in recent decades have chosen to spend their retirement years in Florida, the state presently leads the nation in its proportion of people over sixty-five.)[8] The North Central states' population structure in the nineteenth century reflected its recent and rapid settlement by comparatively youthful people. After 1910, however, the proportion of all people over sixty-five in the region surpassed the national average. Between 1910 and 1950, in fact, more old people lived in the North Central states than any other region. While the West remains the least densely populated section in the country, the region's share of old people has been growing rapidly during the past fifty years. The Pacific states' proportion of persons over sixty-five surpassed the national percentage after 1920, demographers observe, because twentieth-century migrants to the area tended to be in the thirty-nine to sixty-four age range, because previous settlers had remained in the region and were growing older, and because the fertility rate was declining.

The distribution of the aged according to rural-urban residences, moreover, indicates that most old people live where they settled at an earlier stage in life. While some choose to return to their hometown or homeland and others decide to reside in a new location in old age, the elderly as a group move less than younger people. (The interstate migration rate of people over sixty-five in 1970 was only one-sixth as great as that for the five-year age group with the highest rate.)[9] This means that older Americans generally do not keep pace with residential patterns prevailing for the population at large. As in the past, for example, a high proportion (27% in 1970) of the elderly live in small towns. During the past forty years, however, a larger and larger proportion of aged people have been found in places that once constituted the vanguard of the urbanization process. In 1970, 59.3% of all whites and 85.6% of all blacks over sixty-five lived in central cities, particularly in decaying parts. Although older people currently are underrepresented in suburban areas developed after World War II, this too will change in time as predominantly middle-aged, middle-class whites age "in place." In the twentieth century, therefore, the elderly population paradoxically has become increasingly "residentially concentrated and residentially dispersed."[10]

Indeed, relatively recent trends in the aging of America may have changed the status of older Americans. It is conceivable, for instance, that the elderly have become a much larger burden to society since World War I. After all, women, very old persons, and those "stuck" in deteriorating locations now constitute a greater proportion of the aged population than ever before. Long-term changes in age-dependency ratios, moreover, lend additional support to this hypothesis. Table 5.3 reveals that a century ago there were more Americans under nineteen and over sixty-five (age groups considered most likely to depend on others for support) than there were between the ages of twenty and sixty-four (age groups most likely to be fully employed). The dependency ratio has fallen during the past one hundred years, thereby reducing the responsibilities placed on the active work force.

Table 5.3—Age-Specific Dependency Ratio, 1870–1970

Year	Dependency Ratio[a]	Percentage of All Possible Dependents Over 65[b]
1870	111	5.7%
1880	106	6.7
1890	98	7.7
1900	94	8.4
1910	86	9.3
1920	83	10.3
1930	79	12.2
1940	70	16.6
1950	73	19.4
1960	88	19.4
1970	91	20.7

SOURCE: Calculated from U.S. Bureau of the Census data

[a] $\text{dependency ratio} = \dfrac{\text{population 0–19 and population over 65}}{\text{population 20–64}} \times 100$

[b] $\text{possible aged dependents} = \dfrac{\text{population over 65}}{\text{population 0–19 and population over 65}} \times 100\%$

An overall drop in the birth rate accounts for the net decline in the dependency ratio. Simultaneously, however, the proportion of those over sixty-five in the potentially dependent age category has increased significantly. (This is consistent, of course, with the rise in the absolute and relative numbers of old persons in the total population.) On the basis of these data, one might argue that demographic realities have required and will continue to require a greater allocation of national resources to relieve the physical and economic needs of people at the upper end of the life cycle.

This line of reasoning, it is crucial to recognize, rests on the implicit assumption that most people cannot and/or do not support themselves in old age. Yet as late as 1920, most men past the age of sixty-five were gainfully employed. And if a majority of older Americans still maintain their economic independence by remaining in the labor force or by relying on corporate retirement pensions, then one might question whether old age really has caused greater economic hardships in the modern era than in earlier periods of history. To pursue this issue, I shall investigate the twentieth-century changes in the occupational status of the aged.

The Exodus of Older Workers
from the Labor Force

Although the proportion of older Americans in the work force declined very little before 1890, there has been a profound change in the twentieth century, especially during the past fifty years. The withdrawal of elderly workers from the marketplace, according to data in figure 1, has become increasingly pronounced since 1900, when about two-thirds of all men over sixty-five were working: 55.6% of all aged males were in the labor force in 1920, 42.2% in 1940, 28.9% in 1960, and 23.9% in 1970. Furthermore, the percentage of women over sixty-five employed outside of the home has fluctuated, but it never exceeded 10% this century, even though the proportion of gainfully employed women of all ages increased from 18.2% in 1890 to 22.7% in 1920 and 43.4% in 1970. Being over sixty clearly has diminished the likelihood since World War I that older men and women will gain employment or remain in the labor force. This fundamental observation remains true whether one controls for race or place of birth, and it is valid at the regional as well as the national level.[11] In fact, the elderly's employment record in nearly every occupational category also corroborates this conclusion.

Since people over sixty-five years old were more likely to be gainfully employed in farming than in any other endeavor before 1900, I shall begin my examination of the elderly's twentieth-century occupational trends by analyzing continuities and changes in this sector. Agriculture continued to

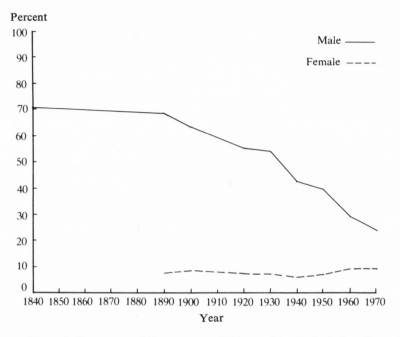

Figure 1. Percentage of Persons over 65 Years of Age in the Labor Force, 1840–1970.

be the occupation in which most elderly men found work between 1900 and 1970. There were persistent variations, however, in the racial and ethnic composition of older farmers: a greater percentage of all gainfully employed blacks than whites were in farming; and elderly native-born white men were more likely to be found in agricultural pursuits than those who were foreign-born (see table 5.4). Not only have most older men who work been more likely to find employment in farming than any other single occupation, but a majority of those who farmed also owned their own land.[12] Once again, there were important racial differences: an overwhelming majority of all white farmers over sixty-five this century have been owners or managers, but the percentage of aged black farm owners did not exceed the percentage of tenants until 1940.

Several interrelated factors account for the concentration of elderly workers in farming.[13] Because age grading is less pertinent to occupational roles in agriculture than in industry, older people physically unable to perform some duties can assume other less demanding but equally necessary chores. "Retirement" on a farm usually connotes reduction—not cessation —of work. Indeed, an elderly farmer may stop performing daily chores but still remain in charge of planning and overseeing major operations as well as

Table 5.4—Composition of the Population Gainfully Employed over 65 Years of Age, 1900 and 1970

1900

Occupation	Native-born White with Native-born White Parents			Native-born White with Foreign-Born Parents			Foreign-born			Black		
	Male	Female	Both	Male	Female	Both	Male	Female	Both	Male	Female	Both
Agriculture	40.4%	4.2%	22.1%	29.0%	2.8%	16.1%	25.4%	1.9%	14.1%	58.7%	10.8%	35.2%
Professional service	3.9	0.2	2.1	3.8	0.4	2.1	1.7	0.1	0.9	0.7		0.4
Domestic or personal service	5.0	2.2	3.6	6.9	2.8	4.9	10.0	2.9	6.6	17.1	17.1	17.1
Trade or transportation	8.6	0.2	4.4	10.6	0.4	5.6	8.4	0.4	4.6	2.6	0.1	1.4
Manufacturing	11.7	1.1	6.3	16.9	1.3	9.2	16.6	0.8	9.0	5.8	0.4	3.2
All occupations	69.7%	7.8%	38.5%	67.2%	7.7%	37.9%	62.1%	6.2%	35.2%	84.9%	28.5%	57.2%

1970

	White		Black	
	Male	Female	Male	Female
Professional service	2.8%	1.4%	1.1%	0.9%
Administrative manager (except farm)	3.3	0.6	0.8	0.2
Sales	2.6	1.1	0.4	0.2
Clerical	1.8	2.2	0.9	0.6
Crafts	3.6	0.2	2.4	0.2
Operative (except transportation)	1.7	1.0	2.2	1.0
Transportation operative	0.8		1.5	0.1
Laborer (except farm)	1.1	0.1	4.1	0.2
Farmer or farm manager	2.4	0.1	1.0	
Farm laborer	0.6		1.7	0.1
Service	3.2	1.7	6.3	2.6
Private house worker		0.9	0.4	6.5
All occupations	23.8%	9.3%	22.7%	12.6%

SOURCE: Calculated from U.S. Bureau of the Census data

NOTE: Due to the rounding off of percentages, the sum of subtotals does not exactly equal the number gainfully employed in *all* occupations.

coordinating other workers' activities. Furthermore, some old people may have stayed active on the farm because they lacked sufficient savings or other income sources to be able to afford retirement. This has been particularly true of women who assumed responsibilities for operating the farm after their husbands died.[14]

Yet while agriculture provided the greatest employment opportunities for men over sixty-five and an important source of livelihood for older women in the twentieth century, it is crucial to observe that the proportion of elderly Americans engaged in farming declined between 1890 and 1970. Roughly 43.0% of all men and 3.4% of all women over sixty-five were engaged in agriculture in 1890; by 1970, the figures were 2.9% and 0.2% respectively. This means that in 1890, 60.8% of all gainfully employed aged men were farmers and that the proportion fell to 12.2% over the next eighty years (see table 5.5). The decline in the percentage of elderly men engaged in agriculture is consistent with a nationwide decrease in the proportion of the population working as farmers. Even allowing for underenumeration, the *absolute* number of men of all ages engaged in farming began to fall after 1910. A technological and organizational revolution, increasingly manifest during the past thirty years, has accelerated the consolidation of small, family-owned farms into a far-flung, highly scientific agribusiness.[15] Consequently, a smaller and smaller proportion of the total work force has been able to produce enough food for the ever expanding domestic and overseas markets.

The diminishing importance of agriculture as a source of jobs, however, has had very different effects on younger and older men. Overall, male labor force participation rates declined very little during the twentieth century as the occupational structure continually evolved to reflect and meet the needs of a complex, expanding, and diversified economy. In 1890, 84.3% of all males over fourteen years old were in the labor force; the figure had dropped to 79.1% in 1940 and to 76.6% by 1970. The proportion of men engaged in nearly every nonagricultural category has risen during the past seventy years. Sometimes, the increase has been spectacular: for instance, 14.0% of all men in the labor force were classified as professional or technical workers in 1970, compared to 3.4% in 1900.[16] And yet, although the rapid expansion of other areas of the economy compensated for reduced opportunities in farming for younger workers, there has not been a significant concurrent upsurge in the proportion of elderly workers in trade, transportation, communication, manufacturing, and mechanical industries as well as a variety of white-collar and blue-collar services. Indeed, even the rise in the proportion of all elderly workers who are professionals (from 4.2% in 1900 to 10.9% in 1970) appears illusory, because the proportion of all older men in the labor force in *any* capacity fell 38.3% during the same period. (See table 5.5.)

Table 5.5—Age-Specific Changes in the Percentage of Americans Working, 1900–1970

1900

Occupation	15–44			45–64			Over 65		
	Male	Female	Both	Male	Female	Both	Male	Female	Both
Agriculture	32.0%	2.8%	17.4%	39.6%	4.2%	22.8%	36.9%	4.0%	20.5%
Professional service	3.1	2.2	2.7	3.8	0.7	2.3	2.9	0.2	1.5
Domestic or personal service	13.7	8.9	11.3	12.5	6.4	9.6	7.8	3.7	5.8
Trade or transportation	17.3	2.5	10.1	15.2	0.1	8.3	8.2	0.3	4.2
Manufacturing or mechanics	22.5	6.0	14.4	22.4	2.3	12.9	13.0	0.9	6.9
All occupations	91.5%	22.5%	56.1%	93.5%	14.1%	56.2%	68.7%	9.1%	38.7%

1930

Occupation	20–44			45–64			Over 65		
	Male	Female	Both	Male	Female	Both	Male	Female	Both
Agriculture	19.6%	1.6%	10.6%	25.4%	2.1%	14.3%	23.0%	1.7%	12.5%
Forestry or fishing	0.6		0.3	0.6		0.3	0.4		0.2
Mining	2.7		1.4	2.3		1.2	0.7		0.4
Manufacturing or mechanics	32.3	4.9	18.6	29.9	2.9	17.0	14.7	1.1	7.7
Transportation	10.2	0.9	5.5	7.9	0.2	4.2	3.1		1.4
Trade	13.3	2.6	8.0	13.0	1.8	7.7	6.9	0.5	3.8
Public service	2.0		1.0	2.5		1.3	2.1		1.0
Professional service	4.6	5.0	4.8	4.4	2.4	3.5	2.7	0.7	1.7
Domestic service	4.4	7.9	6.2	4.7	7.9	6.2	3.1	3.9	3.5
Clerical	5.9	6.5	6.2	3.5	1.3	2.3	1.5		0.9
All occupations	95.8%	29.4%	62.6%	94.1%	18.8%	58.1%	58.4%	8.1%	33.1%

1950*

Occupation	45–64	Over 65
Professional service	5.8%*	2.5%*
Farmer or farm manager	11.0	9.2
Farm laborer or foreman	2.2	1.9
Manager or officer	12.3	4.9

Table 5.5—(continued)

Occupation	Age								
	15–44			45–64			Over 65		
	Male	Female	Both	Male	Female	Both	Male	Female	Both
Clerical				4.8			1.8		
Sales				4.8			2.9		
Crafts				17.4			5.8		
Operative				13.9			3.8		
Manufacturing operative				5.7			1.8		
Transportation operator				1.1			0.4		
Private house worker				0.2			0.1		
Service				6.1			4.0		
Manufacturing laborer				1.9			0.7		
Trade or transportation laborer				3.4			1.6		
All occupations				85.8%			39.8%		

1960*

Occupation	Male	Male
Agriculture	8.0%	5.5%
Professional service	7.0	2.4
Manager	11.8	4.0
Clerical	5.1	1.8
Sales	5.2	2.4
Crafts	18.1	4.1
Operative	10.3	2.8
Manufacturing Operative	5.0	0.9
Trade or transportation operative	0.9	0.2
Private house worker	0.2	0.2
Service	5.6	3.1
Trade or transportation laborer	2.6	0.9
Manufacturing laborer	1.4	0.6
All occupations	85.0%	28.9%

1970*

Professional service	10.0%	6.7%	2.6%	1.4%
Manager or administrator (except farm)	11.9	2.4	3.1	0.6
Sales	6.4	0.4	2.4	1.0
Clerical	5.8	13.8	1.7	2.1
Crafts	19.7	1.0	3.5	0.2
Operative (except transportation)	10.8	7.3	1.7	1.0
Transportation operative	4.9	1.8	0.9	
Laborer (except farm)	4.6	0.4	1.4	0.1
Farmer or farm manager	3.5	0.2	2.2	0.1
Farm laborer	1.2	0.8	0.7	0.1
Service	6.8	7.9	3.4	1.7
Private house worker	0.1	2.4	0.1	1.3
All occupations	85.4%	46.5%	23.9%	9.5%

SOURCE: Calculated from the U.S. Bureau of the Census data

NOTE: Due to the rounding off of percentages, the sum of subtotals does not exactly equal the number gainfully employed in *all* occupations.

*labor force definition used in 1950–70 data

Twentieth-century changes in the status of women over sixty-five years old in the occupational structure reveal a comparable employment pattern. A striking age-specific variation, for example, occurred in the proportion of women engaged as clerical workers.[17] The proportion of all employed women working in clerical positions rose from 3.1% to 20.9% between 1890 and 1930. By 1970, 34.5% of all women in the labor force were clerical workers; 73.6% of all clerical workers were women. A much smaller percentage of older women, however, were employed in clerical positions. As late as 1930, less than 2% of all gainfully employed elderly women were working in that capacity. And while 22% of all working women over sixty-five held clerical positions in 1970, it is worth observing that only 2.3% of all clerical workers were over sixty-five. The growing demand for clerical workers has been a major reason for the overall increase in women's employment during the twentieth century, but few older women have found job opportunities in this area.

The extent to which older Americans withdraw from the labor force, moreover, has accelerated in the twentieth century. Data in table 5.6 reveal that the ratio of men over sixty-five years old in all occupations was 77% as large as that of men working between the ages of forty-five and sixty-four in 1890. It dropped fifteen percentage points over the next forty years and has plummeted thirty-four additional points during the past forty years. Significantly, this long-term trend exists in both the agricultural and nonagrarian sectors of the economy. The rate at which men quit working past the age of sixty-five has quickened in recent decades. Similar, albeit less striking, patterns obtain for women. The ratio of the proportion of all working women over sixty-five to the proportion of women between the ages of forty-five and sixty-four declined from 66% to 20% between 1890 and 1970.

Explanations for and Implications of the Decline of the Aged in the Labor Force

This analysis clearly establishes that the most important exodus of older Americans from the labor force has taken place within the past fifty years. Is it possible that this dramatic transformation in the occupational status of elderly people would have occurred regardless of how Americans perceived the aged's position in contemporary society? The hypothesis is not farfetched: just as the rhetoric and realities of growing old diverged in the nineteenth century, so too changes in the aged's labor force rates could have evolved independently of new ideas about old age during the contemporary

Table 5.6—Rate of Drop-Off from the Labor Force, with Advancing Age, 1890–1970

	Occupation					
	Agriculture, Fishing, or Mining		Nonagricultural Fields		All Occupations	
Year	Male	Female	Male	Female	Male	Female
1890	89%	83%	58%	44%	77%	66%
1900	93	95	59	52	74	65
1920	82	79	53	41	64	47
1930	90	81	52	38	62	43
1940	87	64	44	30	55	32
1950	84	43	38	26	46	27
1960	68	41	30	23	34	24
1970	56	39	26	18	28	20

SOURCE: Calculated from U.S. Bureau of the Census data, which did not include information for 1910.

NOTE: Drop-off ratio $= \dfrac{\dfrac{\text{number over 65 years of age engaged in occupation}}{\text{number over 65 years of age in population}}}{\dfrac{\text{number 45–64 years of age engaged in occupation}}{\text{number 45–64 years of age in population}}} \times 100\%$

era. Thus, one must determine whether the marked decline in the total percentage of gainfully employed older people has been largely the result of structural factors, such as shifting demographic trends or unfolding economic patterns, that arose or became significant in the twentieth century.

One might predict, for example, that the mere presence of more and more people living past the age of sixty-five or seventy-five years old depressed over time the relative number of elderly persons who were gainfully employed, since work force participation rates for men and women tend to decline with advancing years. Available research on this issue, however, suggests that the impact of this demographic trend on the overall proportion of older people at work has been surprisingly minimal. In *The Older Population of the United States* (1958), Henry D. Sheldon demonstrated that changes in the age structure of the elderly population probably reduced the size of the aged labor force by about 1% between 1890 and 1950. According to calculations published in 1969 by William G. Bowen and T. Aldrich Finegan in *The Economics of Labor Force Participation*, even the sharp rise between 1948 and 1965 in the fraction of men over seventy-five in the elderly population caused older male participation rates during the period to decline only 0.8%.[18] The aging of the elderly population, in short, has not appreciably affected the group's relative occupational status.

If the aged's overall health status had been the decisive factor determining their ability to work, it is unlikely that the proportion of gainfully employed elderly men would have fallen off so greatly during the past fifty years. Because of numerous advances and improvements in health care, one would expect a decline in the relative number of people afflicted by infirmities or debilities. However, the proportion of noninstitutionalized men over sixty-five reporting some chronic activity limitation has fluctuated in recent decades; no striking long-term trend yet emerges.[19] Nevertheless, existing evidence compels me to discount a causal relationship between deteriorating health conditions and declining work force rates among the aged during the twentieth century.

Contemporary research also tends to minimize the degree to which the lessening participation in the labor market by elderly men can be explained by the movement of the population from rural to urban areas. A 1958 study by Clarence D. Long found that while a consistently larger percentage of men over sixty-five were employed in rural than in urban locations, rates declined more strikingly in rural areas. The difference between the percentages of older men working in rural and urban settings decreased over time: by 1950, 44.1% of all elderly men were at work in rural places, compared to 40.0% in urban ones. Long also indicated that standardizing for the effect of migration between 1890 and 1950 modified the decline in the total labor force of men over sixty-five "relatively little."[20] The elderly male labor force rate fell another 3% between 1948 and 1965, Bowen and Finegan estimate, due to the persistence of the rural-urban migration pattern. Thus, once again a demographic trend had less impact on the elderly's occupational status than one initially might have anticipated.

The hypothesis that the progressive march of technology has displaced older workers from the marketplace seems credible at first glance. Any technical change is likely to cause some obsolescence of current workers' skills. Continual modifications and innovations, in fact, require a pool of workers possessing skills that enable them to execute new jobs created by more sophisticated technology. As a result, employers tend to recruit recent —and typically younger—entrants to the labor force for jobs.[21] But the effect of technical developments on the aged's chance to stay in the labor force has not been entirely negative. While granting that new techniques make some skills outmoded, several scholars note that employees' working lives may have been prolonged as machines and automation reduced the physical burdens and stress associated with certain jobs in the industrial sector. Bowen and Finegan claim, for instance, that the reduction in the average work week offset the downward spiral of elderly men's labor force rates by as much as 3.5% between 1948 and 1965.[22]

Reformulating the argument, some economists stress that it is not technology per se that discriminates against older people, but rather the elderly's limited education compared to younger job applicants. Advantages in educational background *do* appear to be one reason why younger men and women have been displacing older workers from the twentieth-century labor force.[23] Yet these scholars point out that the phenomenon is not inevitable.

Longitudinal and cross sectional analyses of data published since the 1940s reveal a direct correlation between level of education and labor force participation among the elderly. And, as those with higher and higher median years of schooling (reflecting expanding educational opportunities) approach old age, it is possible in future decades that the aged's decline in labor force participation because of minimal schooling and training will be stabilized, if not reversed.

But industry's preference for younger, better educated workers has not been the major economic factor causing the dramatic decline in the aged's labor force participation. Far more significant have been the invention and extension of alternative sources of support in old age, which have reduced the elderly's need, desire, opportunity, and ability to remain working in recent decades. According to 1967 census survey data, 89% of all persons over sixty-five years of age received money from various retirement programs, and 15% obtained income from veterans' benefits, individual insurance annuities, and personal contributions; 12% of the elderly population relied on public assistance. In contrast, only 27% of all older Americans earned income through wages, salaries, or self-employment.[24] The upsurge in the number of people eligible for Social Security insurance benefits, the rising payment level of these benefits, and the remarkable growth of pension plans and disbursements in both the public and private sectors of the economy have made it financially possible for many older people to afford leisure. Bowen and Finegan conclude, in fact, that increases in nonwage (or salary) income alone contributed to a 9.8% decline between 1948 and 1965 in the fraction of elderly men in the labor force. Furthermore, because compulsory retirement policies generally have been tied to the growing availability of pensions, these two economists claim that mandatory retirement (as distinguished from the pure income effect) caused an additional 5% drop during the period.[25] A segment of the population over sixty-five, in other words, must quit their jobs even if they do not so desire.

In light of this survey, it seems logical to argue that the actual status of the aged in twentieth-century America changed as agriculture ceased to be a major source of jobs, as formal education became a more desirable asset than years of experience, and as pension plans coupled with mandatory retirement spread through business and industry. It appears equally plausible to postulate that these same factors made it increasingly difficult for older Americans to escape poverty through gainful employment, and in turn to propose that the elderly's plight became more and more visible as their numbers grew. Yet the preceding analysis also indicates that examining only demographic patterns and economic trends does not elucidate, much less account for, all the important alterations and developments in older

Americans' situations since 1914. For example, how does one explain the origins of some of the structural determinants themselves, such as the reliance on Social Security benefits and federal public assistance in old age? Do they represent deliberate responses to perceived changes in the elderly's financial resources? In what sense and to what extent do they embody ideas about the aged's assets and liabilities prevailing at the time of their enactment? The sources consulted thus far do not address these matters. To understand and interpret the history of old age in the United States since 1914, therefore, one clearly must explore the dynamic relationship between popular perceptions of older people's worth and their actual place in society.

Needless to say, the interplay between the rhetoric and the reality of being old in America cannot be studied in a vacuum. I dare not assume that people earlier in the century saw things the same way I do, observing the situation in the late 1970s. That Americans in previous decades acted as they might have done under similar circumstances today must be demonstrated, not presumed. Major continuities and changes in the contemporary history of old age, it is crucial to recognize, emerged as the culmination, or at least the byproduct, of broad cultural and social forces that were simultaneously transforming the very nature of American society itself. Because of this, both the meaning and context of growing old in the new land have changed as the United States matured in the twentieth century.

PART III

Contemporary Old Age
in Historical Perspective

The Age Barrier

Cartoon, *The American Labor Legislation Review* 19, December 1929.

CHAPTER 6

Old Age Becomes
a National Problem

Americans between World War I and World War II believed that new theories in the biological and social sciences as well as data gathered by economists, demographers, government officials, and social workers verified negative ideas about the elderly that had emerged during the last third of the nineteenth century. The most recent and authoritative evidence indicated that old age brought pronounced physical decay, mental decline, unpleasant and sometimes deviant psychological and behavioral traits, economic uselessness, personal isolation, and social segregation. "Resent, resist, or ignore it as well as we will, the fact is that once thought of as old, whether because of mental and physical signs or by withdrawal from our wonted sphere of activities, we enter a class more or less apart and by ourselves."[1] By emphasizing this theme, books, magazine articles, and scientific studies, among other sources of information, generally increased the anxiety of those who viewed the aging process with dread.

In fact, Americans between 1914 and 1940 described the status of the aged more pessimistically than their predecessors. Writers between 1865 and 1914 had only claimed that contemporary societal changes were diminishing older people's roles and social worth. Americans after World War I perceived and voiced concern that current demographic and socioeconomic conditions were making old age per se a national problem as well as a personal misfortune. Conditions prevailing in the United States, they contended, rapidly were making the plight of older men and women more visible and acute.

Having redefined the elderly's position to be both unfavorable and problematic, Americans earnestly endeavored to expand existing means of assisting older people. Proposals once dismissed as too expensive, unnecessary, or impractical were seriously considered and acted upon after 1914. The unprecedented belief that the aged's plight now posed a grave societal "problem" and experiments with new "solutions" to remedy the elderly's physical, social, and financial predicaments mark important developments in the history of old age in the United States. In many ways, the outlook and efforts arising after World War I continue to color and shape the current perceptions and treatment of older Americans.

New Studies Reinforce
Americans' Disparagement of the Aged

By seeming to provide qualitatively and quantitatively more impressive evidence than previously existed, research in the natural and social sciences, as well as the sheer force of often repeated derogatory opinions, enhanced the plausibility, persuasiveness, and pervasiveness of the popular belief that old age brought inevitable decline. In retrospect, it appears that investigators and their contemporaries may have exaggerated the degree to which their evidence actually justified such adverse conclusions about the aged. Researchers, for instance, frequently reported innumerable exceptions to the then prevailing tenet that humans automatically deteriorated as they aged, and occasionally admitted surprise that some older men and women did not differ from younger individuals in performance or personality as much as they had anticipated. (Scholarly inquiries conducted after World War II revealed comparable variations but interpreted them in a different manner. Researchers presently cite such variance to support the evolving notion that it can be misleading to describe the aged as a homogeneous group.) Between 1914 and 1940, however, variations within the elderly population were considered far less important than differences between them and other groups. On the basis of their assumptions and evidence, and in accordance with accepted contemporary research standards, commentators before World War II stressed modal patterns in describing the elderly. In so doing they reinforced and amplified the "scientific" basis for the prevailing assumption that old age was a period of pitiful and trying desuetude.

One of the most obvious and frequently mentioned liabilities of growing old was the decline in physical vigor and health. The typical picture of old age drawn from batteries of tests and masses of evidence was "one of dependence and relative helplessness, associated with a restriction of the range of activity, a limitation of voluntary enterprise."[2] It is worth noting, however, that studies published between 1914 and 1940 revealed that the physical conditions of the elderly varied markedly by sex, age, and socioeconomic status. That some people scored higher marks on tests measuring fitness, vigor, and dexterity than much younger subjects clearly indicated that all older Americans were not sick, slow, or clumsy.[3] Nevertheless, researchers generally were less interested in reporting cases of extreme good and poor health than they were in establishing the physical condition considered most prevalent among the elderly. As a result, early-twentieth-century descriptions and examinations of older people tended to confirm a conclusion reached during the last quarter of the nineteenth century: the decline in well-being and vitality that they presumed was associated with old age sharply curtailed a person's ability to keep up with the rest of society.

Elaborate investigations conducted between World War I and World War II into people's ability to learn as they grew older strongly intimated but did not entirely demonstrate that mental as well as physical faculties declined with the years. For instance, Edward L. Thorndike and his associates argued in *Adult Learning* (1928) that "from seventy on, many persons show a notable decline in the amount of learning per year, so that they do not learn as much as they forget and fall back in the amount of knowledge."[4] Such an assertion was made with little proof. Because of the difficulty in assembling "unselected cases of middle age or senescence" and because of the structure of his research design, Thorndike never actually tested the learning capacity of subjects over forty-five. Like most of his fellow investigators, he upheld prevailing opinions about the deterioration of the elderly's mental powers by citing experiments with animals and previously reported research. Thorndike also extrapolated from his own data: having suggested that a person's peak learning performance occurred at twenty-two and then declined about one percent a year until the fifth decade, he considered it unlikely that one's interest in learning could compensate for the "inner degeneration" of an aging body. Other contemporary evidence indicated that people lost their desire as well as their ability to learn. Harry L. Hollingworth, in *Mental Growth and Decline* (1927), asserted that "the learning of new things commonly implies a forward-looking interest which is less characteristic of age than of youth."[5] Thus, while neither Thorndike nor Hollingworth inferred from their evidence that an adult's learning capacity completely ceased in old age, they noted limitations to mental growth and asserted that these strictures became more pronounced with age.

Although researchers like Thorndike and Hollingworth recognized the ambiguous nature of their results, the public generally did not. Most people thought that such studies provided a scientific justification for believing that mental deficiencies no less than physical handicaps diminished the aged's worth. Experiments suggesting that older people did not assimilate new ideas, coupled with real-life instances of "decreased mental and bodily strength and endurance," gave popular writers and their readers reason to doubt that the aged would, or even could, contribute much to society.[6] Such a glum judgment seemed all the more credible because it was consistent with other unfavorable notions about old age.

Commentators after World War I, for example, offered impressive documentation supported by currently avant-garde psychological insights and jargon to prove that older people had undesirable personalities in addition to their mental and physical deficiencies. The nascent professional interest in the psychology of aging generated a novel theoretical and empirical basis for studying and explaining undesirable character traits already recognized to be common among the elderly. On the basis of clinical tests and systematic observations, psychologists by and large agreed that few elderly Americans were either well-adjusted or happy.[7] While admitting exceptions, researchers noted that most old people displayed "unpleasant mental peculiarities" such as dissatisfaction, lack of humor, conceit, suspicion, hypercriticism, bitterness, depression, or slovenliness. Scientists investigated the extent of hypochondria, melancholia, impaired attention, disorientation, and disorders they associated with cases of senile dementia and other mental illnesses. In some cases, they found that "a pathological persecution fixation" and "morbid irritability" became manifest in the aged personality.

Researchers attributed the psychological crises of old age to a plethora of physiological, socioeconomic, and individual factors.[8] Intrinsic changes in the sense organs and nervous system, it was said, affected the elderly's emotional state; diseases and degeneracy were thought to induce hallucinations, neuroses, and strain. Scientists thought that a limiting range of opportunities and experiences also narrowed the aged's outlook on life. In addition, difficulties in facing death and dying made older people's psychological well-being all the more precarious. By indicating that many aspects of the aged personality surfaced only in the later stages of life, scientific inquiries into the psychology of old age thus lent additional justification for believing that personal handicaps diminished the social value of the elderly.

Besides cataloging the elderly's idiosyncracies, writers itemized ways that behavior of the aged deviated from that of other people. "Old age is simply a mass of bad habits."[9] Writers not only condemned older Americans for having disagreeable or peculiar habits but they also perpetuated earlier injunctions prohibiting senior citizens from normal adult activities. Consider, for example, attitudes toward aged sexuality. In the *Psychology of Sex* (1933) as well as in his previous multivolume studies, Havelock Ellis argued that by engaging in intercourse at advanced ages, men risked heart attacks, cerebral hemorrhages, and even death; an efflorescence of sexual activity past sixty often was accompanied by egotism, callousness, exhibitionism, homosexuality, or child abuse. Paradoxically, however, Ellis reported that total abstinence made older men feel like eunuchs.[10] Because cultural pressure to disengage from sex in old age was so pervasive by the 1940s, Alfred C. Kinsey and his associates stressed that the most important generalization to be made about the sexual behavior of older males seemed "astonishing, for it is quite contrary to general conceptions of aging processes in sex." After studying the case histories of thousands of men between fifteen and sixty years old, Kinsey found that sexual activity did not decline sharply at advanced ages, but rather waned throughout the adult stages of the life cycle.[11] Kinsey might have "scooped" the sex experts of the 1960s by emphasizing that older men's sexual life and interest was not as dormant and futile as many supposed or hoped it would be, but because he had so few elderly subjects and was more interested in other matters anyway, he did not pursue the issue. Instead, he attributed the aged's decrease in sexual responsiveness to physiological decline and psychological fatigue. In so doing, Kinsey actually corroborated rather than undermined existing ideas about older men's sexual behavior.

Everything seemed to reaffirm and embellish the belief that one's value faded in old age. Unless a person was mounting a rising tide of success, it seemed doubtful that any conceivable benefits of growing old would out-weigh its physical, mental, psychological, and behavioral liabilities. "We have become accustomed to associate old age with thoughts and visions of senility, decrepitude, uselessness and burdensomeness."[12] In light of the overwhelming and impressive support for such an opinion, it becomes perfectly understandable why Americans after World War I resented, resisted, ignored, and dreaded the coming of age.

Observers Claim That the Aged Constitute a Societal Problem

Commentators did more, however, than investigate and elaborate upon the ways that people deteriorated as they grew older. Americans after World War I claimed for the first time that contemporary conditions were making the elderly themselves a serious social "problem." Basically, they argued that current ideas and evidence about old age interacting with demo-graphic factors and socioeconomic developments were causing the elderly's plight to evolve into a national predicament. The situation seemed parti-cularly grave because the continued interplay of cultural trends and structural forces was sharply reducing opportunities for older people to support themselves and to participate meaningfully in American life. As Corra Harris observed in a 1926 issue of *Ladies Home Journal*,

> Old people are not so much prisoners of their years and their infirmities as they are of their circumstances, after they are no longer able to produce their own circum-stances, but are obliged to adjust themselves to conditions made for them by people who belong to a later generation in a new world. It is worse than if they became foreigners in their old age, because they are in the midst of familiar scenes, but obsolete, like fine old words erased from the epic of living.[13]

Because of the way they perceived the situation, Americans increasingly redefined the obsolescence of old age to embrace its broadening personal implications and societal importance.

Demographers, economists, and other writers postulated that the number of elderly persons in the United States made old age a "problem" in modern American society. In part, they predicated their argument on recent census data and other population studies indicating that the proportion of the population over sixty-five years old was growing in the twentieth century. Not only did Americans rightly recognize that the relative size of the elderly population was increasing, but they also correctly predicted that the proportion would increase. In forecasting a "nation of elders in the making," many speculated that an older population might alter national production, consumption, and inheritance patterns; some warned that the trend might even threaten America's economic prosperity and political institutions.[14] The fears expressed in such predictions suggest that Americans were not reacting just to the absolute and relative increase of old people in their midst. They also were grounded in the belief that a person's chronological age increasingly determined his or her role in society. "In no other country does the basis of age alone furnish so definite a line of demarcation between a portion of the population recognized as economically efficient and socially attractive and that part of it which is neither useful nor particularly attractive."[15] Commentators argued that America's age-grading system, which not only affected nearly every dimension of life after World War I but also reflected the prevailing bias against the old, compounded the predicament of the elderly.

Older people's positions were becoming more vulnerable, observers contended, as the United States continued to evolve into a predominantly urban and industrial nation. According to rural sociologists, the mass migration from the country to the city had not eroded the elderly's status until relatively recently.[16] Prior to 1920, most aged men and women lived on farms or in a rural setting where they had jobs, participated in civic and church functions, and could rely on community support when necessary. Researchers postulated that the situation changed as more and more older Americans lived in cities: they discovered that food, housing, and recreation in an urban environment were expensive and they experienced difficulties in finding and keeping a job. Furthermore, as urban mores and modern technology transformed the countryside, it was predicted that the process would even undermine the responsibility, roles, and respect accorded aged people who stayed on the farm.

Articles in popular and scholarly journals and help-wanted newspaper advertisements appearing after 1914 clearly reveal that the elderly's presumed value and apparent status in the labor market were steadily deteriorating. Careful examination of pertinent literature suggests, moreover, that both opponents and advocates of age-discrimination practices evinced little sympathy for workers seeking employment after the age of sixty.[17] Surveys of specific occupational groups (including professionals) revealed that earnings declined after the age of fifty-five.[18] Women, it was found, encountered sex as well as age discrimination: years of experience and skills guaranteed neither job security nor high wages. But unlike her male industrial, clerical, and domestic counterpart, a woman was an "older worker" at a comparatively young thirty-five.[19] Americans often justified their disesteem for elderly workers by citing evidence that age impaired a person's productivity. New findings corroborated previous data "proving" that the elderly were less efficient than personnel in their twenties, or even late forties, and that they also caused morale problems.[20]

And yet, social theorists who hypothesized that the continued growth of the economy adversely affected the aged's employment worth went beyond rehearsing late-nineteenth-century observations about the factory system's prematurely wearing out employees and making older workers appear inefficient. The sheer growth of big business and industry itself, economists and popular writers noted, reduced the elderly's economic prospects. Establishments once considered "cushions for the scrap heap" were declining in importance. Industries with advanced technologies and sophisticated production processes made little effort to recruit and retain older employees.[21] In addition, more and more corporations were implementing and expanding policies—such as group insurance plans and retirement programs—and establishing personnel departments armed with batteries of psychological tests and "job analysis" profiles to standardize recruiting procedures. Though these innovations in some respects were clearly improvements over previous practices, they also tended to ease people over sixty out of the work force and they created obstacles to their reentry: cost and efficiency considerations generally made older job applicants seem less attractive and useful than younger ones. A federal study of *Recent Social Trends* (1933) noted that "there is much evidence to support the growing belief that industry is honeycombed with strict hiring limits."[22] Accordingly, most writers projected that the percentage of elderly Americans supporting themselves through gainful employment would continue to decline.

Decreasing employment opportunities for the aged after World War I raised fundamental questions about the ability of older people to support themselves in later life, and thereby stimulated new interest in old-age dependency. Social workers, professional reformers, scholars, business groups, civic organizations, the U.S. Bureau of Labor, and more than a dozen state legislatures conducted surveys between 1914 and 1940 that focused on the causes and dimensions of financial hardships among the elderly. One common theme emerging out of the welter of statistics and rhetoric was that urbanization, industrialization, and the shortened working period of life among other things were making old-age dependency different from what it had been in former times. "Poverty in old age can no longer be made impervious by mere hard work, frugality and good habits. Our fortune

has become dependent on altogether too many forces beyond our control."[23] Modern conditions, Americans increasingly claimed, were creating
a situation in which economic insecurity threatened a large segment of the
elderly population.

In fact, many thought it impossible to discuss the problems of old age
without referring to old-age dependency. Robert Kelso, a respected researcher of poverty, claimed in 1929 that "old age, merely by that name, is a
synonym for poverty."[24] It is imperative to recognize that Kelso's state-
ment, because it conveys a sentiment often expressed between the world
wars, reflects a fundamental shift in ideas about old-age dependency. Before World War I, most Americans did not think that industrial and urban
conditions per se caused many cases of indigency among the elderly; infirmity and intemperance seemed more significant sources of hardship.
Writers after 1914 acknowledged that traditional factors contributed to the
problem. But they also placed unprecedented emphasis on evolving societal
forces beyond people's control that severely hampered and sometimes precluded their best efforts to maintain themselves in old age.

Furthermore, contemporary observers pointed out that recent developments in the economy and in society at large strained existing means of support. For instance, although it remained a cultural norm that the family was
and should be an older person's primary source of assistance, caring for parents seemed to be more problematic than it once had been. Writers increasingly noted that multigenerational living arrangements elicited com-
plaints and feelings of resentment among young and old alike.[25] Personality
differences were not the sole cause of domestic travail. Economic matters
fueled tensions. Surveys conducted in the 1920s suggested that legislators
underestimated children's difficulties in assisting their aged parents. Pre-
occupied with their own family responsibilities, many sons and daughters
could not take on the additional burden of supporting dependent parents.[26]
In addition, the fact that recently constructed homes had fewer but larger
rooms may have exacerbated the situation. Eliminating the spare bedroom
reduced the space potentially available for grandparents without diminishing the premium Americans placed on privacy in the home.[27] Influenced by
their own reflections on such psychological, economic, and logistical considerations, commentators frequently suggested that it was better for the old
to live meagerly but independently than to dwell in a child's home.

No one seriously recommended, however, that elderly persons seek
refuge in the local poorhouse unless there was no other alternative. Filth,
shocking treatment, mismanagement, and especially the social stigma attached to it made the almshouse an undesirable option for the aged poor.
"The word 'poorhouse,' " concluded a 1926 survey funded by the Fraternal Congress and Loyal Order of the Moose, "has become the threatening
symbol of one of humanity's great degradations."[28] Yet despite the growing

conviction that healthy and self-respecting older men and women did not belong there, the absolute and proportional size of the aged population in almshouses continued to rise. The situation was clearly tragic.

In short, Americans after World War I increasingly concluded that contemporary demographic trends and socioeconomic developments were making old age per se a problem fraught with alarming national significance. In some instances observers may even have overstated the degree and extent to which recent structural forces adversely affected older people. The rising number of persons over sixty-five in society was, after all, a long-term phenomenon just beginning to accelerate. Industrialization's impact on elderly workers was neither entirely negative nor wholly irreversible: wartime exigencies, for instance, had required recruiting presumably superannuated veterans back to production lines.[29] Intergenerational tensions and the elderly's preference for maintaining independent households, moreover, were not new; such feelings existed before the twentieth century. Nor was this the first time that the plight of older people in the poorhouse had been deplored. Nevertheless, what really matters at this point in the narrative is that after 1914 more and more essayists, social and natural scientists, and other writers perceived and interpreted the aged's social position in an unprecedented manner. Having determined that "modern" conditions made the personal hardships as well as the societal implications of growing old a matter of grave concern, Americans then proceeded to act on the basis of their ideas.

Salvaging Old Age

Keenly aware of the pervasive animus against old age, different groups after World War I attempted to mitigate or even eliminate the liabilities of being old and to reaffirm its advantages in order to improve the status of the elderly in the United States. Advice columns, poems, and essays often repeated hoary maxims reminding readers over sixty to exercise moderately, remain cheerful, maintain relationships with younger people, keep abreast of new developments, and seek the comfort of religion, among other things.[30] Some writers, moreover, updated the perennial suggestion that people should stay useful and busy as long as possible in order to make it reflect modern circumstances more closely. Recognizing that "as the world is organized now, there seems to be no niche" for older people, writers tried to help the aged find satisfying alternatives to gainful employment. They advised men to prepare for their retirement years early in life by acquiring hobbies and interests that would remain stimulating and they recommended that women take up quilting and other crafts that the world still valued but no longer spent the time or effort to create by hand.[31] Indeed, a

spate of books attempted to mold more favorable identities and constructive livestyles for older Americans. Works such as Walter Pitkin's *Life Begins at Forty* (1932), Elmer E. Ferris's *Who Says Old* (1933), and Lyman
Pierson Powell's *The Second Seventy* (1937) were immensely popular.

At first glance, the self-help books and literature published between 1914
and 1940 might seem unduly optimistic or unrealistic. Yet, in retrospect,
they clearly are just as much a product of the era as the grim images of old
age they sought to counterbalance. They expressed a theme found
frequently in government reports, scholarly studies, and a variety of popular writings: people could protect themselves against premature decay and
possibly make valuable contributions if they continued to grow mentally and
psychologically beyond middle age. The eminent psychologist G. Stanley
Hall, for example, speculated that "intelligent and well-conserved senecti-
tude has very important social and anthropological functions in the world,
not hitherto utilized or even recognized, the chief of which is most compre-
hensively designated by the general term synthesis, something never so
needed as in our very complex age of distracting specialization."[32] Hall, of
course, grossly inflated the originality of his proposal: one of the major roles
of older people before the Civil War had been to offer the wisdom garnered
over many years. The significance of Hall's proposition lies not in what he
said, but rather in its underlying assumption that older Americans could
improve their situations by mobilizing their own resources and potential.

In this context, it is worth noting that fresh ideas and new methods of
coping with the difficulties of aging were often the inspirations of elderly
men and women joining forces to deal with the fact that they were "old." Dr.
Lillien J. Martin, a retired head of Stanford University's psychology department, opened an Old Age Center in San Francisco and wrote numerous
articles and books to help older people who had lost their desire to live life
fully. Building on her professional opinion and personal belief that most humans could learn at any stage of life, Martin urged her fellow older Americans to reform their thinking and acting. "What the old must do to salvage
themselves, to prevent themselves from being pushed into the background,"
she conceded, "is no easy task, but one that is rich in returns."[33] Another
retired educator, Dr. William McKeever, operated a "school for maturates"
in Oklahoma City in the 1930s to teach those over seventy years old to enrich their lives and outlooks. Local clubs founded by and for older persons
sprung up throughout the nation during the period and served as informal
organizations for educational and social activities. Somewhat later in the
century, the elderly began to form "gray lobbies" to press for special old-age
legislation. Hence, older Americans themselves after 1914 took an
originally small but ultimately significant step in "salvaging old age." While
aged men and women have always had to deal with their individual difficulties in some manner, these first old-age centers, clubs, and schools consti-

tute the elderly's initial organizational efforts to deal with their situation collectively.

Medical researchers also made important headway in their attempts to alleviate, and even save, people from the physical deterioration of advancing years. Sometimes scientists derived their inspiration from late nineteenth-century pioneers. Serge Voronoff and Eugene Steinach, for example, based their research on Brown-Séquard's hypothesis that the degeneration of reproductive and other ductless glands caused old age: independently they tried grafting glands of young animals to older ones as a means of restoring youthfulness.[34] Others tested different methods. Pierre Delbet in the 1930s pursued Elie Metchnikoff's notion that one could ward off old age through antidotes, but he prescribed an intake of magnesium chloride instead of lactic acid. Still others believed recent inventions could restore vigor in old age. Dr. William Bailey proposed (but did not prove) that ionizing an elderly person's endocrine cells with radioactive elements of the thorium family would make the patient feel younger.[35] Even though all these attempts proved to be dismal failures, it is important to recognize that between the world wars there remained considerable evidence and professional support for claiming that the last stage of life was characterized by pathological degeneration and hence could be "cured." Those who considered old age a disease, or thought that senile deterioration could be arrested or reversed, strongly defended such experiments and occasionally lauded the effort to apply new discoveries in radiology and endocrinology to an age-old malady.

At the same time researchers were working on the assumption that old age was a curable pathological disorder, other scientists were investigating the possibility that old age resulted from natural developmental processes. Two early-twentieth-century spokesmen of this emerging school of thought, Charles Sedgwick Minot (an embryologist) and Charles Manning Child (a cytologist), believed that old age resulted from cumulative changes in the properties of cells and tissues as an organism matured.[36] Proceeding along similar lines, Dr. I. L. Nascher sharply contrasted "senility" and "senile pathology," a distinction he felt too many researchers blurred. He contended that old age was not a pathological state of maturity but a distinct physiological stage of life, because "the aged individual is in fact an entirely different individual from the one who was formed from the ancestors of the late cells."[37] Accordingly, Nascher recommended that doctors treating senile disease try to restore a patient's body to a state of health normally found in later life, and not to one associated with middle age. He also pointed out that doctors should consider the effects of an elderly patient's mental outlook and attitudes about his physical and social condition.

Besides insisting that scientific researchers view old age from a broader perspective than they were accustomed, Nascher also urged his colleagues to consider the study of senility and senile pathology a legitimate medical specialty, complete with its own theories, areas of research, and professional standards. Nascher gave the discipline its name, "geriatrics." He also published the most important study on old age since Charcot's landmark—a book not surprisingly called *Geriatrics* (1914)—and served as the first president of the New York Geriatrics Society, founded in 1915.

Yet recounting red-letter dates in the fledgling field's early history tells only part of the story. Actually, Nascher and his theories met with considerable resistance during most of the period. Finding a firm willing to publish his work proved very difficult. As late as 1926, Nascher admitted that he knew no other scientist who described himself or herself as a full-time specialist in geriatrics.[38] Until his ideas gained credibility, the nation's only practicing geriatrician was able to contribute little more than a name, a book, and enthusiasm to his cause. Developments in medicine after 1914 eventually did lend Nascher's views an aura of respectability that they initially lacked. Cytologists amassed impressive evidence indicating that old age was a discrete and inevitable stage in the life cycle of cells and tissues. Endocrinologists began to define "senility" as the last major "endocrine epoch" before natural death. Even some pathologists rejected older hypotheses and described old age as a stage of physiological retrogression inherent in an organism.[39] In so doing, experts in a variety of scientific areas corroborated the plausibility of Nascher's theories.

Despite the fact that the study of old age was gradually acquiring the characteristics distinctive of every legitimate medical specialty and despite all the technological and conceptual advances in medicine itself, scientists did not discover a remedy for the biological aspects of growing old. Indeed, between the world wars, two radically different conceptions of old age vied for acceptance in the medical profession. One school considered "senility" a pathological disorder; the other described it as a normal physiological state. In 1941, it remained "a major problem for science to determine which is correct."[40] Paradoxically, the future course of action for researchers was less certain than it had been in former times because they perceived the baffling complexities of senescence more sharply.

Coping with the Aged's Economic Insecurity before 1929

As popular and academic writers advocated ways to salvage older people's self-esteem and social worth, and as scientists sought methods to arrest or even vanquish the deterioration associated with growing old, still others grappled with financial aspects of the old-age problem. Americans after World War I attacked the problem of economic insecurity from two complementary directions: on the one hand, they tried to provide a means of income for elderly workers once they retired; on the other hand, they attempted to relieve those aged men and women who currently were in straitened circumstances.

Probably the most important new retirement plan inaugurated during the period was the compulsory old-age and disability insurance program enacted by the federal government in 1920 for its half-million civil-service employees. Workers contributed part of their salaries to a general fund; the government assumed all other expenses. Connecticut, Maine, Massachusetts, New Jersey, New York, and Pennsylvania also enacted retirement systems for civil servants before 1929.[41] In addition, retirement policies were extended at the municipal level: nearly every city provided pensions for retired police and firemen, and most gave benefits to teachers.

Retirement plans were expanded in the private as well as the public sector. In 1929, for instance, 140 industrial plans, covering nearly a million workers, paid out $6.67 million to 10,644 beneficiaries; labor organizations disbursed $3.35 million to 11,306 recipients. A few corporations—such as Westinghouse, General Electric, and Eastman Kodak—provided their pensioners facilities and equipment so that they could spend their leisure time creatively and possibly make discoveries or inventions valuable to their former employers.[42] Yet without belittling either the concern or generosity reflected in these retirement provisions, it is important to recognize that most new retirement programs did not really guarantee workers any greater measure of security than earlier plans had provided. Like their predecessors, corporations established and expanded pension policies because they hoped to increase efficiency, promote worker morale, and combat labor turnover. Furthermore, most employers still did not provide universal coverage for their workers; they maintained strict eligibility requirements and reserved the company's right to discontinue paying benefits at any time.[43] The actual benefits superannuated employees might have derived continued to be of secondary importance to those who designed and implemented retirement programs.

Just as private pension schemes after World War I essentially built upon existing practices and ideas, so too Americans prior to the Depression tended to deal with indigency in old age by applying traditional methods and concepts. The family's responsibility to aged relatives, for instance, was reaffirmed in new legislation: five more states enacted statutes enforcing the moral duty of children to support their elders; eleven other jurisdictions made failure to care for destitute parents a criminal offense.[44] In addition, more and more private organizations built facilities to care for older people. The Bureau of Labor Statistics reported that there were 1,270 old-age homes in 1929. In explaining why they preferred relying on old-age homes rather than the almshouse in helping needy people, Americans reiterated earlier judgments that the private institutions tended to be cleaner, more comfortable, and did not rob residents of their dignity.[45]

Efforts after World War I to cope with poverty among the aged were not simply elaborations of previously established norms and precedents, however, for it was during this period that legislators first began to consider publicly funded cash assistance for the aged needy as a realistic and legitimate alternative to the almshouse. In so doing, government officials clearly were responding to mounting evidence that the elderly's overall financial situation had become a serious "problem." Commissions appointed by state legislatures to investigate the extent of old-age dependency in a given jurisdiction typically found "a state of need . . . far beyond what had been anticipated or is realized by the general public."[46] Old-age pensions, moreover, became the leading issue of social insurance lobbyists after World War I. The movement's most articulate and prolific spokesmen offered somewhat different assessments of the problem, but estimated that at least 40% and possibly as many as 67% of all older Americans in the 1920s could not support themselves.[47] Diverse groups—such as the Fraternal Order of Eagles, the United Mine Workers of America, and the American Association for Labor Legislation—also attempted to make the public aware of the inadequacy of current means of caring for the elderly in general and of the horrors of the almshouse in particular. Abraham Epstein, who had served as research director of the Pennsylvania Commission on Old Age Pensions and had been associated with the Fraternal Order of Eagles, established the American Association for Old Age Security in 1927. Governors, including Pennsylvania's Gifford Pinchot, added their political clout. Opposition to public old-age assistance, therefore, was increasingly eroded by the growing opinion "that the state should make it possible for those reduced to poverty by age to spend their remaining years in self-respected privacy, free from anxiety and the stigma of pauperism, living independently in their own surroundings instead of being massed in institutions."[48]

As a result of public clamor and organized pressure after 1914, old-age assistance programs operating at the state level became a new means of relieving needy older people. Initial legislative victories, it is worth mentioning, proved somewhat illusory. Measures passed by Nevada, Montana, Colorado, and Wisconsin in 1923 and 1924 generally remained inoperative: none of these laws *required* county officials to establish old-age pensions, and few chose to implement the option. The Pennsylvania Supreme Court in 1925 nullified the commonwealth's two-year-old law on technical grounds, but noted that it was not ruling on the principle of giving old-age assistance to the needy.[49] This unfavorable decision, however, proved to be the last major setback. Six states had old-age pension laws in effect by the end of 1928. That twelve more states passed legislation between 1929 and 1931 alone suggests that the first phase of the Depression did not inaugurate but clearly accelerated the trend toward publicly funded financial assistance for elderly citizens in difficult circumstances.[50]

Examining the specific measures enacted reveals considerable differences among various states' old-age assistance programs. The minimum age of eligibility in nine jurisdictions was sixty-five and seventy in the other nine. New York required that recipients be wholly incapable of supporting themselves. Most states set income and/or property limits, but three established no means tests (an eligibility criteria based on demonstrable economic need). Pensions could not exceed $250 per year in Kentucky; Massachusetts set no limit; the typical old-age pension was worth $365 annually. Procedures for processing claims and administering benefits varied from place to place. Thus there was no uniform approach to the problem of old-age dependency in the 1920s, even among states that passed public assistance laws to relieve needy older persons.

Indeed, although the legislation initiated and implemented in the 1920s established crucial precedents for more ambitious governmental old-age relief programs in the 1930s, the fact that most states did not yet pass any measures underscores the lack of unity in efforts after World War I to improve the elderly's situation. While most Americans were willing to believe that economic insecurity in old age was a "problem," they disagreed profoundly on the precise number of older persons in need and even on their degree of deprivation. For instance, the respected actuary Louis I. Dublin, in sharp contrast to some of his contemporaries' far more grim estimates, suggested that only one-sixth of all elderly Americans were in difficult circumstances. A 1928 National Civic Federation survey of 13,785 people over sixty-five years old living in eleven northern cities and two villages also minimized the extent of old-age dependency, claiming that only 20–25% of the sample, which included professionals as well as blue-collar workers, depended on others for support. The study also predicted that the proportion would decline as a result of recent immigration restrictions.[51] These findings clearly challenged more dire assessments of the elderly's needs set forth at the time by Epstein, Rubinow, and others pressing for new old-age measures. In the absence of "definitive" data, Americans could select from a wide range of estimates in order to bolster their particular case for or against new efforts to assist older citizens.

Radically divergent perceptions and definitions of the aged's socioeconomic plight, however, were not the only obstacles confounding large-scale efforts to address the financial problems of being old. In the midst of the dazzling prosperity of the 1920s, it was hard to convince a majority or even an influential minority of Americans that a fundamentally different approach was necessary. In fact, many feared that any significant departure from the status quo designed to relieve the elderly's hardships might threaten or even destroy the social framework, processes, and values that provided financial security to most members of society. Conflicting political and economic interests in society at large no less than organizational and personal rivalries within reform circles further complicated the situation.[52]

In the face of such formidable opposition, Americans after 1914 tended to supplement and expand rather than rethink and replace traditional methods of dealing with economic insecurity among the elderly. Indeed, it is telling that the federal military pension program—which clearly was designed to provide gratuities for military services to veterans and some of their dependents, but not to operate as a universal public old-age subsistence plan—remained the primary source of relief to older men and women who were poor or disabled. In 1929, 82.3% of all beneficiaries of any public or private pension plan were recipients of war-related survivor and disability pensions; 80% of all money distributed through pensions came from this source.[53] Like their predecessors, therefore, Americans before the Depression continued to cope with the aged's financial difficulties in an indirect and piecemeal manner.

One can draw two lessons from the preceding analysis. First, the degree to which old age became a national problem after World War I was as much a function of cultural assumptions as of statistical realities. Sociologists, demographers, and other commentators did not need the perspective gained from hindsight to recognize that the proportion of people over sixty-five years old was increasing at the very time that older workers' employment opportunities were diminishing and that circumstances beyond an individual's control were altering the dimensions of old-age dependency. They were quite alert to the actual changes in older people's status occurring in front of their eyes. Yet the ways that Americans perceived "reality" depended on the manner in which they interpreted such trends and weighed the liabilities and assets of old age itself. These judgments, in turn, hinged not simply on empirical observations but on a host of factors, including the dynamic interaction of cultural norms and values, scientific ideas, and conventions, as well as personal biases and attitudes prevailing at the same time.

Furthermore, the extent to which Americans believed that old age had evolved into a serious problem with ominous implications in large part determined how willing they were to move beyond the ideas and practices of their predecessors. Public officials, business and labor leaders, scholars and researchers, and the public at large considered broader alternatives and implemented new ways of dealing with the personal and societal dimensions of being old only when and insofar as they considered existing methods insufficient and decided that conditions warranted a different approach.

"Solutions" to the "problems" of old age, therefore, took place at the interface of cultural assumptions and statistical realities. Precisely because the parameters of that interface were shaped simultaneously by a particular societal environment and distinctive social milieu, actual American achievements in "salvaging" the social, biomedical, and economic woes of growing old—the ultimate significance of their innovations notwithstanding—were modest in comparison to the changes that took place in the following decades.

FIRST PENSION RECIPIENT
FIRST TO GET AID INCREASE

LUDLOW, Vt., Oct. 3 (AP).—Miss Ida M. Fuller, 76, first person in the United States to receive an old-age insurance check, today was the first in the nation to receive her increased benefit check under the new Social Security law.

Miss Fuller received serial check 00-000-001 Jan. 17, 1940. Under the new law she was given an increase of $18.75 a month, making her monthly check now $41.30.

Ida M. Fuller, the first person to receive a Social Security check. (Courtesy of the Social Security Administration.)

CHAPTER 7

Social Security: A Novel Solution for the Problem of America's Aged

The Great Depression of the 1930s provided the context in which prevailing ideas about older people's status and their actual conditions forcefully combined and caused Americans to create a novel solution to the plight of growing old. While most Americans in 1929 already recognized that the economic situation of the elderly was problematic and had taken some steps to remedy the situation, the severity and intensity of the Depression years proved that all citizens, and especially the aged, needed an alternative means of insuring their financial independence and securing assistance when necessary. And yet, it proved to be one thing to call for governmental action for older Americans and quite another to enact legislation that would satisfy the demands and needs of many different groups. Drafting a social security bill required molding an amalgam of familiar and innovative but sometimes conflicting ideas and practices into a workable policy that reflected the harsh realities of the decade rather than the optimistic hopes of the 1920s.

The Impact of the Depression on Popular Attitudes and Current Means of Assisting the Aged

Had the prosperity most people enjoyed after World War I lasted beyond 1929, Americans probably would have been reluctant to consider or implement a new way of dealing with the problem of economic security among the aged. Existing methods seemed reasonably adequate and always could be expanded. Remaining in the labor force as long as possible and then relying upon individual savings undoubtedly would have remained the basic sources of financial independence in old age. The number of private insurance policies providing old-age annuities would have continued to grow. As retirement systems covered an increasing number of employees in the private and public sectors of the economy, the likelihood of becoming indigent during retirement gradually might have been mitigated for a greater proportion of workers. Americans presumably would have treated old-age dependency in the prevailing manner with innovations instituted as needed. For those elderly men and women who did find themselves in straitened circumstances, the family would have remained the primary source of support. Alternatives to the almshouse for those without kin and friends would have multiplied. The size and number of private old-age homes and charitable relief programs would have expanded. More and more states would have emulated the pacesetters and provided some old-age assistance to its helpless senior citizens. A considerable segment of the aged population would have continued to claim their right to benefits under the federal military pension program. It is possible that an old-age assistance and/or insurance scheme would have eventually passed both houses of Congress. There already were people calling for various types of federal programs; it is conceivable that a growing number of financially vulnerable, elderly voters would have been able to mobilize sufficient political pressure to get some sort of measure enacted that embodied the welfare concerns and economic considerations of the day. But it is much harder to speculate about when, why, or how the federal government might have changed its posture and begun to help solve the problem of financial insecurity in old age at the national level.

The United States, of course, did not enjoy uninterrupted prosperity after 1929. The Great Depression of the 1930s disrupted the lives of all Americans. At least twenty-five percent of the labor force was unemployed between 1929 and 1933; ninety thousand businesses failed; eighteen million Americans sought emergency relief in order to subsist. "While the intensity of falling prices and monetary contraction was not at all unprecedented, the intensity and duration of unemployment was new and shocking."[1] Bank failures as well as the declining value of personal and real estates wiped out many people's savings and at the very least strained the financial resources of countless Americans. A sizable proportion of the purportedly prosperous middle class personally experienced the tragic nature of dependency for the first time in their lives.

The Depression was a wrenching experience for everyone, but it had a particularly devastating effect on the elderly. The proportion of older people forced to leave the labor force exceeded the extent of unemployment among other age groups: for example, the Massachusetts Census for Unemployment for 1934 indicated an average unemployment of 25.2%; the percentages for those aged sixty to sixty-four and sixty-five to sixty-nine were 27.2% and 29.8% respectively.[2] Savings that had been minimal even in flush times proved grossly insufficient during the economic catastrophe.

The Depression disrupted most pension programs. Forty-five plans, covering one hundred thousand employees, were discontinued between 1929 and 1932; other plans, lacking an adequate fiscal base, curtailed benefits. In 1932, only 15% of all wage earners in industry and commerce were covered by pension schemes. Trade union pension plans fared no better: the New York Old Age Security Commission reported in 1930 that only twelve out of more than one hundred organizations had pension programs; most of these were on the verge of bankruptcy.[3] Children, friends, and relatives who previously had borne a major part of the cost of caring for the aged found the burden unbearable as they tried to provide for their immediate families. Not only did straitened circumstances increase the need for many old people to seek public or private assistance, but many predicted that the Depression inevitably would exacerbate the problem because it wiped out people's savings and deprived millions of older workers of jobs without guaranteeing that they would reenter the labor force.[4]

The various hardships endured during the Depression did more than expose deficiencies in existing means of providing financial relief to the average citizen. Commentators frequently observed that the catastrophe "increasingly convinced the majority of the American people that individuals could not themselves provide adequately for their old age and that some sort of greater security should be provided by society."[5] Thus the economic crisis also revitalized interest and fostered support for alternative measures of protecting people against economic misfortunes, particularly in their later years.

Americans sometimes seized upon utopian schemes proposed by visionaries who called for dramatic changes in governmental policies. Two grassroots movements deserve special mention.[6] Upton Sinclair in 1933 promulgated a program that he promised would "end poverty in California." Included in Sinclair's twelve-point EPIC panacea were plans to make people on relief self-supporting and to grant pensions worth fifty dollars a month to all needy persons over sixty who had resided in California for at least three years. Almost simultaneously, Dr. Francis E. Townsend of Long Beach, California, launched a movement to restore economic, social, and psychological security in the United States. He recommended that all Americans over sixty receive a monthly sum of $200 on the condition that they not engage in gainful employment and that they spend their pension within thirty days; a two percent tax on all business transactions was to pay for the plan. Townsend claimed that his measure would relieve suffering among the elderly as it restored full employment and economic prosperity, reduced taxes, and balanced the budget. Although these plans originated on the West Coast, they quickly attracted attention and support throughout the nation.

The Depression experience also aroused unprecedented support for government-supervised social insurance systems that some social workers, academics, professional reformers, and humanitarians had been advocating unsuccessfully since the 1920s. New and renewed interest in unemployment and old-age insurance systems, in turn, led to the formation of centralized organizations to coordinate reformers' efforts. Abraham Epstein's American Association for Old Age Security (founded in 1927), for instance, became the American Association for Social Security in 1933 and joined the fight for unemployment insurance.[7] Reform groups called for a wide-ranging and coherent program to protect Americans from some of the unforeseen and inevitable tragedies of life.

In addition, organized labor changed its attitude toward the role government should play in providing social security. Reversing its previous stand, the American Federation of Labor in 1932 officially endorsed state-funded unemployment insurance "and the supplementing of such state legislation by federal enactments."[8] Thereafter, labor union officials became increasingly active supporters of legislation calling for unemployment insurance and old-age assistance at the state and federal level. Labor unions shared the belief expressed by reform organizations and grassroots movements that a broad program of public assistance and social insurance was necessary.

Besides galvanizing public support for the idea that the federal government should assume a new role in protecting citizens from the hardships accompanying involuntary unemployment, especially those associated with growing old, the crisis also made public officials more willing to act upon such demands. This does not mean, however, that the economic crisis required the national government to assume an extraordinary responsibility for ensuring the public welfare or that it necessitated a radical reworking of bureaucratic operations at the state and federal levels.[9] The writings of Lester Frank Ward, Richard Ely, Louis Brandeis, and John R. Commons, among others, offered philosophical justification, and previously enacted social welfare bills provided legislative precedents for guaranteeing citizens a measure of social security in old age. Hence, in pushing for specific legislation to meet the present crisis, congressional leaders and executive policymakers were able to cite and build on an existing political tradition. The reorganization and expansion of federal and state operations between 1914 and 1932, moreover, prepared the way for implementing a variety of new policies. Because most governmental bodies operated with a budget and had come to rely on a cadre of technicians, coordinators, and administrators, the creators of New Deal legislation were able to propose means of financing and regulating their measures compatible with already established and relatively sophisticated bureaucratic networks and techniques.

Between 1930 and 1932, Senator Clarence Dill offered several bills proposing that Congress promote old-age assistance at the state level by authorizing federal grants-in-aid equal to one-third of a state's total expenditure for such relief. Representative William Connery, Jr., jointly sponsored similar bills during the 1933–34 legislative session. Senator Robert Wagner and Representative David J. Lewis introduced a bill in February 1934 designed to accelerate states' efforts to enact unemployment insurance laws.[10] Largely because the Roosevelt administration neither initiated nor actively supported the Dill-Connery and Wagner-Lewis bills, the seventy-third Congress failed to take any affirmative action. Before adjourning, however, it listened to the executive branch's ideas on the subject.

President Franklin Delano Roosevelt addressed Congress on 8 June 1934, and announced his intention to appoint a special committee to devise ways of protecting Americans against some of the conditions that threatened their financial well-being:

> If, as our Constitution tells us, our Federal Government was established among other things, 'to promote the general welfare,' it is our plain duty to provide for that security upon which welfare depends. . . . Hence I am looking for a sound means which I can recommend to provide at once security against several of the great disturbing factors in life—especially those which relate to unemployment and old age.[11]

For the first time in American history an incumbent president advocated legislation and initiated efforts in the executive branch to provide public assistance against old-age dependency and to promote unemployment insurance. In outlining a general program of social security, Roosevelt expressed his desire that funds necessary for such a measure would be raised through contributions rather than by increasing general taxation. The president avowed his belief that this legislation should be national in scope, with states and the federal government sharing responsibility for its implementation. The federal government was ready to act.

A Delicate Balance:
The Creation of the Social Security Act

Although the Depression experience fomented a sense of urgency about devising ways to relieve and to prevent various forms of economic insecurity, the crisis did not eliminate or wholly resolve obstacles that had impeded earlier attempts to involve the federal government in a publicly funded program of old-age assistance or social and unemployment insurance schemes. One of the most serious practical difficulties facing the Committee on Economic Security, which drafted the legislative particulars, was the lack of reliable data identifying who needed help and how much assistance the target population(s) required. State surveys conducted during the 1920s on the extent and degree of old-age dependency were considered suggestive but inconclusive because the statistics differed widely. Needless to say, everyone recognized the difficulty in estimating the cost of any program for which as little as one-sixth and as much as two-thirds of all Americans over sixty-five might be eligible. It was generally assumed, moreover, that the Depression had increased the proportion of old people who sought and/or needed relief. Under the circumstances, the committee developed an elaborate old-age security program premised on the explicit assumption that at least fifty percent of all aged men and women presently alive were dependent.[12]

Just as the staff and committee members who formulated the Social Security Act had to make a reasonable guess about the proportion of old people in need on the basis of a wide range of opinions, so too they had to piece together a viable program in the face of political pressure from diametrically opposed groups. Some social philanthropists, believing that state-sponsored old-age pensions were un-American and ineffective, advocated that Washington do nothing except permit private charitable agencies to continue developing their own ways of assisting elderly people.[13] At the other extreme, visionaries proposed a host of utopian tax schemes and panaceas for the aged. Dr. Francis Townsend, for example, claimed in 1935 to have five million supporters and at least sixty congressmen sympathetic to his measure alone, despite mounting contemporary evidence that Townsend exaggerated the effectiveness of his scheme while underestimating its cost and administrative difficulties.[14] To defuse such public clamor, the federal government clearly had to enact some sort of program.

As they struggled to reach a consensus about the best way to relieve old-age dependency, the executive and legislative branches grappled with complex philosophical and procedural questions. Was it the government's responsibility to prevent as well as to relieve destitution? Should the United States provide straight government pensions, as many Scandinavian countries did, or should it institute a contributory insurance system for wage earners, as Germany, Austria, and France did, or should it follow England's example and inaugurate both an insurance and an assistance program for old age? Should there be a single federal system or merely an aggregate of state plans? If an insurance program were established, should it be voluntary or compulsory, universal or selective?

In addressing such questions, an even larger issue concerning the underlying function of social insurance had to be faced. Two sharply divergent theories had prevailed in the United States since at least the 1920s.[15] One tradition, promulgated by John B. Andrews and John R. Commons, as well as the American Association of Labor Legislation, with which they were closely identified, stressed that preventing economic insecurity was the primary function of social insurance. To achieve collective security the "American plan" stressed business's cooperation rather than compulsory state action and depended upon capitalistic motives and methods rather than a deliberate measure to redistribute income. Over time, it became increasingly apparent that this approach conflicted with a theory of social insurance being developed in somewhat different fashions by I. M. Rubinow and Abraham Epstein. Both Rubinow and Epstein asserted that it was the government's duty, regardless of overall economic conditions, to provide income maintenance for that portion of the population that was in need. Epstein, in fact, went beyond most of his contemporaries' positions and urged governmental leadership to use social insurance as a way to redistribute income. As I shall show, the creators of the Social Security Act tried to reconcile these two traditions into a workable policy as they debated and later amended the intent and provisions of the act's old-age insurance plan. For the moment, however, it is sufficient to recognize that there was no basic consensus even among those who advocated government-supported social insurance.

If political realities and philosophical differences caused the framers of the Social Security Act to approach the entire matter of social insurance with extreme care, cost considerations ultimately played a critical role in determining the program they developed. Committee members argued that the cost of federal subsidies for old-age assistance would be enormous if a nationwide contributory annuity system were not simultaneously implemented. Actuaries estimated that the cost to the federal government of public relief for the elderly would be $1.3 billion in 1980 without an old-age insurance program; if such a system existed, expenditures would not exceed $500 million.[16] Comparable cost calculations influenced other decisions about financing social security and determining benefit levels.

Not only did executive and legislative committee members endeavor to weigh the political feasibility, philosophical implications, and economic practicality of many public assistance and social insurance programs in designing the Social Security Act, but they also were quite sensitive about possible constitutional challenges as they deliberated alternatives. All proposed measures had to be scrutinized in light of the 1935 Supreme Court decision that the Railroad Retirement Act (1934), which established contributory old-age annuities for employees, contravened the due process clause of the Fifth Amendment.[17] In drafting legislation, committee members tried to minimize the possibility that the Supreme Court might also find grounds to rule the Social Security Act unconstitutional.

Examining successive drafts of titles I and II reveals how legislators and policy makers tried to deal with the practical difficulties, the philosophical and political choices, and the constitutional and economic considerations confronting them as they sought to establish a national system of old-age assistance and insurance. Precisely because they were an amalgam of familiar and innovative ideas and practices, the titles of the 1935 Social Security Act directly affecting the elderly were, paradoxically, simultaneously ambitious and narrow in scope yet broad and restrictive in their intended effect. Indeed, the very wording of the text appears to have set crucial parameters in the measure's actual ability to relieve and present old-age dependency.

Title I initially appropriated $49,750,000 "for the purpose of enabling each State to furnish financial assistance, as far as practicable under the conditions in such State, to aged needy individuals." The title delineated precise requirements for grants-in-aid.[18] A state's old-age assistance program had to be mandatory and in effect in all subdivisions. States could not transfer financial responsibility entirely to localities but had to furnish some of the funds. Federal funds could not be used to pay for the grants to aged people in public institutions. State plans had to provide an independent agency that directly administered (or supervised local administration), guaranteed the right of appeal to those denied assistance, and submitted prescribed reports to the Social Security Board. A federal board was created to establish broad guidelines on age, citizenship, and residency requirements for applicants.

In anticipation of proposed federal aid, many states passed new laws or amended existing legislation so that it would be consistent with the Social Security Act.[19] Between 1 January and 15 October 1935, eight states (Alabama, Arkansas, Connecticut, Illinois, Missouri, Oklahoma, Rhode Island, and Vermont) and the District of Columbia passed mandatory old-age assistance laws; Florida's new law was pending approval by referendum; Oregon's act became operative as soon as federal funds were available. During the same period, sixteen states and two territories altered existing statutes in order to conform to anticipated federal guidelines. Some made previously optional programs mandatory; others established administrative units, liberalized residency and citizenship requirements, or enacted legal provisions for state financial participation on a matching basis. In 1936, New York substituted "assistance" for each reference to "relief" in its law and lowered eligibility requirements to sixty-five. Thus, the provisions of a bill drafted at the federal level reduced some variations in the ways different states administered relief for their aged poor.

Yet the Social Security Act did not eliminate all differences in old-age assistance from state to state. For all its specificity, Title I permitted considerable flexibility in several areas. The original draft, for example, stipulated that states provide a "subsistence compatible with decency and health." Dr. Edwin Witte, who chaired the Committee on Economic Security, defended the phrase by citing as precedent the language in the Massachusetts and New York laws.[20] Witte and his colleagues clearly hoped to establish minimum national standards for helping needy older Americans. But Senator Henry Byrd denounced the provision as an infringement on a state's sovereignty. The president of the U.S. Chamber of Commerce, other senators, and corporate executives shared Byrd's reservation and noted difficulties in defining or implementing "decency." The final version of Title I deleted the controversial provision.[21] Instead, it pledged that the federal government would match state expenditures up to a maximum of $15 per person, and it permitted each state to determine the precise financial award in light of its own circumstances. Consequently, the Social Security Act did not guarantee all old people in the United States equal amounts of assistance. In December, 1936, for instance, the average national monthly allowance was $18.36. The average per recipient in Mississippi was $3.92; in California it was $31.36. States' old-age assistance laws also continued to vary considerably in the maximum amount of personal and real property and income an aged person could possess and still qualify for assistance. Some states, in fact, retained a clause stipulating that those whose relatives could support them were ineligible for assistance. Finally, the federal aid appropriated in Title I was an inducement, not a compulsion, for state assistance. Arizona, Georgia, Kansas, North Carolina, South Carolina, Tennessee, and Virginia still had not enacted old-age assistance statutes by 1937. Older people in Nevada could not qualify for federal assistance because the state's pension law remained optional at the county level.

The provisions of Title I thus mark a significant but circumscribed departure from existing methods of relieving indigency in old age. By appropriating a large sum of money to match state efforts and by establishing guidelines and regulations that states had to follow in order to qualify for federal grants, Congress mandated the need to supervise a national problem at the federal level. By generating funds and stimulating efforts at the state level, it provided some sort of immediate relief for the elderly. Above all, by permitting applicants to appeal administrative decisions, the federal government made old-age assistance a right that could be legally enforced. Public relief in old age was no longer a gratuity. Yet the limitations of the original title are as important as its innovations. The federal appropriation for old-age assistance was not designed to wipe out old-age dependency. Furthermore, since it granted states considerable flexibility in setting requirements and the actual amounts of assistance to be given to needy old people and allowed states the option of not applying for federal assistance, Title I precluded any federal government effort to ensure that old-age assistance be either uniform or equitable throughout the nation.

Similarly, the provisions of Title II reflect a deliberate effort to effect a profound but not radical alteration in the means by which Americans could insure their financial independence in old age.[22] The title authorized the Department of Treasury to set up an "Old Age Reserve Account." Into this account, an employee and his or her employer would contribute equally a prescribed percentage of the first $3000 of that wage earner's salary; the federal government would appropriate additional funds sufficient to pay current old-age benefits. (To preclude a possible constitutional issue, the authors of the Social Security Act separated titles pertaining to revenues and those related to appropriations. Hence, employee and employer taxes actually were levied in Title VIII, not Title II.) The exact amount of benefits, initially scheduled for disbursement beginning on 1 January 1942, was determined by the wages received in any employment and any service performed in the United States, Alaska, or Hawaii, up to a maximum monthly payment of $85.00.

Policy formulators and legislators hoped that ultimately Title II would provide universal coverage to all workers and thereby significantly reduce the threat of old-age dependency in the future. They were unwilling to jeopardize the future success of the program, however, by making coverage universal at the outset.[23] Because of the difficulties foreseen if, initially, all occupational categories were covered, the title specifically excluded farm laborers, domestic servants, and government employees, among others. Administrative considerations, therefore, necessitated that at least 9.4 million wage earners were not covered by the act. Yet it was not wholly clear how many workers would be participating in the program, since the law did not require "employers" to make personal contributions to insure themselves. Economists estimated that as many as seven to eight million people at the time were intermittently or simultaneously employers and employees.[24] The scope of the title would not be known and its effectiveness could not be assessed, in short, until it was actually implemented.

It is crucial to point out, however, that the original actuarial calculations, target population, and philosophical underpinning of the old-age insurance program were profoundly altered before the first benefit was ever paid. Amendments to the Social Security Act in 1939 affected Title II in the following ways. Monthly benefits became payable two years earlier, on 1 January 1940. More people, including employees of banks and loan associations and seamen, were to be covered by the program. Perhaps the most significant change was that the emphasis "shifted from the worker as an individual to the worker as breadwinner for the family group."[25] To promote family security, the amendment provided payments not only for retired wage earners at age sixty-five but also for their wives at the same age or for their dependent children. In addition, benefits were granted to widows, dependent children, and, under certain circumstances, dependent parents of workers who died.

The 1939 amendment reflected the priorities and assumptions of the times. In expanding the scope of Title II to ensure the importance and integrity of the family in social legislation, Congress significantly broadened the Social Security Act's welfare function. By providing family members as well as contributors at least a minimum guaranteed income, they gave greater emphasis to the "social adequacy" (or income support) aspects of social insurance than had appeared in the 1935 version of the title. Expanding the number of potential beneficiaries, moreover, led to scrapping initial plans for a large old-age insurance trust fund and instead financing the insurance program largely on a pay-as-you-go basis. This procedural change seemed justifiable in light of the Keynesian economic principles then coming into vogue: experts argued that there was no overriding macroeconomic reason for enormous trust fund accumulations in the late 1930s or the foreseeable future.[26] And yet, the amendment did not nullify the concept of "equity" (or earnings replacement) implicit in Title II. Benefit protection was still related to the amount a wage earner had contributed over time. Furthermore, the amendment provided coverage only for those women and other "dependents" who qualified because of their relationship to a wage earner who had contributed to the program. The 1939 amendment liberalized existing provisions without making federally supervised old-age insurance a universal right.

Not only did the creators of Title II try to strike a balance between the kind of actuarially determined payments provided by private insurance companies and the type of benefit levels proposed by income-redistribution advocates like Abraham Epstein, but they also hoped to give workers more options than they had previously enjoyed. Consider, for example, the way they sought to administer a program of income maintenance in old age without denying people over sixty-five the right to work. Tracing the successive drafts of the 1935 and 1939 social security acts indicates that lawmakers did not use the provisions of Title II to establish a compulsory retirement scheme.[27] In fact, Congress rejected proposals requiring workers to retire in order to qualify for old-age benefits. Title II of the 1935 measure stipulated that "under regulations prescribed by the Board," a recipient would forfeit one month's worth of old-age benefits for any month in which he or she received wages from "regular employment." The wording was deliberately vague, but its intent was clear. Although they did not want to preclude older people's opportunity to work if they so desired, the authors of Social Security did want to devise some sort of retirement test because they thought that old-age benefits under Title II should primarily replace lost earnings. In 1939, the Social Security Board recommended that the law be amended by imposing a ceiling on monthly earnings. Congress listened to arguments urging the elimination of all retirement clauses, but followed the board's recommendation and permitted eligible people to receive benefits if their earnings in covered employment were less than $15.00 a month. (Later amendments prorated benefits according to an employee's annual earnings.) Once again, policy makers hoped to give the aged some options about working. Yet they restricted the range of choice because they shared a fear prevalent in labor, business, and insurance circles that subsidizing older people's wages might depress the overall wage structure.

In sum, the Social Security Act quite literally was an invention of the times. The measure established old-age assistance and insurance as a right, not an act of benevolence. Titles I and II sanctioned an elaborate institutional framework that went beyond any existing American program in potential scope, cost, and effectiveness. At the same time, however, the act sought to avoid creating a bureaucratic leviathan by incorporating precedents and building on existing programs whenever practical. The federal government also deliberately restricted the program's initial impact by limiting its coverage and making many of its crucial provisions optional. Nevertheless, the very existence of Social Security profoundly affected the subsequent history of old age in the United States.

The Emergence of an Institutional Framework to Coordinate Efforts to Help the Aged

Because the Social Security Act was a delicate balance of programs pieced together with a sense of urgency in the spirit of pragmatic compromise, it is not surprising that it was alternately condemned for doing too little or too much. Leaders of older people's grassroots movements assailed the measure because they did not believe that the old-age pension features were sufficient. Townsendites and other organizations continued to fight for broader programs: approximately eighty old-age welfare schemes bid for support during 1937 and 1938 in California alone.[28] Businessmen also expressed severe reservations about the Social Security Act. The National Association of Manufacturers, for instance, attacked the payroll tax on employers. Some managers and shopkeepers in small communities like the Lynds' "Middletown" remained hostile to the idea of old-age pensions in any form.[29] Finally, titles I and II disappointed reformers such as I. M. Rubinow, Eveline Burns, and especially Abraham Epstein, who had not been invited to help prepare the legislation. They faulted the program for being inadequately and/or unsoundly financed, for covering a sector of the population that was too narrowly defined, and for seeming to be more concerned with complicating administrative procedures than with liberalizing benefits. For all of their objections, however, Epstein, Rubinow, and Burns acknowledged that the fundamental aims of titles I and II were well intentioned, and in time could be remedied.[30]

Indeed, despite criticisms and reservations raised at various points in the political spectrum, the provisions of the Social Security Act affecting the elderly seemingly enjoyed immediate and overwhelming popular support. Of all those asked in a December 1935 Gallup survey, 89% favored old-age pensions for needy persons. Two years later, 73% of all respondents approved the present Social Security tax on their wages. Eighty-five percent rejected the suggestion that employees pay the whole amount of the tax.[31] While there clearly was widespread support for federal disbursements to the aged needy during the latter years of the Depression, it is impossible to draw a firm conclusion about whether people preferred the insurance or the assistance provisions of the measure. The difficulty goes beyond ambiguities in the ways pollsters phrased questions. It is quite likely that the public did not fully understand the difference between old-age insurance and old-age assistance. Edwin E. Witte, among others, decried the public's miscomprehension of the act they so overwhelmingly endorsed: "Despite the numerous articles which have been written . . . the two parts of the old age security program are confused and many of the essential features have been grossly misrepresented."[32] Hence, Americans initially may have accepted Social Security, not because they fully understood its operation, but because they accepted the principle that the federal government's program provided a necessary means of alleviating if not eliminating the problems associated with old age.

Although the extent of initial public acceptance of the distinctive features of Title II remains a moot issue, there can be no doubt that the judicial branch of the federal government seriously weighed the legality of the act's old-age insurance provisions. Litigation against several provisions of the Social Security Act began within a year after President Roosevelt signed the measure. The Supreme Court upheld the constitutionality of Title II in a landmark decision. Delivering the majority opinion on 24 May 1937, Mr. Justice Cardozo noted that because the problem remedied by old-age benefits was "plainly national in area and dimensions," Congress had the right to appropriate money to promote the "general welfare."[33] The Supreme Court would not rule on the wisdom of Title II, but it did certify its constitutional legitimacy. The court thereby removed a serious potential obstacle to further government efforts to relieve the aged's economic predicament.

Even as the Supreme Court deliberated the constitutionality of the Act's old-age provisions, administrators in the executive branch sought to justify governmental responsibility for the elderly's economic situation. In fulfilling its "duty of studying and making recommendations as to the most effective methods of providing economic security through social insurance,"[34] the Social Security Board, a duly appointed federal agency, broadened current definitions of old-age dependency to include not only those who were in need but also those who potentially might be in need.

> The dependent person . . . will be defined as one who is dependent wholly or partially on others for support. Such a definition is not greatly at variance with previous concepts, but simply broadens the coverage to include those persons who are without means of support and who are potential dependents on public assistance or private charity.[35]

On the basis of this definition, the board in 1937 compiled existing data and contended that no more than 34.7% of all persons over sixty-five—those supporting themselves through earnings, savings, pensions, and annuities—were financially secure. Another 19.8% of the aged population were recipients of public or private assistance. The other 45.5% were dependent by definition, the board claimed. It derived the figure by subtracting the number of people it classified as self-dependent and the number of people on relief from the total aged population.[36] Because of the way it conceptualized the problem, the board did not have to show that the remainder of unaccounted-for people were *actually* dependent on others for help; what mattered was that they *could* be. The Social Security Board then cited its finding to underscore the necessity of recent legislation. Assuming that old people posed a serious social problem in the present and probably would continue to do so in the future, the board cautioned against relying solely on public assistance and asserted that the insurance program created under Title II offered a "reasonable solution" to the problem of offering economic support to the elderly.[37]

The social security system immediately evolved an internal dynamics independent of the society that had created it. Although federal administrators did not presume that their perception of the aged's plight was the only way to define the situation, it was the Social Security Board that presented evidence for the first time in American history purportedly demonstrating that a majority of people over sixty-five years old in the United States were dependent. Government officials did not claim that Title I, operating in conjunction with Title II, provided the only or even the most important way to tackle the economic problems of old age. Nevertheless, the board's recommendations made the social security system more than a passive agent reflecting the federal government's priorities. The system itself was beginning to affect attitudes toward the elderly, and the basis for their economic security.

And yet, as Americans clearly recognized, the Social Security Act embodied a response to only one aspect of a multifaceted situation. Having enough money to live was a necessary but not a sufficient precondition for well-being in old age. "The time has come," writers observed, "when for social security we must think about the problems of the aged in terms of what they really need."[38] A better understanding of the elderly's needs and desires, it was hoped, would lead to more satisfactory solutions to their plight.

Private foundations sponsored the first large-scale projects investigating noneconomic aspects of growing old. Research in the medical and biological sciences was among the earliest to benefit from this new institutional support.[39] The Josiah Macy, Jr., Foundation published the first collaborative progress report, entitled *Problems of Aging*, in 1933. In 1937, the Macy

Foundation, along with the Union of American Biological Sciences and the National Research Council, sponsored the first conference on aging in the United States. These groups underwrote special work-study sessions in subsequent years. Around the same time, private hospitals in Boston, New York, and Brooklyn opened clinics to offer coordinated medical and social services for the elderly and to foster the study of geriatrics.

The federal government soon joined efforts to promote and coordinate research into the biological and social aspects of aging. In 1940, Surgeon General Thomas Parran appointed a National Advisory Committee on Gerontology. In the same year, with the encouragement of the Macy Foundation, the National Institute of Health (which then was a division of the Public Health Service) organized a unit whose chief aim was to serve as a clearing house for studies on the aged. The new governmental agency immediately conducted a survey of current and contemplated research in order to "emphasize the urgent need for greatly augmented support for systematic studies of these vitally important problems of senescence."[40] The federal government's decision to assume a primary role in directing and funding systematic, interdisciplinary analyses underscores its belief that the social and biological no less than the economic aspects of old age had to be recognized as a national problem requiring immediate if undetermined solutions.

The passage of the Social Security Act marks a crucial watershed: it opened a new chapter in the history of old age in the United States by establishing the first nationwide institutional structure to assist older Americans. Large-scale organizations henceforth played an independent and significant role in transforming popular attitudes about the elderly's status and in generating new ideas about the physical, mental, psychological, and behavioral aspects of senescence. They also provided or led to the establishment of unprecedented options for those who were old as well as for those preparing for their old age, and thereby affected the aged's actual status in society. The creation and subsequent expansion of governmental bureaucracies, private agencies, and professional bodies to deal with the elderly's problems at the national level, in fact, have been instrumental in shaping many of the distinctive features of growing old in America today.

Maggie Kuhn, founder of the Gray Panthers, reflects the new political activism among older Americans. (Courtesy of the Gray Panthers.)

CHAPTER 8

Old Age in the United States since Social Security

Since the passage of the Social Security Act, the growth of institutions to help the aged as well as the continued interplay of large-scale cultural trends and structural developments have altered both assessments of the elderly's situation and the actual circumstances associated with growing old in the United States. Organizations in the private and public sectors representing and/or catering to older Americans have had a profound effect as they multiplied in numbers and augmented their scope and services over time. A nationwide institutional approach to the problems of old age has helped to improve elderly people's overall financial situation and has enhanced their opportunities to contribute to society. Such institutions have also sponsored and supported surveys and scientific research that gave rise to more optimistic perspectives on the capabilities and worth of the aged than existed earlier in the century. Unfortunately, however, despite all the positive and encouraging changes, serious difficulties remain. A significant number of older men and women are impoverished, and the economic resources of an even larger percentage are barely adequate. Furthermore, most Americans ignore more recent findings and continue to subscribe to wornout, negative conceptions of old age.

And yet, the nature and parameters of the old-age predicament have become strikingly different from those of forty years ago. The income resources, demographic characteristics, and perceived needs of the population over age sixty-five have changed. "Solutions" conceived in the midst of the Great Depression, subsequent legislative decisions, and additional administrative regulations intended to remedy program deficiencies or increase policy effectiveness often have created and/or necessitated an unanticipated set of new "reforms." In addition, many of the aged's present and projected difficulties result from and reflect larger national crises and broader challenges that have become more apparent or acute in recent times. Current efforts to address specific aspects of the elderly's plight, moreover, immediately raise fundamental issues about how Americans have allocated social roles and rewards in the past and continue to discriminate on the basis of race, sex, and age. Consequently, old age generally remains a serious "problem" in the United States today, but the ways in which contemporary Americans define and grapple with it are historically novel.

The Growth of Institutions to Help the Aged

A vast and complex institutional framework to assist Americans over the age of sixty-five has arisen in this country. While its origins are to be found in events prior to 1935, its most dramatic growth has taken place since the New Deal. Seventy years ago, there was no nationwide apparatus that offered any direct means of old-age insurance or assistance, nor did any federal body seek to improve older Americans' health care and general welfare. Today, every elderly person is affected by one or more programs providing an ever-expanding variety of benefits and services.

Developments in the Social Security system illustrate this dramatic institutional growth in the public sector. More than 40% of the labor force initially was excluded from the federal government's old-age insurance program because the original provisions covered only employees in commerce and industry. During the 1950s and 1960s, compulsory coverage was extended to agricultural and domestic workers, military personnel, and the self-employed; other groups, including state and local government officials, could elect to join the program. The system now approaches universal coverage. As the program has matured and expanded, the proportion of people over sixty-five eligible for insurance benefits under Title II has risen from 20% in 1941 to 93% in 1974; since 1964 all Americans over seventy-five have been entitled to benefits.[1] Furthermore, early retirement benefits at age sixty-two (with an actuarial reduction) were established for women in 1956 and men in 1961 to give those approaching old age more options in preparing for the future. Finally, monthly benefits have been rising: the average monthly benefit for retired workers was $23 in December 1940 and $207 at the end of 1975. This increase has been significant in terms of actual purchasing power: retired workers on the rolls in 1975, for instance, received benefits worth roughly 40% more than those their counterparts got a decade earlier.[2] Income security transfers, in fact, have constituted the fastest growing share of the national budget since 1960.

The federal government has evolved into a major clearinghouse for ideas about the elderly and old age. In response to public demand, the Federal Security Agency sponsored a National Conference on Aging in 1950. White House conferences on aging in 1961 and 1971 set forth policy recommendations concerning nutrition, transportation, and spiritual matters, among other things.[3] In addition, Washington has greatly augmented its commitment to encourage investigation into the dynamics of aging and the ramifications of being old. The departments of Labor, Commerce, and Agriculture, and especially various bureaus and advisory councils within the Department of Health, Education and Welfare have directed and/or funded important research during the past decades. In an effort to centralize and coordinate some of these efforts, the National Institute on Aging, the eleventh national health institute, was established in 1974. Created out of existing branches and agencies and given a fresh mandate, this institute promotes and sponsors intramural studies (mainly at the Gerontology Research Center in Baltimore) as well as projects (primarily in the natural and social sciences) throughout the United States.[4]

Besides extending its earlier commitments to provide economic assistance and research incentives to aid the elderly, the federal government during the past four decades, and especially since the 1960s, has enunciated a more ambitious set of goals and has created, in turn, more elaborate and far-reaching social welfare programs. Whereas relieving economic insecurity was the foremost goal of the 1930s, Americans by the 1960s were declaring a full-scale "War on Poverty." Authors such as John Kenneth Galbraith, in *The Affluent Society* (1958), and Michael Harrington, in *The Other America* (1963), provided compelling arguments to justify the federal government's use of its then seemingly boundless resources and influence to make fighting poverty a national priority. To a greater extent than their predecessors, postwar Americans explored and sought remedies for the emotional, intellectual, environmental, and psychological conditions of the poor. By the mid-1960s, "relative poverty" concerned Americans in general and government officials in particular almost as much as abject deprivation. In this milieu, professional and popular writers increasingly detailed "the culture of aged poverty."[5] The predicament of older Americans aroused special concern.

It is worth noting that the aged were not always the prime targets or chief beneficiaries of legislation considered in the latter months of the Kennedy administration or enacted during the first thirty months of Johnson's term. In an eclectic, daring, and often impulsive effort to eradicate poverty from many different directions simultaneously, policy formulators drafted measures to provide job training, legal services, civil rights, opportunities for community action, and compensatory education programs for youth, unskilled heads of household, and other disadvantaged persons.[6] In many instances, the policies that were designed and implemented ignored or bypassed the special concerns and needs of elderly men and women. Nevertheless, from the perspective of the late 1970s, it appears that the elderly as a constituency ultimately benefited more than any other age group from the legislative achievements of the past decade. For example, despite persistent and considerable opposition since the 1940s to a comprehensive national health insurance program, Congress at last was persuaded that older Americans needed help in defraying at least part of their medical costs. Two measures passed in 1965, largely to assist the old, represent the first truly major breakthrough in this area. Medicare provided a hospital insurance program for old-age insurance beneficiaries and a supplementary, voluntary insurance plan to help the aged cover some of the costs of physicians' services. Medicaid provided assistance for poor people of all ages.[7] Like the Social Security Act on which they were modeled and grafted, Medicare and Medicaid constituted both a new direction in national policies affecting the elderly and a deliberate decision to adopt an incremental approach for establishing new programs.

In the same session, Congress enacted the Older Americans Act, which pledged governmental support for projects designed to facilitate and afford the elderly new employment opportunities or a meaningful retirement as well as "freedom, independence and the free exercise of individual initiative."[8] This broadened commitment to the elderly was further underscored by the establishment of the Administration on Aging (1965) as a central agency coordinating efforts to deal with the older person's income, health, housing, legal, and social needs. It was also reflected in the growing importance of the Senate Special Committee on Aging (formed in 1961), which evaluates and prepares old-age proposals for legislative consideration. Addressing the elderly's needs became a rising national priority that went far beyond the steps first taken in the midst of the Depression. In this context, the 1972 law enacting a Supplementary Security Income program for the aged deserves special mention. The federal government now guarantees older Americans a minimal income, financed directly from the U.S. Treasury. This legislation not only replaced the method of old-age assistance established in 1935 under Title I but set a potentially significant precedent for a universal income-maintenance program.[9]

Indeed, it appears in retrospect that identifying and solving the problems of old age in an incremental manner has been advantageous in three ways.[10] First, by formulating new programs and liberalizing existing measures, legislators and administrators have attempted, though not always successfully, to adjust the social security system and a host of other nationwide old-age programs to meet ever-evolving purposes and priorities. Yet for all of the framework's flexibility, policy makers generally have been careful neither to vitiate the strengths of existing programs nor to abrogate longstanding norms and rights. This mixture of innovative conservatism, in turn, has made reform efforts politically feasible in an arena rife with vested interests too often bent on expediency.

Not only has Washington reshaped the scope of its old-age programs, but in the process it has revamped the relationship between federal and state agencies serving the aged. Ten regional offices currently handle much of the federal administration of old-age programs. Amendments to the Older Americans Act in the early 1970s, moreover, authorized states to plan, develop, and evaluate programs in their local areas and to act as "brokers" in coordinating social services to elderly people. In reaction to this development and in response to their own set of priorities, most state and local governments now have commissions on aging; a few have cabinet-level departments on elder affairs.

Burgeoning interest in the problems of the elderly and efforts to deal with them at all levels of government have paralleled and in some instances promoted activities in the private sector. There has been an extraordinary growth of citizens' organizations for older people.[11] Groups like the National Association of Retired Federal Employees and the National Retired Teachers Association/American Association of Retired Persons claim to represent hundreds of thousands of voters as they lobby for increased pension benefits and other legislation; the National Council of Senior Citizens, organized by some participants of the 1961 White House Conference on Aging, currently has more than three thousand senior citizen club affiliates. The Gray Panthers and the National Caucus on the Black Aged command far wider media coverage and wield more political clout than their numbers and budgets might otherwise suggest. In addition, large-scale organizations perform countless other functions. Perhaps the most important is the National Council on the Aging (NCOA), established with Ford Foundation support in 1950, which now represents more than 1,400 autonomous groups, including public and private health, recreation, community-action, and social-work agencies. Roughly three hundred other national organizations, not federated with NCOA, operate aging programs for their members.

Professional interest in the study of the biological and socioeconomic aspects of old age, which had begun to grow before Social Security, also has developed tremendously. In the 1940s, the areas of research receiving greatest attention were the anatomical, endocrinological, and pathological changes associated with senescence; the nutritional problems of the elderly; and the psychology of adjustment and older people's attitudes.[12] Since 1950, there has been a comparable efflorescence of primary research by economists, political scientists, anthropologists, and humanists as gerontology has emerged into a legitimate and increasingly popular field of inquiry. Growing professional interest in the aged has led to the creation of new organizations: the American Geriatrics Society and the Gerontological Society were founded in 1942 and 1945 respectively. Groups such as the American Medical Association and the American Psychological Association established committees to coordinate studies of aging within their professional ranks. Scholars started attending national, hemispheric, and international conferences on aging and contributed to an ever-growing list of specialized journals. Colleges and universities in nearly every state began to sponsor training, research, and service institutes of gerontology and to offer courses for those interested in life-long learning.

Finally, the complex connections among business, industry, labor, and government have led to the spectacular growth of one other old-age institutional resource in the private sector. Although most corporate and union pensions went bankrupt during the Depression, several developments since the 1930s have made the proliferation and expansion of pension trust funds a major economic trend.[13] The passage of the Social Security Act stimulated interest among American workers and particularly labor unions in all sorts of supplemental retirement benefit schemes. From management's viewpoint, creating and enlarging pension plans made sense: for the relatively low net cost of liberalizing fringe benefits, corporations could reduce taxes (due to favorable laws), augment investment portfolios, and plausibly justify a wage freeze. In retrospect, a 1948 National Labor Relations Board ruling and other court decisions making pension plans subject to collective bargaining, as well as General Motors president Charles Wilson's offer to establish a pension fund during his 1950 negotiations with the United Auto Workers, also appear to have fostered the pension boom.

Over time, the proportion of workers eligible for old-age benefits from private pension plans has soared. In 1930, no more than 9.2% of the entire civilian labor force were covered by programs; only 15% were protected twenty years later. By 1970, 37.2% of the civilian labor force were covered by industrial and business pensions. The 1974 pension reform law, by requiring minimum vested benefits and permitting "individual retirement accounts" under certain circumstances, undoubtedly extended coverage even more. One economist estimates that workers, through their pension plans, presently own at least a quarter of the nation's total equity capital.[14] Funds technically invested to pay for workers' retirement benefits thus constitute one of the greatest sources of financial power shaping contemporary American society.

Needless to say, the phenomenal growth of an institutional approach to the elderly's problems during the past four decades has been a most significant development in the history of old age in the United States. Organizational case histories and statistics, however, tell only part of the story. Sometimes directly, sometimes indirectly, and sometimes unintentionally, the institutions Americans erected, expanded, and supported in attempts to assist the aged have reformed the elderly's societal position and re-formed perceptions of the aging process.

Old-Age Programs Reform
the Elderly's Place in Society

One immediate and obvious effect of the institutional apparatus constructed to help older Americans has been the growing societal significance of the chronological age sixty-five. A decision by the framers of the Social Security Act largely accounts for that birthdate's significance; another age just as reasonably could have been chosen.[15] The Committee on Economic Security determined that at least six other birthdays (60, 62, 68, 70, 72, and 75) were used as an eligibility criterion in public and private schemes operating in the 1930s. Nor was sixty-five the only age considered in drafting the original measure. But in light of available cost estimates as well as existing actuarial data, and in the spirit of compromise, legislators decided that only people at least sixty-five years old could be eligible for federal old-age programs.

This administrative line has gained profound importance by marking the age at which a person becomes "old" enough to receive categorical benefits. Since 1935, more and more private companies have adopted age sixty-five as one eligibility requirement. The proliferation of these policies, in conjunction with federal laws, greatly influences older people's options. For instance, men and women who are not yet sixty-five are not entitled to many old-age privileges and perquisites. Occasionally, benefits are possible at an earlier age, but then payments are reduced to conform to the sixty-five-year baseline. Some workers must quit the labor force at sixty-five because of mandatory retirement policies; others must decide whether they want to continue working or collect the benefits they have already earned. Thus even though physiological old age defies precise chronological definition, sixty-five increasingly denotes the onset of socioeconomic old age as more and more older Americans retire with income from Social Security and other pension plans. (This may change in the future. Amendments to the federal age-discrimination law, effective with certain exemptions on 1 January 1979, raise from sixty-five to seventy the age at which most employees can be forced to retire. While it is useful to forecast the impact of this new measure on social attitudes and behavior, it is too early to evaluate its actual effect on the significance of age sixty-five as a benchmark.)

The increasing availability and size of retirement payments as well as the ever greater proportion of people who are eligible for old-age insurance and assistance benefits, in turn, have resulted in a fundamental change since 1935 in the ways that Americans over sixty-five support themselves. During the past four decades, intergenerational transfers have become the major source of support in old age. Prior to Social Security, earnings generated an overwhelming proportion of the total income available to people over sixty-five; by 1967, however, those sixty-five and older as a group received 46% of their aggregate income from retirement benefits, 29% from employment earnings, 15% from assets, and 10% from all other sources. Changes in income sources even during the past twenty-five years underscore the growing significance of retirement benefits as a source of income.[16] In 1951, pensions represented the principal source of income for only 23% of all couples over sixty-five, 26% of all unmarried aged men, and 15% of all unmarried elderly women. According to the most recent national survey (1968), 49% of all elderly couples, 71% of all unmarried men over sixty-five, and 75% of all aged unmarried women do not derive any income from working and rely on retirement benefits as their primary means of support. Hence, as the creators of the Social Security Act anticipated, old-age insurance and assistance provisions have become the basic—and in some instances, the sole—means of support for more and more older Americans.

Not only have benefits generated in the private and public sectors become the elderly's major source of income, but the overall economic situation of a majority of the aged has improved since the 1930s, when it was estimated that at least 50% of all older Americans were dependent. The number of persons receiving old-age assistance payments dropped below the number receiving old-age insurance benefits for the first time in August 1951. And "had it not been for OASDHI benefits," Social Security Administration researchers contend, "two to three times as many beneficiary couples would have been classified as poor in 1967—more than half of all the beneficiary couples—instead of one-fifth."[17] Indeed, the proportion of older people below the poverty line established by the federal government has declined. The percentage of Americans over sixty-five with low incomes fell from 35.2% to 24.6% between 1959 and 1970. By 1974, despite a worsened national economy, the proportion of old people below the poverty line dropped to 15.7%. Experts outside of the government concur that the cash transfer system has reduced the incidence of old-age poverty and that its effectiveness has increased since the 1960s.[18]

Yet while there has been an overall improvement in the elderly's economic position, there remain extreme differences in the amounts of financial resources available to various groups within the aged population. Survey data since the 1950s consistently have indicated that older men or women with earnings as their principal source of income have the highest average level of receipts. Older persons not in the labor force, who supplement social security benefits with income from savings or pension funds, have been better off than those who relied solely on federal old-age insurance or assistance.[19] Furthermore, institutional mechanisms do not yet ensure retirement incomes above the low-income level. Poverty is a fact of life for a considerable number of older Americans and a real threat to many more. In 1974, 11.6% of all U.S. citizens had incomes below the government's poverty line, compared to 15.7% of all older persons. In the same year, the incomes of 36.4% of all blacks over sixty-five fell below the low-income level. A third of all older women who lived alone were poor.[20] Despite victories in the "War against Poverty," old-age dependency remains a serious predicament, especially for minorities and women.

Besides providing the elderly new means of support and altering their general economic circumstances, the expansion and extension of old-age assistance and insurance programs has changed the roles and relative importance of other institutions catering to the aged. For example, the wording of the original Social Security Act indirectly accelerated the decline of the poorhouse and the rise of the nursing home. The authors of the act, who by and large rejected the almshouse method of providing for aged dependents, drafted and successfully defended a provision denying direct assistance to poorhouse inmates. A hitherto unnoticed private institution, the "rest home," benefited from the situation because it could offer a residence and care for old people on public assistance without contravening Title I. Many former (or potential) poor farm residents thus relocated in proprietary homes.[21]

The enactment of Medicare and Medicaid in the 1960s gave further impetus to the growth of commercial nursing homes. The promise of good return on investments, rather than altruism, created a nursing home boom. As a 1966 article in *Business Week* described the situation:

> One of Wall Street's regular chores is watching legislation that comes out of Washington to see what the biggest of the big spenders—the U.S. government— is going to do next. . . . The real action, say the analysts, will come in real estate deals for nursing homes—a complex and little-understood field that in the past has been characterized by converted ramshackle dwellings and old movie theatres, fast-dealing entrepreneurs and occasional scandals.[22]

The characterization regrettably has proven accurate. To be sure, there are some good proprietary convalescent centers. In addition, not all nursing homes are commercial ventures. Twenty-one percent of America's institutional homes are nonprofit organizations concentrating on residential and personal rather than nursing care; these homes tend to perpetuate the service ideals of the earlier philanthropic old-age homes. Nevertheless, conditions in many nursing homes are disgraceful. Recent exposés indicate in tragic detail why people consider them "halfway houses somewhere between society and the cemetery."[23] Hence, the proprietary nursing homes replaced the almshouse after 1935 as a place where old people sometimes reside. The demise of one old-age institution, however, has not eliminated the sense of dread and fear elderly people feel as they enter the alternative fostered by social welfare programs.

In addition to the direct and indirect effects that growth of an institutional approach to old-age problems has had on shaping the elderly's position in American society since 1935, it has also played an unanticipated role in altering several other aspects of older people's situations. Consider, for instance, the initial impact of federal programs on children's attitudes toward caring for their parents. Existing evidence is tantalizing, even if fragmentary and difficult to interpret. (Any possible changes wrought by Title I would not have occurred uniformly, since states' old-age assistance laws varied concerning familial responsibilities for the elderly.) A few early surveys found that the enactment and availability of public assistance provided a "certain liberation for kinfolks, usually heavily burdened by their own economic problems, and the provision of greater happiness, self-respect, and joy of life for a larger number of men and women."[24] If so, Social Security may have reduced tensions between the generations and provided an additional source of security. A 1944 study, however, reached a less sanguine conclusion. After attempting to prove that the obligation to care for needy parents was no longer well established in the mores, the investigation proceeded to suggest that the means test required in many states for assistance heightened old people's anxiety: "The result is that parents who are in doubt about being helped by their children sometimes are equally uncertain about being able to qualify for assistance from the state or look upon it as an unacceptable alternative."[25] More research must be done to determine whether and how the original provisions of Title I may have altered children's willingness or need to offer their parents support. Yet it is worth noting that any change was unplanned, given the language of the provisions and expressed aims of the act's architects and administrators.

The subtle and mixed effect of old-age legislation on intergenerational relationships within the family, which became apparent almost at once, has persisted to the present day. Changes in the types and amounts of income available to older people occasionally appear to influence residential patterns: demographers note among other things a dramatic upsurge in the number of older persons sharing quarters with an unrelated elderly adult of the opposite sex; the proportion of unmarried women living alone is far greater among those with incomes above the poverty line than those with much lower incomes.[26] Furthermore, restrictions in recent old-age legislation sometimes force an older person to calculate the relative economic advantages of living alone compared to residing with kin. The availability of extrafamilial services, moreover, generates a variety of confusing, and often conflicting, feelings about what the older and younger generations expect of one another.[27] Hence the enactment and proliferation of regulations and laws have complicated the elderly's choices in living arrangements although this has rarely been their primary purpose or foreseen result.

I hope that even this brief survey illustrates how dramatically public and private old-age policies, facilities, and services have changed the ways that older Americans live. An institutional approach to the economic, medical, and social problems of old age has had a remarkable impact on the aged's options and circumstances. The indirect and unintentional effects of old-age programs, no less than their direct successes and failures, underscore this conclusion.

Recent Studies Re-form Ideas about Elderly's Worth

The growth of old-age programs not only has provided services and benefits that make the aged's life experiences different from those before the Depression, but it also has supported research that is altering our present understanding of the aged's worth and potential usefulness. Americans between World War I and World War II stressed modal patterns in describing the elderly: theories and data presented by natural and social scientists confirmed the then prevailing popular and professional opinion that old age was a period of pronounced physical decay, mental decline, undesirable psychological and behavioral traits, economic uselessness, personal isolation, and social segregation. Research conducted during the past four decades, however, has undermined the scientific basis for such an interpretation.

For example, recent inquiries into the physiological and pathological manifestations of aging have exposed serious deficiencies in the manner in which research was conducted and data were interpreted in medical and biological circles during the first decades of the twentieth century. Experts today are becoming particularly sensitive to the possibility that their precursors overstated the extent of degeneration in old age because they tended to base their ideas and facts on cross-sectional observations of older subjects who were institutionalized and/or disabled. Studying only these subsets of the elderly population, it is now believed, can be misleading, because less than five percent of all older Americans actually are institutionalized and because most severely incapacitated elderly persons are over seventy-five.[28] To gain a different perspective and to correct possible sample biases in previous work, recent investigators at gerontology centers, government institutes, and elsewhere have deliberately focused on patterns of "normal" aging among healthy people who remain in the community. In addition, an explicitly multidisciplinary approach has facilitated efforts to analyze interrelationships among the anatomical, metabolic, neurological, endocrinal, genetic, molecular, and cellular changes occurring throughout an organism's life cycle.[29]

While scientists still have not formulated a theory that adequately explains the complexities of the aging process, new approaches to the study of senescence have necessitated a reformulation of many basic ideas. Like their predecessors, researchers have found that visual acuity, hearing, and other physiological functions tend to decline over time. Unlike their predecessors, however, contemporary investigators emphasize that there are greater differences in physical conditions and capabilities among the elderly than in any other age group. Current survey data indicate that 57.7% of all people over sixty-five are not physically prevented from working or performing any basic tasks. Another 5.2% suffer some restrictions, and an additional 20.7% experience major limitations due to chronic conditions; the remaining 16.4% are unable to carry on primary activities.[30] Discussing only modal health tendencies among the elderly, in short, does not convey the total picture. Nor does it seem axiomatic any longer to claim that older people are physically unable to do good work. Increasingly, scientists are referring to the compensatory mechanisms and capacities of an aging body. For instance, it is now believed that older people typically perform at a slower pace than younger workers because their motor response is less efficient. Yet this deficiency is generally offset when the elderly's output is measured in terms of accuracy and quality.[31]

Currently available evidence, therefore, does not lend scientific credibility to the belief that the decrement in health and other physical capabilities associated with aging necessarily make old people useless burdens to society. Studies of workers' performance in industry reveal among other things that older employees can keep up with younger people in terms of their attendance, continuity of service, and output per hour.[32] Such findings suggest that an elderly worker's ability must be judged on its individual merits and not on the basis of age.

Not only has research published since World War II undermined the empirical basis for assuming that older people invariably are physically incapacitated, but it also has overturned all previous justifications for believing that learning and creativity inevitably cease with advancing age. In the 1920s, it will be recalled, psychologists using a battery of IQ tests and other measures postulated a curvilinear relationship between age and intelligence, and inferred that a human's innate mental degeneration accounted for his or her "lost" intelligence over time. Recent studies have demonstrated, however, that these earlier cross-sectional studies of age differences in intelligence confounded age and cohort effects. It now appears clear that earlier studies were actually measuring differences in educational levels and cognitive processes among various age groups, but were not proving that physiological changes in old age diminish mental capacities.[33]

Indeed, new studies indicate that if a person stays healthy and uses his or her skills, there is a measurable maintenance and sometimes even an improvement in intelligence into at least the seventh decade. One of the earliest works to set forth this new perspective in aging was Harvey Lehman's influential *Age and Achievement* (1953), which found that "the typical creative thinker . . . continues to produce quantitatively during most of his life."[34] Later research generated comparable results in tests involving less famous "creative thinkers" than Lehman analyzed. To be sure, scholars have been careful to note that old people as a group exhibit more diverse patterns of performance than the young. Some aged men and women cannot or do not learn new things. Older persons who suffer extensive brain damage, for instance, often experience a precipitous drop in intelligence; those who make no effort to maintain or broaden their social contacts find that their world becomes smaller and smaller. Nevertheless, most people can continue to grow mentally and develop their creative potential throughout their lives.

Just as recent studies have uncovered a wide variety in physical and mental capacities among elderly persons, so too they have documented considerable differences in the aged's personality traits.[35] Mounting evidence has undermined early-twentieth-century interpretations that described negative qualities found among older subjects as if they were universal and inescapable tendencies. Although psychologists today do not discount the effect of intrinsic physiological changes on an old person's outlook, they are far more inclined than their predecessors to invoke alternative developmental theories and to emphasize the impact of past, present, and anticipated experiences in their analyses of old people's personalities. Few, in fact, describe the psychology of aging as a monolithic process. Cross-sectional research projects have indicated significant variance in old people's general life satisfaction and overall psychological well-being. Longitudinal studies have confirmed that individual differences in later life do not decrease with age.

Besides confirming that variations in personalities exist among the aged as well as in younger age groups, recent research also has determined that old and young people share the same sorts of values, goals, fears, and needs, even though they may express these feelings in very different ways. Aging does not inexorably alienate older people from the dominant values and prevailing beliefs of their society.[36] The elderly generally want to be as independent and autonomous as they were at earlier stages of life. They fear illness and lack of sufficient income, but such anxiety is hardly unique to the old. The need to be respected and to maintain one's self-esteem does not decline with age. Furthermore, contemporary interpretations present a far more intricate and subtle analysis of generational differences than were common earlier in the century. Researchers no longer seize upon the rigidity of opinion or "fogyism" apparent among some old people as a causal explanation for differences between the young and old. Instead, they describe generational differences in terms of either the effect of being at different points in the life cycle or the impact of being socialized at different times; sometimes they integrate a developmental model and a historical approach. Regardless of their model, most researchers make allowances for differences among the elderly.

Professional discussions of aged sexuality illustrate both contemporary researchers' fundamental divergences from previous scientific studies of old age and their deliberate efforts to describe the important diversity in older people's life styles and attitudes.[37] Although confirming an earlier finding that sexual activity and interest tend to wane over time, scientists have become less willing to explain this decline by referring to a marked and inevitable reduction in the intensity of a person's sexual drive. Variations within the elderly population, researchers now believe, result from subjects' previous sex histories as well as their physical condition, marital status, and psychological make-up. Analysts also pay particular attention to cohort differences that might reflect changes in cultural norms. Given such an orientation, it is not surprising that researchers eschew cosmic generalizations about the elderly's attitudes and behavior.

Recent surveys of the elderly's actual life experiences, in fact, provide a striking contrast to descriptions earlier in the century that characterized old people as basically lonely, ignored and resented by their kin, or idly waiting to die. Results of independent nationwide studies reported in the 1970s, for example, indicated that less than an eighth of all older Americans experienced loneliness for extended periods of time; 84% of the population over sixty-five live less than an hour away from at least one of their grown children. Family visits occur often, and apparently provide ample opportunity for emotional, economic, and social interaction between the young and old.[38] And while most people withdraw from the labor force at about the same point in the life cycle, the impact of and adjustment to retirement vary according to a person's situation and personality. Roughly a quarter of all retired workers admit feeling obsolete; retired women often express this feeling more intensely than men. Most, however, report no significant sharp decline in life satisfaction, health, and activity after retirement.[39] Furthermore, those who are financially and psychologically prepared for retirement often find new challenges and rewards. When their previous roles as breadwinners and parents become less time-consuming and demanding, many older men and women assume greater responsibilities in church functions, local politics, and informal social groups and take advantage of educational and recreational opportunities. The civic, cultural, and commercial activities and achievements made by Americans chronologically past their "prime" forcibly remind one that old age these days is not invariably a period of obsolescence.[40]

Researchers during the past thirty years, in sum, increasingly have rejected ideas about senescence that had been elaborated by popular observers and scientists before World War II. On the basis of new theories and survey data, investigators in the natural and social sciences have undermined the credibility of believing that the aged, considered individually or collectively, are physically, mentally, and psychologically incapable of making worthwhile contributions to society. Current evidence persuades most gerontologists, in fact, that the very diversity of experiences and abilities among older people make their advice and services valuable and necessary. Thus, researchers increasingly have begun to describe as "myth" those conceptions of old age that their predecessors once asserted accurately described "reality."

Current Circumstances
Create a New Set of Old-Age Problems

As my analysis thus far suggests, a nationwide institutional approach not only improved the elderly's overall financial position and provided vital services, but it also broadened the understanding of the aging process and undermined unfavorable assumptions about the elderly's inherent capabilities and potential worth. Nevertheless, its undeniable and laudable achievements notwithstanding, the prevailing method of defining and dealing with the aged's needs in recent years has come under tremendous fire. Occasionally, critics are reacting to the fact that some of the economic circumstances and social factors that made old age a problem in the 1930s persist in the 1970s: commentators note that, despite all of our efforts and expenditures, many older Americans are desperately poor and without minimal health care and other basic services. Discontent with the system itself, moreover, is rampant.[41] Some advocate scrapping all existing programs or at the very least demand a major overhaul. Others recommend adhering to an incremental approach in correcting inherent faults and apparent shortcomings.

One of the most obvious deficiencies with the current system arises from the way we define and measure poverty in general and its incidence among older people in particular. After 1945, the Bureau of Labor Statistics and the Department of Agriculture, among other federal agencies, devised indices to determine the minimal cost of certain basic essentials deemed crucial for a healthy, productive existence. In the early 1960s, Mollie Orshansky, an economist in the Social Security Administration, designed a poverty index, based on money income only, as a research tool. Orshansky's endeavors attracted wide attention, because her work was being discussed in official circles at the very moment the architects of fledgling antipoverty programs were groping for a suitable measure of the extent of need in the United States. Orshansky's index, which was later modified to include even more specific income thresholds depending on the size and location of the family as well as the sex and age of its head, became an important government yardstick by the end of the decade. Economists have subsequently pointed out, however, that this particular measure is biased because it does not count public and private in-kind transfers (such as food stamps and fringe benefits), which have increased in relative importance to lower-income people during the past ten years. Other indices used by different agencies also are sensitive to the particular income definition used, and generally ignore year-by-year changes in individual and family financial resources.[42] Ironically, therefore, we are as unsuccessful as our predecessors in establishing a rationally acceptable or accepted measurement of deprivation, even though we have far more sophisticated survey tools and voluminous data available than existed when the creators of Social Security were forced to estimate the proportion of Americans requiring old-age assistance.

The lack of integration among various types of antipoverty programs enacted since the 1930s also contributes to the "welfare mess." Although we cannot fully determine either the precise degree of overlapping benefit coverage or the extent of gaps in coverage, it is painfully apparent that poor people with similar needs are not entitled to the same amount of assistance: depending on the program, a family with a female head may get more than one with a male head, or vice versa. Furthermore, programs often work at cross purposes. [43] The twenty percent increase in Social Security benefits in 1972, for instance, placed many elderly men and women over the poverty line, thus making them ineligible for Medicaid and food stamps: having more money paradoxically impaired many older Americans' economic situation. In addition, the sheer complexity of eligibility criteria and the welter of administrative details raise operational costs, increase the chance for inefficiency and error, and decrease prospects that agencies can—or will—regulate themselves.[44]

Needless to say, evaluating the strengths and weaknesses of existing programs is difficult under such circumstances. Major shortcomings in a new large-scale federal program often do not become manifest until that program has been set into operation. Even then, different perspectives on the situation occasionally arise. For some, protecting jobs and procedures assumes greater importance than honestly assessing cost-to-benefit ratios in light of stated objectives and anticipated impact. For others, attacking specific measures proves easier than proposing alternatives.[45] Divergent standards of judging a program's effectiveness further complicate the evaluative process. Advocates for a new program sometimes promise more than they can possible deliver, thereby making it hard to determine what a "realistic" assessment entails. It is becoming increasingly clear, moreover, that the "War on Poverty" escalated expectations about what the federal government should do to achieve a society in which everyone has access to certain minimal resources as well as basic goods and services. It also inflated hopes about what government at all levels could do to achieve this end. As a result, demonstrable "successes" often have been dismissed as "failures" by those who judge programs in light of newer and ever grander goals.[46]

Yet the aged's plight in contemporary America is not simply the result of limitations and failures in current old-age programs. In large part, the drawbacks reflect and are caused by broader structural and cultural changes in the evolution of society itself. Some of these problems have long existed, but now appear in a new form. Others are age-old predicaments that have assumed unprecedented or heightened urgency. Still others are the unique product of the present era.

In the past several decades, for instance, Americans have become more and more sensitive to the ways that their culture and society once perpetuated, and to a lesser extent still permit, systematic discrimination against various segments of the population. The recrudescence of the civil rights movement after World War II, and especially the dramatic events of the 1960s, forced Americans to acknowledge and respond to the fact that blacks have not been allocated, or enabled to achieve, an equal and decent position in society. In 1971, for example, the average monthly social security benefit for retired blacks was equal to only four-fifths the amount received by whites. In part, the gap in average benefits reflects cumulative differences in prior earnings among blacks and whites. As a group, blacks generally have experienced more job discrimination and have worked in lower paying jobs. In part, however, the source of the present disparity is an artifact of administrative decisions that made sense on certain levels yet, in retrospect, clearly operated to the particular disadvantage of blacks. Employment in agriculture and domestic service jobs was not covered initially because officials in the legislative and executive branches hoped to reduce some of the bureaucratic difficulties anticipated during the early stages of implementing the Social Security program. But because blacks in the 1930s and 1940s were heavily concentrated in these occupations, many "lost" earnings credit and benefits that they otherwise would have received if they had been employed in other areas. Furthermore, striking racial differences have been uncovered in the utilization of government health-care programs. Experts such as Sar Levitan and his colleagues report that blacks benefit proportionately less from Medicaid than from cash public assistance; a smaller proportion of eligible nonwhites use Medicare benefits than their white counterparts.[47] The unavailability of medical care facilities, the cost of various programs, and the complexity of government applications help to explain why blacks, relatively speaking, do not take full advantage of available services. Not surprisingly, researchers are also beginning to document that elderly Spanish-speaking, Indian, and Asian-American subsets of the population face comparable obstacles in seeking to provide for their economic and physical well-being.

The most recent phase of the women's liberation movement, in turn, has riveted attention on the disadvantages of and prejudices against women in past and present times. Like blacks and certain other minority groups, women have been, and continue to be, penalized because their typical working history and earning records diverge from the modal patterns for Caucasian, white-collar men. For example, the Social Security Administration currently determines retirement benefits by averaging all of a person's annual earnings except for the five lowest years—a procedure clearly more beneficial to men than women. Because a woman leaving the labor force to raise children receives no credit for housework and child rearing, all but five years of a woman's zero earnings are averaged with her salaried working years, thereby reducing her retirement benefits. Commentators have demonstrated, moreover, that current social policies are discriminatory insofar as they operate on the historically conditioned assumption that most women remain married to the same partner for at least ten or as many as twenty years (depending on which eligibility criterion applies in a given instance) and are "dependent" on his income for support.[48] Such notions about the dynamics of marriage and the role of women, which more accurately characterize earlier circumstances than contemporary conditions and projected trends, permit inequities that handicap the sex with the longer life expectancy.

Since the mid-1960s, government officials and the public at large have become increasingly sensitive to the ways that racism and sexism accentuate the difficulties encountered at later stages of life. More and more Americans have concluded that certain groups within the aged population deserve better treatment, and they have begun to demand government action. Constructive steps, in fact, have been taken. Furthermore, some of the egregious inequities presently existing should become less significant in the future as the gap between the income, education, and employment attainments of the currently disadvantaged and the more favored groups in society narrows. Nevertheless, visions of a utopian America in the year 2001 are definitely premature.

Counterbalancing optimism about the future is the sobering realization that other developments and trends simultaneously jeopardize the nation's ability and threaten its pledge to improve older Americans' overall situation or to remedy the predicament of those in particularly straitened circumstances. Changes in the means by which older people support themselves coupled with current and projected economic patterns, for example, have raised considerable concern about the societal costs and implications of present methods of allocating income and work through the life cycle. The relative economic position of the aged increasingly has been determined by the magnitude of intergenerational income transfers and the real monetary worth of old-age pensions. The cost of supporting old people in this manner has been and continues to be determined by the relative size of the elderly population and the amount of money guaranteed to them by law. Experts point out, however, that inflation and unemployment—two nemeses of the post–World War II economy—significantly raise the costs of this financial arrangement and adversely affect the aged more than other groups.[49] Because the level of a major component of old people's income (Social Security benefits) is established by legislation rather than in the market-place, inflation tends to erode the elderly's buying powers at a faster rate than Congress can remedy the situation. Because private pensions and savings, unlike Social Security, do not generally have cost-of-living clauses, inflation seriously depreciates the value of all other sources of income in old age. In addition, a rise in nationwide unemployment diminishes the likelihood that older men and women can find work, thereby forcing them to live on savings and supplemental income. Significant declines in the proportion of all Americans in the labor force by necessity increases the contributions those who are working must make for retirement programs, unless Congress chooses to reduce Social Security benefits, to raise the maximum earnings base for contributions and benefits, or to introduce government contributions derived from general revenues into the system.

Furthermore, the continued aging of the population greatly influences policy options about Social Security and other old-age programs. There are presently about three persons of working age for every one over sixty-five. This ratio will fall when the post-World War II babies reach retirement age. If current fertility patterns persist, the relatively small number of children born after the "war babies" will have to assume an ever-growing pension burden during their working lives.[50] Hence, existing and expected demo-graphic patterns strongly suggest that the cost of current programs will have to rise sharply if they are operated and financed in the same way in the future.

Perhaps more than ever before, therefore, recent social, economic, and demographic developments necessitate an immediate and thoughtful ap-praisal of the implicit values and actual impact of current means of providing and distributing income, work, and social services throughout a person's lifetime. In some ways, the times are becoming more and more propitious for systematic, interdisciplinary efforts to investigate the relationships among national priorities, societal values, and public policies. Americans in the 1970s are gradually realizing that government at all levels must distinguish between what it can deliver and what it cannot achieve. Civic leaders, officials, scholars, and the public at large are slowly but increasingly joining in serious analyses and dialogues about the values laden in their institutions and programs.[51] But such an enterprise, it must be recognized, is fraught with obstacles that go far beyond the predictable complications arising from political realities, economic exigencies, and professional and personal rivalries. Precisely because ours is a pluralistic society with broad, overlapping and often contradictory value sets, it is difficult to articulate the beliefs and shape the norms we hope our policies will reflect. Reifying value systems in symposia is an ever-present danger. Clashes also will occur among different groups concerning the relative importance of desirable but seemingly incompatible goals: proposals for nondiscrimination legislation, for instance, are not easily reconciled with the expressed commitment to equality of opportunity on the one hand and individual choice on the other.

The troubles typically besetting value-oriented policy discussions are particularly acute in those concerning the aged. Americans must decide whether and how they want to improve the elderly's position in the future. Steps might be taken to facilitate the voluntary reentry of older workers into the labor force on a full-time or more flexible basis. Alternatively, older people might be provided with more substantial retirement incomes so that they can enjoy their leisure and provide services for which they will not be paid. Any decision will hinge not only on economic, demographic, and political considerations, but also on the attitudes that Americans espouse. Estimations of older people's inherent qualities and potential worth greatly affect our options and action. After all, it only makes sense to encourage the elderly to seek gainful employment or volunteer their services if it is believed that older Americans can make meaningful contributions. "Social policy in aging, as in anything else, represents the synthesis of competing objectives, contending within the framework of a social philosophy conditioned by a value system or systems."[52]

It is for this very reason that prospects for a dramatic change in the aged's status seem slight at this writing. In his Pulitzer-prize-winning analysis of being old in contemporary America, *Why Survive?* (1975), Dr. Robert N. Butler, who became the first director of the National Institute on Aging in 1976, argues that there exists a profound prejudice against the elderly that extends beyond the classic fear of growing old. "Ageism can be seen as a systematic stereotyping of and discrimination against people because they are old, just as racism and sexism accomplish this with skin color and gender."[53] The ways that people currently view and treat the elderly compound the problems of growing old.

Americans by and large continue to disparage the elderly's usefulness even though recent research lends substantial support for a concept of old age that recognizes the diversity in older person's abilities and conditions and that emphasizes positive as well as negative aspects of senescence. According to a Louis Harris study on attitudes about old age (1975), most still subscribe to images of old people that prevailed earlier in the century. Regardless of their income, education, sex, race, or age, Americans generally do not consider the aged very active, alert, efficient, or contented.[54] There is, moreover, a tremendous discrepancy between what old age is expected to be like and the actual experiences elderly Americans say they have. Even those whose life in old age is far better than anticipated consider their situation exceptionally lucky and atypical.

Inaccurate assumptions about the elderly exist in all areas of society. Television, newspapers, and other molders of public opinion regrettably foster erroneous images of old age. "Media coverage of the elderly poor, the elderly sick, the elderly institutionalized, and the elderly unemployed or retired," Harris suggested in his 1975 survey, "may be protecting and reinforcing the distorted stereotypes of the elderly."[55] Several independent surveys of the portrayal of older persons in television programs and commercials substantiate this finding. The few exceptional characters in family dramas, detective stories, and situation comedies notwithstanding, most aged men and women are represented as one-dimensional, peripheral types who lack (or are denied) the full range of human feelings and foibles expressed by younger actors. In light of their actual numbers in the population, Americans over sixty are disproportionately found in commercials recommending health aids or geared to nostalgia buffs, but they almost never sell cars or clothing. The media, of course, are not the only creators and promoters of ideas about being old that contradict empirical observations and scientific theories and that hamper efforts to understand the aged's current predicament. Gerontologists, among others, have become very sensitive to the possibility that their own research inadvertently may perpetuate fallacious notions about the meanings and realities of old age.[56]

In this context, it is not wholly surprising that age discrimination persists in legislation designed to combat it. Administrators and politicians sometimes act as if funds allocated for the aged inevitably reduce monies for youth programs, rather than seeing both age groups competing together for a larger share of the total pie. In other instances, viewing older persons as a group with very special needs and inevitably debilitating limitations leads to well-intentioned but misguided laws.[57] For example, two years after it explicitly made "opportunity for employment without age discrimination" a principal objective for older Americans, Congress enacted the Age Discrimination in Employment Act of 1967. Ironically, ten years after its passage, the measure still applied only to people under sixty-five. A December 1977 Supreme Court decision, moreover, declared that corporate retirement and pension programs in effect before 1967 were not covered by the act. This ruling permits yet another major exemption to a measure already replete with problems. Indeed, as this book goes to press, one of the most important questions to be faced is whether chronological age per se is a socially desirable, much less a morally relevant, criterion for distributing services and allocating roles in society. It is impossible to predict how Americans will grapple with this issue. It is not even altogether clear that they really will try to address the matter.

Yet the future is not hopeless. Current awareness of the aged's assets and liabilities as well as the present understanding of the broader cultural trends, social forces, and structural factors that affect the elderly and all other Americans require us to recognize that some of our ideas have become outmoded and that some of our approaches to problem solving have grown obsolete. If we are willing to adjust our perception of the elderly's situation and the way we seek to change it, we can improve conditions for older citizens. Nevertheless, it remains to be seen whether Americans can or will meet the challenge of enhancing elderly persons' status under ever-changing conditions.

Toward the Year 2001

We have reached a critical juncture in the history of growing old in the new land. Ideas about older people's inherent worth and perspectives on their actual place in American society are in flux. Problems unforeseen and crises unimaginable even a decade ago make us question, and occasionally regret, previously enacted old-age policies. In attempting to determine where we are going, we sometimes seek to understand where we have been. We turn to the past, not to recapture a world we have lost but to learn the lessons of history.

In this context, I believe that historians have an unprecedented opportunity to play three crucial roles in writing the next chapter in the history of old age in the United States. They can work with other social scientists and humanists to formulate interpretations of the past that facilitate rather than complicate our ability to assess the elderly's current conditions and future prospects. Second, I think that they should also assume a somewhat unfamiliar but increasingly significant task: historians ought to apply their expertise in trend analysis and actively engage in establishing and evaluating old-age priorities and policies. At the same time, however, they dare not forget that history is both an art and a science. Accordingly, they must continually sensitize themselves, other gerontologists, and concerned citizens, as well as the public at large, to the dynamic ways that implicit and explicit values shape our thoughts and influence our actions concerning old age.

Historians as Social Scientists

Nearly all available analyses of older Americans' situations in past times directly or tangentially address a fundamental theoretical issue: to what degree does the process of "modernization" describe and explain continuities and changes in the history of old age? The appeal of modernization models arises, I suspect, from their presumed ability to demonstrate how a wide range of undeniably significant long-term developments—including, among

other things, increased life expectancy at birth, urbanization, industrialization, bureaucratization, and secularization—have affected the elderly over
time. Mainly because modernization seems to be such a comprehensive
concept, researchers to date have employed it alternately as an organizational device for recounting the key points in their narrative, as a theoretical construct for explicating and predicting social and cultural trends over
time, and as a heuristic typology to help disclose vital questions. As they
have generally been formulated, however, modernization models actually
may confound efforts to study the aged in history because practitioners have
often failed to appreciate their inherent conceptual problems and operational limitations.

In this regard, historians already have performed a useful function.
Although their interest in old age per se is somewhat belated when compared to other social scientists, they have identified various problems with
the overall "modernization" concept. It is clear, for instance, that because
underdeveloped and/or nonwestern societies do not invariably conform to
patterns of growth associated with the experiences of many European countries and the United States, we must squarely recognize the cultural biases
of the modernization thesis. Most scholars, moreover, acknowledge that the
societal changes associated with modernization have occurred in a slow and
incremental manner. Hence they increasingly recommend expanding
instead of shortening a project's temporal parameters and they challenge
two-stage models that present a dramatic and complete break from a "traditional" order and the emergence of a radically different "modern" one.
Yet liberating themselves from simplistic and deterministic models generally fuels more, not less, controversy.

Historians vehemently disagree about how to periodize the evolution of
American society, in part because they articulate various conceptions of
what features of social change were most important and because they reach
different conclusions about when new structural and cultural configura-
tions arose and/or displaced prevailing patterns. In large measure, however,
the plethora of interpretations attests to the complexity of the process of
modernization itself. That industrialization, bureaucratization, and urbanization were simultaneously reshaping society at a given moment does not
necessarily mean that the impacts of these social forces were identical.
Rarely has one aspect of modernization altered America to the same extent
and at the same rate as another component. Furthermore, there have been
important differences both in the timing and in the degree to which large-
scale forces and cultural patterns impinge on various groups in society.
These generalizations, in turn, lead to one final observation: teleological
concerns too often erroneously intrude into analyses. Since the impact of
modernization has been neither inevitable nor inexorable, it is risky as well
as naive to write an epic tracing Americans' fall from grace or manifest destiny from a remote point in our development.

Not surprisingly, then, my research reveals that special care must be exercised in studying old age in past times. The history of growing old in America did not, and could not, neatly conform to the major lines of development in the prolonged and protracted process of modernization itself. There have been too many surprises, ironies, and exceptions to claim that changes were ever uniform, one-directional, or irreversible. Some aspects of old age have remained constant over time while others have changed. Trends within the elderly population (especially those related to blacks, women, and, at some points in history, possibly immigrants) have diverged considerably from the modal patterns of the population over sixty-five at any given moment. Therefore, cautions about modernization's teleological implications definitely apply to the history of old age. The situation of the elderly simply has been too diverse and complex in preindustrial America and during subsequent phases of evolution to permit facile generalizations. Inevitably, older people's circumstances improved in some aspects and deteriorated in others with the passage of time.

It is also important to note that the processes associated with modernization affected perceptions of elderly Americans' worth in different ways and at different times than they altered the aged's actual experiences. There has never been a revolutionary shift in the process of change since 1790. No period(s) or decade(s) looms as *the* transitional stage(s). Indeed, the occasional dysfunction between the rhetoric and realities of old age is one of the more striking motifs of my analysis. A basic discontinuity between prevailing images and the actual experiences of growing old remains an unfortunate feature in the current history of old age: most Americans still subscribe to negative conceptions of older people's intrinsic and extrinsic characteristics that once seemed to make sense but that no longer have much basis in fact.

The place of the elderly in American society has changed along with those of other groups as the United States evolved, but certainly not in the same ways or for the same reasons. Older Americans sometimes proved quite successful in partially adapting to developments occurring in their midst while tenaciously clinging to traditional roles and arrangements. And although the aged were among the last to become "modern" in America, the present insights, demands, and efforts of older men and women attempting to enrich their lives may lead us all into the "postindustrial" era. It seems very likely that those who are, or shortly will be, over sixty-five will be among the first to experience widely forecasted developments. For instance, by pressing for flexible job schedules and demonstrating imaginative uses of retirement time, our elders can provide models for more healthful and sensible work-and-leisure arrangements throughout the life cycle. Indeed, as Americans increasingly comprehend that diminishing energy resources and unceasing international crises undoubtedly will force us significantly to reorder our priorities and alter our lifestyles, we should prepare to follow the aged's example and learn to make more out of less. If the human lifespan can be significantly extended through medical technology and genetic research, as some predict, then the current and following generations of older Americans will be the ones who will discover firsthand how the quality of later life improves and/or deteriorates in its prolonged form.

I believe, therefore, that scholars will find reformulated modernization models useful in studying the history of old age. They probably will be most pertinent in interpreting the aged's relatively recent past, the implications of which will become more fully apparent in the proximate future.[1] They should enhance analyses of changing perceptions of the immediate and cumulative impacts of broad-scale forces on the status and potential usefulness of old age. In addition, more sophisticated modernization models will permit researchers to evaluate the extent to which older persons themselves adapt(ed) deliberately or involuntarily, and adjust(ed) hesitantly or wholeheartedly to an ever changing world and world view. Applying insights from such studies will also enable investigators to describe and explain the dynamics of the age structure itself as it evolved in the United States. Ultimately, therefore, reconstructing the history of (old) age will reveal much about the long-term development of American culture and society itself.

Historians as Policy Analysts

Since the past shapes the present and affects the future, discussions of the meanings of history cannot be confined to the classroom or to professional gatherings. Historians need to join broader based efforts to create a reliable historical perspective with which to assess the elderly's current conditions and on which to premise projections and expectations about the situation for older Americans in the years ahead. In particular, they must convince experts in other disciplines, policy makers, and legislators that the temporal aspects of all policy discussions and decisions affecting the aged are just as important as demographic, socioeconomic, political, and ideological considerations.

Creating policies to help and benefit the elderly, a group that has diverse and varying characteristics, requires far more than remedying existing deficiencies and satisfying present goals. Policies must also make sense in light of well-established patterns, current attitudes and practices, and anticipated trends. While it is humanly impossible to forecast with absolute certainty the next steps and major developments in the story of growing old in the United States, a historical understanding of the events and forces that have led to the aged's present situation offers a fresh perspective worth utilizing as we seek to improve older Americans' status and conditions.

The preceding analysis, in fact, suggests three points that policy makers should heed:

1. Precisely because older Americans' present conditions differ considerably from conditions in the past, we cannot assume that the elderly's situation will remain the same in the future as it is today. The aged's demographic and socioeconomic circumstances, ideas about old age's worth, and definitions of the nature and extent of old-age dependency have never been static and undoubtedly will continue to change in the future. Institutions to serve the elderly, which are products of the milieu in which they were created and amended, will also evolve in new and different ways. The future, in short, will not simply be the present writ large.

2. Generally speaking, therefore, we should continue to institute changes and implement reforms on an incremental basis. We should pay closer attention to anticipated short-range patterns than long-term predictions, since in all probability they are more accurate. We should recognize that we stand a far greater chance of attaining goals set for the immediate rather than the distant future. An incremental approach, in fact, has two advantages. On the one hand, we reduce the likelihood that, in scrapping one major program for another, we are destined to discover in untried approaches problems that are more pernicious than those found in existing measures. On the other hand, we maximize the possibility that some long-standing philosophies and methods, which currently have fallen into disfavor or disuse, might be revitalized without necessitating a radical readjustment in all other policies.

3. This does not mean, however, that a conservative stance in policy development is always the best course of action. We must accept the fact that major reforms are periodically necessary and ultimately constructive. The Depression experience forcibly reminds us, for instance, that our predecessors were willing to consider options they had once dismissed as unnecessary and un-American when a dramatic and unanticipated turn of events seemed to give them no other choice. We, too, must remain flexible and sensitive to important disjunctures in historical development and societal context. Under certain circumstances, novel approaches and unprecedented activities are the most feasible and desirable options. For regardless of the estimates we make and the hopes we espouse, unexpected crises or opportunities as well as limitations in both our current understanding of the aged and judgments about what should be done next may force us to adjust our priorities and policies at any moment.

Historians as Humanists

As we become more and more alert to temporal biases in the stated principles by which and the established manner in which we allocate services and resources to the elderly, we will find it increasingly necessary to evaluate the short-term efficacy and long-term impact of various old-age programs in the most comprehensive framework possible. As I have shown, we must investigate the interplay of many diverse factors that impinge(d) on attitudes about growing old and determine(d) the aged's environment. Above all, I think, we must examine and be honest about the fluid nature of value judgments that prevail(ed) in the United States concerning the aged's worth and potential usefulness.

Needless to say, the relationships among human values, ethically bound social systems, and old age are difficult to investigate. But this does not diminish the importance and urgency of the task. Specialists in the humanities must inspire the humanist and nurture the humaneness in all of us. They must convince people that gerontology, for all of its technical jargon and arcane methodologies, is really the study of the opportunities and challenges associated with the last stages of human existence. Historians, as heirs to Clio, must do their part to convey this basic message and to shape the way in which it is presented. They must demonstrate that our perceptions of "reality" are products of the perennial paradoxes of growing old and the elderly's eternal experiences, as well as the cultural tendencies, value systems, and structural forces pervading society at any given moment.

The historical record reveals that since 1790, our dominant conceptions of old age have neither faithfully mirrored the aged's actual circumstances nor automatically shifted as new ideas arose and conditions changed. Rather, our ideas about the functions and overall worth of being old have a dynamics of their own, and thus exercise a significant—and often unanticipated and ironic—impact on our outlook and actions. For example, the comparatively favorable estimates of old people's worth articulated before the Civil War cannot be dismissed as idealized sentiments simply because they may be compatible with the pious ruminations of ministers or prescriptions contrived by writers hoping to combat dangers and to control excesses they perceived in the infant republic. The intellectual origins of admonitions to heed the elderly's wisdom or of recommendations to rely on their talents have deeper roots: acknowledging the aged's value made sense because it meshed with the exigencies of nation building and the dominant beliefs of pre–Civil War America. Yet even in this milieu, there were divergent patterns of thought that did not accurately reflect older Americans' "real" conditions. On the one hand, popular but sentimental images of old age ignored or glossed over the acute physical, psychological, and social problems of later years. On the other hand, the intense preoccupation with the tragedies of old age in a "romantic" impulse to heighten the presumed merit of living a long life appears, in retrospect, to have sown the seeds for less sanguine interpretations in the future.

In fact, one might plausibly argue that old age was not really as grim as some commentators claimed in the past. The growing belief that elderly persons were becoming obsolescent after the Civil War appears to have been more of a response to new theories, events, and conditions transforming American culture and society at large than a function of significant shifts in the "objective" demographic and socioeconomic status of the aged, at least insofar as it can be reconstructed through census records and other statistical data. And even when changes in the elderly's relative numbers and occupational and financial position did become more discernible, after World War I, it seems clear that writers sometimes misstated and exaggerated the trends occurring in their midst because of the intellectual paradigms and conventions, and social mores and expectations that shaped their perspective. Nevertheless, the extent to which reformers, scholars, government officials, the general public, and the elderly themselves perceived old age to be a "social problem" clearly influenced the nature of their response and the "solutions" they forged—as the initial and continued debates over Social Security and the "war on poverty" legislation, among other things, reveal.

Precisely because previously held judgments about the meanings and experiences of being old do shape current thinking, historians are not invariably seduced by present-mindedness when they join other humanistically oriented scholars in showing that some of our ideas have now become out of date and some of our methods have grown ineffective. The time is ripe, I think, for discarding the now inappropriate but still prevalent notion that older Americans are "problems" and for concentrating instead on the problems they have. Furthermore, if we are to reduce the likelihood of becoming victims of our own excessive sentimentality, sensitivity, or cynicism and pawns of institutional priorities or academic predilections, we must increase our number of experts in gerontology. The twentieth-century record indicates, in my opinion, that we can and must rely on the insights and resources of both the aging and the aged public. Yet, in offering these recommendations, I am keenly aware of the ways in which my own viewpoints are colored to some degree by the issues and vocabulary of the day: even historians must remember that their studies of old age become anachronistic in due course.

It is difficult to scrutinize our assumptions about old age; it is harder still to discard ones that we discover are wrong. It is often very painful or at least quite inconvenient to acknowledge that the values and the society in which we live are constantly changing, thereby ever forcing us to challenge prevailing verities and precedents and to rethink the way we perceive and deal with old age in this country. Yet it can be done if we hope to address the elderly's real needs and desires instead of our own preconceptions. And it must be done if older Americans—and ultimately ourselves—are to have roles that ensure meaningful lives and dignity.

APPENDIX

Sources and Procedures Used
To Study Conceptions
About the Elderly's Status

My analysis of American perceptions of the position of older people in society rests primarily on evidence found in popular and scientific periodicals, books for the aged or about old age, dictionaries and other reference works, and statutes and miscellaneous public records. Each source has its distinctive advantage. Magazine articles are useful barometers of changes and continuities in ideas because the medium reached beyond the local community, and because journals survived mainly on their ability to shape and/or satisfy readers' ever-changing tastes. Literature ranging from medical and economic treatises to self-help and Social Security tracts not only embodied prevailing assumptions about old age per se but also gave clues about the larger society in which the elderly lived. Editors of encyclopedias, almanacs, and dictionaries made considerable efforts to update material and revise entries so that references would be (or at least appear) definitive and current. Such materials thus conveyed an aura of authority that contemporary periodicals did not presume and had a serialized lifespan that books did not enjoy. Finally, laws, congressional hearings, census records, national and state surveys, and other public documents reveal the priorities, concerns, and assumptions that officials and citizens expressed about the elderly's worth as well as their presumed and actual status. Such documents also provide important insights about the institutional framework created over time to help older Americans.

While these sources offer considerable insights into the history of ideas about growing old, they do not tell everything. Relying primarily on printed sources, I have excluded the ideas of the inarticulate and the lower classes and concentrated on definitions of the roles and worth of older Americans as expressed at the national level by a predominantly white, middle- to upper-middle-class population. Since I used mainly sources that were published in English, I could not determine whether conceptions of old people's status varied among native-born and foreign-born groups. Although I tried to be sensitive to regional and urban-rural variations, I did not attempt to capture the diverse richness of circumstances that surely existed in local settings. On the basis of my evidence, I have not been able to probe the feelings that writers may have confided in private but not expressed in public; except in the published cases of a few distinguished Americans, I could not trace people's ideas as they grew older. In the future, others will want to consult autobiographies, diaries, private letters, newspapers, oral histories, and data in ethnic archives. While analyses of these data will necessitate revisions in the arguments presented here, my work nevertheless should provide a useful starting place.

Furthermore, methodological considerations dissuaded me from tracing the history of old age in America from 1607 onward, even though at one stage I had hoped to investigate the colonial experience. I confined my attention to developments after 1790 because I wanted to study national trends using data that were relatively accessible and comparable over the longest period of time possible. Accordingly, 1790 seemed a reasonable starting point, since the first federal census was taken that year and since most of the pertinent books, periodicals, reference works, and federal records dealing with old age or the aged were published after that date. (It is worth noting that I did examine those works included in the Evans microfiche collection, *Early American Imprints*.) To study the colonial era in depth, however, different materials (such as town and county documents, court records, sermons, and private letters) would have been more appropriate; yet it seemed too awesome a task to analyze these types of records systematically over the course of 370 years. The pre-Revolutionary heritage, especially in the middle and southern colonies, obviously deserves far more attention than it has received to date. But on the basis of currently available or soon to be published hypotheses and evidence, I believe that future interpretations of the colonial experience will enrich rather than invalidate the crux of the arguments presented here.

The value of this monograph, however, depends not only on the sources used but also on the way I used the sources. I began by consulting the classic bibliographic sources, and read works cited that seemed pertinent to my subject. I then checked the indexes and tables of contents of fifty-six periodicals, which I considered representative of the times or which catered to an important group of readers. (The actual periodicals surveyed are listed in the bibliography.) I proceeded to read all relevant articles, poems, letters, or editorials in these periodicals, volume by volume, throughout the life of the journal, or at least for those years that fell between 1790 and 1940. In reading an article, I copied the essential point(s) the author made about growing old and the aged. I also wrote down adjectives, phrases, and sections that seemed characteristic of the selection. Each time I came across a reference to an article or a book on old age that I had not yet consulted, I noted it and tried to read the source in its original form. I followed the same procedure in surveying the encyclopedias, dictionaries, and almanacs listed in the bibliography. Although time consuming, this procedure was feasible because the total material on old age contained in these sources prior to 1940 was not awesome. Obviously, had I chosen to study the development in ideas about "democracy" or "success" rather than "old age," I would have had to devise a sampling procedure. Indeed, the extraordinary increase in articles and works about old age since the passage of the Social Security Act made it impossible even to try to read all the pertinent material. (Hence I base my conclusions about recent trends in ideas concerning the elderly largely upon evidence in the most frequently cited works in gerontology and geriatrics published since 1935, published popular opinion polls, and upon insights derived by reading retrospective articles on the "state of the field.")

About halfway through the process of gathering data, I decided to investigate whether the trends I thought I was finding would survive a systematic examination of the material I had accumulated. I devised (and refined as I proceeded) a codesheet arranged into six major categories with detailed subtopics. These categories were: overall estimates of the aged's worth; evaluations of the aged's position in society; physical, mental, psychological, and behavioral characteristics of old people; economic uses of the elderly; noneconomic functions of the aged; and old-age dependency. Next, I arranged my data according to the decade in which it originally was published; items that were republished in a later decade were noted and credited to that decade. I then sorted the data according to the categories on my codesheet. This exercise was repeated four more times, to control for the possible effect of a given author's sex, age, or regional bias and to determine whether data from diverse types of sources produced widely different results. This analysis revealed dramatic differences in perceptions of the elderly, but no one decade or period emerged as *the* decisive turning point. The evolution was gradual. I found variations in descriptions of older men and women's roles and in comparisons of youth and age; medical and nonmedical sources often differed in tone and substance. I did not detect important differences, however, in the ways that people of different regions or different age groups or different sexes described the elderly or evaluated their worth and uses. (It is worth noting in this regard that a 1975 Louis Harris poll also found that the overall image of older people did not vary by income, education, race, or age.)

I incorporated these preliminary results into my subsequent analysis. I searched for evidence that might refute or at least force me to qualify judgments about the patterns that seemed to be emerging. I also found it necessary to draw sharper distinctions than I had made originally. Furthermore, I tried to compensate for biases in this procedure and to reduce the extent to which my predilections distort the results. Discussions with friends, teachers, and other scholars working in the field helped immensely. The most important checks I have performed, however, were designed to determine whether the patterns I describe make sense in terms of the context in which they actually evolved. For instance, I traced meanings of key words (such as "senility" and "retirement") over time; the overall trends I delineate are consistent with the patterns generated by this exercise. In addition, I tried to verify that changes I believed were occurring in medical, economic, legal, and social conceptions of old age made sense in light of broader developments in medicine, industry and business, law, and society at large.

Finally, in the course of revising my dissertation for publication, I had an opportunity to participate in a project, sponsored by the National Endowment for the Humanities, at the Institute of Gerontology in Ann Arbor, which traced images of old age found in American prints, etchings, photographs, and other graphics since 1790. While this independent research revealed to me how much the medium itself shapes ideas about being old, it also increased my confidence that I have accurately described some of the significant continuities and changes in conceptions of older Americans' worth and status. Far more research must be done, however, before we can understand the total picture.

Some Problems in Using Federal Census Data in Longitudinal Analyses of Old Age

The Underenumeration of the Aged in the 1870 and 1880 Occupational Statistics

One of the canons of historical analysis is that the credibility of an interpretation depends in large part on the reliability and quality of the data a researcher uses. Every bit of evidence must be examined for internal and contextual discrepancies. Very often a historian can cope with deficiencies he or she detects by making adjustments or estimates and by being sensitive to the ways in which biases in sources can distort the mathematical and theoretical interpretations of the analyses performed. Occasionally a researcher finds evidence so flawed, however, that it is useless.

Occupational statistics for men and women over sixty years old in the 1870 and 1880 federal censuses are a case in point. Although constituting the earliest age-specific statistics on the number of older people gainfully employed, the figures arouse suspicion: the percentages for men over sixty reported as engaged in all occupations in 1870 and 1880 were 64.2% and 64.3% respectively; in 1890, however, 73.2% of all men over sixty-five were listed as employed. These statistics seem curious because work force participation generally tends to decline with advancing age. In fact, on the basis of internal evidence in various federal documents as well as a comparison of federal and state census statistics on the work force participation rates of elderly men and women in Massachusetts and New York during the latter part of the nineteenth century, I determined that the 1870 and 1880 old-age data were grossly underenumerated.[1]

Changes in instructions to enumerators taking the census in large measure may explain why census returns on the percentage of elderly men and women working at gainful jobs were less accurate before 1890 than after. While enumerators were told that inquiring about people's profession, occupation, or trade was "one of the most important questions" of the 1870 and 1880 schedules, there was no specific instruction *requiring* that occupational data be gathered.[2] More importantly, no fines were levied if such data were *not* collected. This ambiguity was eliminated in 1890, when the census office required enumerators "to obtain each and every item of information and all the particulars.[3] Information relating to age, sex, and race, on the other hand, *had* to be gathered for every person; no return would be accepted whenever these data were missing. As a result, the occupational status of every member of every household was recorded in 1890. This practice continued in subsequent years, so information on this item should be reasonably complete.

Other Census Data Problems

The problem of underenumeration, needless to say, is not limited to occupational statistics in the 1870 and 1880 censuses. For instance, canvassers often overlooked certain segments of the population (notably blacks, immigrants, and urban dwellers) in doing surveys. This means that the totals for various subsets of older Americans in a given census year, especially in the nineteenth century, might have been greater than reported.[4] Often those interviewed tainted the reliability of information gathered. The number of persons who said that they were sixty years old or older probably differs from the number who actually were that precise age. A few people guessed because they did not know how old they really were. Other people lied about their age; the reasons motivating them were so diverse, however, that it is impossible to determine the net direction of the distortion. Age heaping—resulting from people's tendency to round off their ages to the nearest five-year interval or decade—compounds the problem.[5]

In addition, systematic alterations in the way that the categories were defined and the survey itself was conducted make it difficult to trace changes over time. Before the Civil War, census officials classified all slaves and free blacks over forty-five together as one age group, thereby preventing comparison of the aged by race in the antebellum period. Analyses of aged blacks are further hampered by a bureaucratic decision to classify all blacks, Indians, and Orientals as "colored" in 1880 and 1890. (Although it is reasonable to suppose that nearly all "colored" people in the South at the time were blacks, such an assumption is not warranted for the rest of the nation.) Occupational data are particularly sensitive to definitional and procedural changes. For example, in 1890 and 1900, the federal census was taken during the month of June. In 1910 and 1930, the population was enumerated in April. In 1920, however, the census was taken in January, a slack period for farmers. The Brookings Institution estimates that more than half a million agricultural workers were underenumerated in 1920 simply because of the change of month in scheduling the census.[6] Furthermore, the introduction of the "labor force concept" in 1940, to replace previous definitions of "gainful employment," greatly affected occupational statistics: data for the percentage of gainfully employed older workers between 1890 and 1930 must be adjusted slightly downward to make them compatible with 1940 and subsequent census data.[7]

Finally, the evolution of American society itself affects the comparability of census data over time. This is particularly apparent when one considers the multiplication of new occupations resulting from innovations in technology, transportation, bureaucratic practices, and large-scale industrialism. In 1890, census officials classified every occupation into one of five groups: agriculture, fishing, and mining; professional service; domestic and personal service; trade and transportation; and manufacturing and mechanics. There were thirteen major categories of occupations by 1940, including such new classifications as construction, finance, business, and government workers. The schema has been revised several times since then to reflect subsequent changes in the labor force. The growing complexity of the occupational structure becomes problematic because of its effect not only on the numerical size of any given occupational category but also on the age structure within occupational groupings.

Cataloguing deficiencies in the census statistics and citing possible methodological problems in comparing such data over time should not lead anyone to the conclusion that it is foolhardy to analyze the material available in the decennial census volumes. Rather, recognizing the data's limitations makes one wary of attaching too much significance to dramatic changes in demographic or economic rates from one decade to the next. Abrupt shifts may reflect a new direction in census definitions or procedures, not an important change in actual behavior. Therefore, what is essential is that the student of history try to grasp the meaning of long-term trends that gradually emerge over time.

Estimates of the Aged Work Force before 1890

Estimate of the White Work Force over 65 Years of Age in 1840

In order to estimate the 1840 work force participation rate of whites over 65 in the United States, I made assumptions, derived estimates, and reached calculations according to the following procedure.

1. Because the 1840 census did not list the number of whites over 65, I had to estimate the proportion of people between the ages of 60 and 70 who were over 65. On the basis of these estimates, I assumed that the number of white Americans in 1840 over 65 was no less than 341,369 and no more than 369,171, and that the number of white Americans between the ages of 10 and 65 was no less than 9,604,805 and no more than 9,632,607.

2. I estimated that the ratio of the proportion of gainfully employed people over 65 to the proportion of gainfully employed people between 10 and 65 fell within the following ranges:

Occupational Category	Low	Best Guess	High
ʳAgriculture	.95	1.20	1.60
ʳManufacturing	.54	.63	.70
ʳTrade or transportation	.37	.49	.60
ʳDomestic service	.50	.58	.66
ʳOther	.48	.54	.60

These ratios were derived by calculating the drop-off ratios for the same fields in 1890, 1920, and 1940 and by projecting trends backward.

3. Knowing the proportion of all workers in a given occupational category that were between the ages of 10 and 65 between 1890 and 1940, I estimated the minimum and maximum numbers of people between 10 and 65 who were engaged in the same occupational group in 1840.

4. I then calculated the number of white Americans over 65 who were

gainfully employed, using the following equation:

$$r = \cfrac{\cfrac{\text{number of people over 65 years old engaged in occupation}}{\text{total population 65 years old}}}{\cfrac{\text{number of people between 10 and 65 years old engaged in occupation}}{\text{total population between 10 and 65 years old}}}$$

On the basis of these calculations, I compute that the actual figure lies between 26.1% and 48.8%. My best estimate is 38.1%.

Estimate of the White Male Work Force over 65 Years of Age in 1840

I repeated the procedure outlined above in estimating the white male work force over 65 in 1840, but had to make an additional assumption, namely, that the same male-female ratio that existed for a given occupational category in 1890 obtained in 1840 as well. I thereby estimated the number of white males over 65 gainfully employed in 1840 to be:

Occupational Category	Low	Best Guess	High
Agriculture	77,161	84,627	91,351
Manufacturing	9,505	11,710	12,166
Trade or transportation	6,993	9,221	10,236
Domestic service	1,883	2,253	2,352
Other	8,661	10,827	12,631
Total	104,203	118,638	128,736
Percentage of the aged population employed	61.6%	70.1%	76.6%

Estimate of the White Male Work Force over 60 Years of Age, Massachusetts, 1840

Estimates of the white male work force over 60 in Massachusetts in 1840 are based on data available in the 1885 Massachusetts census. Using the same procedures outlined above, I derived the following figures:

Occupational Category	Low	Best Guess	High
Agriculture	8,725	12,387	15,664
Mining	21	21	21
Manufacturing or trade	3,430	3,430	3,430
Transportation	1,015	1,015	1,015
Professional service	165	165	165
Total	13,356	17,018	20,295
Percentage of the aged population	58.5%	74.6%	88.9%

NOTES

Notes

INTRODUCTION

1. Since the publication of Philippe Ariès's classic *Centuries of Childhood* (New York: Random House, 1962), the bibliography on the histories of early stages of life in the United States has grown enormously. Particularly recommended are the works of John and Virginia Demos, Philip Greven, Tamara Hareven, Joseph Kett, and Maris Vinovskis. A splendid model of research using cohort analysis is Glen Elder's *Children of the Great Depression* (Chicago: The University of Chicago Press, 1974).

2. See ch. 4 and 5, *infra*, for further discussions on this matter. See also Bernice L. Neugarten and Robert J. Havighurst, eds., *Extending the Human Life Span* (Washington, D.C.: Government Printing Office, 1977).

3. This generalization is based on a systematic analysis of the year(s) suggested for old age that appeared in the literature examined from 1790 to the present.

4. This distinction is found in medical and popular dictionaries throughout American history, although the terms used to distinguish the two stages have varied. The meanings of medical terms, moreover, change over time. As I shall show in Part 1, for instance, tracing the meaning of "senility" in the nineteenth century offers clues about medical definitions of old age. The distinction between "young-old" and "old-old" was advanced by Bernice Neugarten, an eminent gerontologist, in "Age Groups in American Society and the Rise of the Young-Old," *Annals of the American Academy of Political and Social Science* 415 (September 1974): 187–98.

5. See Bernice Neugarten, ed., *Middle Age and Aging* (Chicago: The University of Chicago Press, 1968); Robert H. Binstock and Ethel Shanas, eds., *Handbook of Aging and the Social Sciences* (New York: Van Nostrand, 1976); and Leo W. Simmons, *The Role of the Aged in Primitive Societies* (New Haven: Yale University Press, 1945).

6. See Walter Moss, ed., *Humanistic Perspectives on Aging* (Ann Arbor: Institute of Gerontology, 1976); Mary Sohngen, "The Experience of Old Age as Depicted in Contemporary Novels," *Gerontologist* 17 (February 1977): 79–85. Forthcoming essays from the 1975–77 "Human Values and Aging" project, directed by David D. Van Tassel, will further elucidate this point. See also the catalog from the exhibit, *Images of Old Age in America: 1790 to the Present*, researched by W. Andrew Achenbaum and Peggy Ann Kusnerz under the auspices of the Institute of Gerontology at the University of Michigan.

7. On the early American situation, see the essays by John Demos and Daniel Scott Smith to be published in the Van Tassel collection. For conditions in preindustrial France (and subsequent developments), see Peter N. Stearns, *Old Age in European Society* (New York: Holmes and Meier, 1976). For conditions in England, see Peter Laslett, "Societal Development and Aging," in *Handbook of Aging and the Social Sciences*, ed. Robert Binstock and Ethel Shanas (New York: Van Nostrand, 1976). Jack Goody's "Aging in Nonindustrial Societies" in the Binstock and Shanas collection is also worth reading.

8. David Hackett Fischer, *Growing Old in America* (New York: Oxford University Press, 1977), p. 113. For critiques of the strengths and weaknesses of Fischer's argument, see Lawrence Stone, "Walking over Grandma," *New York Review of Books*, 12 May 1977, as well as my remarks in "From Womb through Bloom to Tomb," *Reviews in American History* (June 1978).

9. I have two reasons for distinguishing between "perceptions" and "attitudes" in this monograph. First, the materials I investigated constitute written definitions and observations intended for public consumption. While a historian obviously must pursue the assumptions and

rationale inherent in such documents, it would be reckless to assume that examining only this type of evidence enables a researcher to probe the private (and often inchoate) notions or range of attitudes of a person he/she has never met, much less interviewed. Second, I decided to trace ideas about old age and the aged that went beyond idiosyncratic notions about a particular aged individual. Hence I mention specific cases primarily to illustrate overall patterns of thought or to highlight important deviations from the prevailing trends under consideration. (See also appendix technical note A.)

CHAPTER 1

1. *Niles Register* 28 (30 July 1825): 346.

2. Henry Adams, *History of the United States during the Administration of Thomas Jefferson* (1889; reprint ed., New York: Albert and Charles Boni, 1930), p. 1. See also Richard D. Brown, *Modernization* (New York: Hill and Wang, 1976), pp. 95–96, 100; and Robert F. Berkhofer, Jr., "From Colonial Communities to Modern Mass Society: A Social Evolutionary Model of American History" (Paper delivered at the 1976 American Historical Association convention, Washington, D.C., 29 December 1976).

3. Stow Persons, "The Cyclical Theory of History in Eighteenth Century America," in *The American Culture*, ed. Hennig Cohen (Boston: Houghton Mifflin Co., 1968), p. 121; see also Henry Steele Commager, *Empire of Reason* (Garden City: Anchor Press/Doubleday, 1977), esp. ch. 4.

4. See, for example, Christopher Wilhelm Hufeland, *The Art of Prolonging Life* (1797; reprint ed., New York: Thomas O'Kane, 1873), p. iii; Anthony F. Willich, *Domestic Encyclopedia,* 2d American ed., 3 vols. (Philadelphia: Abraham Small, 1821), 2: 453, 480; Wooster Beach, *Family Physician*, 16th ed. (Boston: B. B. Mussey Co., 1854), p. xli; H. Holland, "Human Longevity," *Living Age* 53 (25 April 1857): 203–6.

5. Quoted in James H. Cassedy, *Demography in Early America* (Cambridge, Mass.: Harvard University Press, 1969), p. 263.

6. William Barton, *Observations on the Progress of Population and the Possibilities of the Duration of Life, in the United States of America* (Philadelphia: Aitken, 1791), p. 20.

7. This observation is based on a survey of more than a hundred different almanacs, published between 1790 and 1860 in diverse parts of the nation, housed in the Clements Library at the University of Michigan, Ann Arbor.

8. For illustrative examples, see *Niles Weekly Register* 9 (1815): 98, 300, 402, 404, 430; ibid. 14 (1818): 151, 296; ibid. 23 (1823): 145, 354; and ibid. 41 (1832): 448.

9. John Bristed, *Resources of the United States of America* (New York: James Eastburn & Co., 1818), pp. 20, 453.

10. Jeremy Belknap, *History of New Hampshire,* 3 vols. (Boston: Bradford and Read, 1813), 3: 171–73, 188–90.

11. Benjamin Rush, "An Account of the State of the Mind and Body in Old Age," in *Medical Inquiries and Observations,* 4 vols. (1793; reprint ed. Philadelphia: Thomas Dobson, 1797), 2: 300.

12. William Godwin, *Enquiry concerning Political Justice, and Its Influence on Morals and Happiness,* 2 vols. (1793; reprint ed., Toronto: University of Toronto Press, 1940); Antoine-Nicolas de Condorcet, *Outlines of an Historical View of the Progress of the Human Mind* (Ann Arbor: Edwards Brothers, [1795]); Thomas Malthus, *On Population* (1798; reprint ed., New York: Modern Library, 1960). For an essential discussion of these writers and attitudes about longevity in general, see Gerald J. Gruman, *A History of Ideas about the Prolongation of Life: The Evolution of Prolongevity Hypotheses to 1800* (Philadelphia: The American Philosophical Society, 1966).

13. Willich, *Domestic Encyclopedia*, 2: 453, 480.

14. *The New Encyclopedia,* 3 vols., 3d ed. (London: William H. Hall, 1797), s.v. "longevity"; *Encyclopedia Brittanica*, 1st American ed., s.v. "longevity"; Frederick Marryat, *A Diary in America* (1839; reprint ed., Bloomington: Indiana University Press, 1960), pp. 121–22; Daniel Harrison Jacques, *Hints toward Physical Perfection* (New York: Fowler and Wells, 1859), pp. 209–14.

15. John Bell, *On Regimen and Longevity* (Philadelphia: Hasnell & Johnson, 1843), pp. 389–91; Jacques, *Physical Perfection,* p. 219; Elliot G. Storke, *The Family Farm and Gardens* (Auburn: Storke, 1859), pt. 2, p. 249. Marriage, it was said, also promoted longevity.

16. Charles Caldwell, *Thoughts on the Effects of Age on the Human Constitution* (Louisville: John C. Noble, 1846), p. 19. See also "Oldest Negro Yet," *Frank Leslie's Illustrated* 3 (20 December 1856): 44.

17. Lester Snow King, *The Medical World of the Eighteenth Century* (Chicago: The University of Chicago Press, 1958), pp. 193–226, 263–96; Richard H. Shryock, *Medicine and Society in America, 1660–1860* (New York: New York University Press, 1960), pp. 61–66; Barbara G. Rosenkrantz, *Public Health and the State* (Cambridge, Mass.: Harvard University Press, 1972), ch. 1–2.

18. Charles E. Rosenberg, *The Cholera Years* (Chicago: The University of Chicago Press, 1962), pp. 73, 154–157; Richard H. Shryock, *Medicine in America* (Baltimore: The Johns Hopkins University Press, 1966), pp. 72–89; Joseph F. Kett, *The Formation of the American Medical Profession* (New Haven: Yale University Press, 1968), pp. 156–57.

19. Hufeland, *Prolonging Life,* pp. i–ii, 104.

20. Thomas Bailey, *Records of Longevity* (London: Darton and Co., 1859), pp. 4–5. See also David Ramsay, *History of South Carolina*, 2 vols. (Newsberry, S.C.: David Longworth, 1809), 2: 233; Belknap, *New Hampshire, 2: 174; Niles Weekly Register* 29 (10 September 1825): 27; *Atkinson's Casket* 12 (May 1835): 282–83; *North American Review* 55 (July 1842): 272; Andrew Jackson Davis, *Harbinger of Health* (New York: A. J. Davis & Co., 1842), pp. 180–81; Joel Pinney, *How to Attain Health and Long Life* (London: S. Highley, 1839), p. 138.

21. Caldwell, *Effects of Age,* p. 22; Bell, *Regimen,* p. 387; Robert B. Thomas, *Farmer's Almanac for 1853,* p. 37; idem, *Farmer's Almanac for 1858,* p. 38; Bailey, *Records of Longevity,* pp. 4–6, 29, 33; "The Length of Human Life," *Littell's Living Age* 41 (7 July 1855): 3–8.

22. Abraham Shoemaker, *U.S. Almanack* (Elizabeth-town, N.J.: Abraham Shoemaker, 1797).

23. Orville Dewey, *The Problem of Human Destiny*, 2d ed. (New York: James Miller, 1854), p. 122. See also Thomas Bernard, *The Comforts of Old Age,* 5th ed. (London: John Murray, 1820), pp. 31–32; *Cramer's Pittsburgh Almanack* (1807), p. 10; G. G. Foster, "The Old Man Returned Home," *Graham's Magazine* 20 (April 1842): 225; "Youth and Age," *Littell's Living Age* 49 (1856): 99.

24. Benjamin Rush, *Medical Inquiries and Observations, upon the Diseases of the Mind* (1812; reprint ed., New York: Hafner Publishing Co., 1962), p. 297.

25. On this point in general, see Gordon Wood, *The Rising Glory of America* (New York: George Braziller, 1971), pp. 1–22; Arthur M. Schlesinger, Jr., "America: Experiment or Destiny," *American Historical Review* 82 (June 1977): 507–14.

26. The first quotation comes from Senex, "On Education," *Balance, and Columbian Repository* 1 (1802): 370; the second quotation comes from S. Reed, "A Review," *North American Review* 24 (January 1827): 56–57. Reed did not limit this role to the old.

27. Cortlandt Van Rensselaer, *Old Age: A Funeral Sermon* (Washington, D.C.: By the author, 1841), pp. 10–11; Albert Barnes, *Life at Three-Score: A Sermon,* 2d ed. (Philadelphia: Parry and McMillan, 1859), p. 9.

28. Dewey, *Human Destiny*, p. 123. See also "Youth and Age in America," *Harper's Magazine* 20 (January 1860): 264–67; "Life's Lessons," *Knickerbocker Magazine* 21 (June 1842): 505; E. Gallaudet, "Youth and Old Age," ibid. 26 (November 1845): 414; James Pritchett, "The Old Man and the Children," *Littell's Living Age* 51 (October 1856): 256; L. Maria Child, *The Mother's Book,* 6th ed. (Chicago: C. S. Francis & Co., 1844), pp. 114–15.

29. James Fenimore Cooper, *American Democrat* (1838; reprint ed., New York: Alfred A. Knopf, 1931), p. 146; William Mountford, *Euthanasy*, 2d ed. (Boston: W. Crosby and H. P. Nichols, 1850), p. 2; "Outlived Her Usefulness," *Littell's Living Age* 48 (January–March 1856): 317; T. S. Arthur, "The Old-Time Grandfather," *Godey's Lady's Book* 56 (April 1858): 320–21.

30. *An American Dictionary of the English Language*, 1st ed., s.v. "venerate." The definition of "venerate" did not change in successive editions of Webster's dictionary for fifty years. Richard M. Rollins ("Words as Social Control," *American Quarterly* 28 [Fall 1976]: 415–31) argues that Webster used his dictionary as a vehicle to express his concern about social authority and control. This may be so, but it should not be inferred from this important finding that Webster was the only person who described the aged as "venerable" or that his contemporaries necessarily shared his fears or his philosophy. For other examples of "venerable," see *North American Review* 2 (November 1815): 142; *Niles Register* 17 (30 November 1819): 192; ibid. 19 (9 December 1820): 225; ibid. 22 (18 May 1822): 192; Robert B. Thomas, *Farmer's Almanac* for 1805 and 1812, and the *Orwigsburg Almanac for the Year of Our Lord 1830*, p. 50.

31. Maria Leach and Jerome Fried, eds., *Dictionary of Folklore, Mythology and Legend,* 2 vols. (New York: Funk and Wagnalls, 1949), 2: 818; George Lyman Kittredge, *The Old Farmer and His Almanack* (Boston: William Ware and Company, 1904), pp. 333–35.

32. Eugene Genovese, *Roll, Jordan, Roll* (New York: Vintage Books, 1974), pp. 522–23; Mitford M. Mathews, *A Dictionary of Americanisms on Historical Principles,* 2 vols. (Chicago: The University of Chicago Press, 1951), 2: 52, 1793; Leslie H. Owens, *This Species of Property* (New York: Oxford University Press, 1976), pp. 139, 203, 209; Herbert Gutman, *The Black Family in Slavery and Freedom* (New York: Alfred A. Knopf, 1976), esp. ch. 2–4. This does not mean, however, that whites who referred to aged blacks as "Uncle" or "Aunt" invariably did so out of respect. Bertram Wyatt-Brown has suggested, in "The Ideal Typology and Ante-bellum Southern History," *Societas* 5 (Winter 1975): 17, that such possessive labels may also have signified a black person's powerlessness. (See also Owens, *Property*, pp. 47–48 on this point.) Clearly, far more work must be done before we can establish whether respect for aged blacks mollified racial animosity.

33. Caldwell, *Effects of Age,* pp. 6, 14–18; Oliver Wendell Holmes, *Autocrat of the Breakfast Table* (1858; reprint ed., Boston: Houghton Mifflin Co., 1883), pp. 150–63. See also Robert B. Thomas's *Farmer's Almanac* for the years 1846 (p. 25), 1857 (p. 39), and 1864 (p. 2).

34. Kittredge, *Old Farmer*, p. 313; Jedidiah Morse, *The American Universal Geography*, 7th ed., 2 vols. (Charlestown: Lincoln & Edmands, 1819), 2: 291–92. See also Robert Thomas's *Farmer's Almanack* for February 1813, July 1815, December 1820, September 1822, February 1824, and December 1827. "The Contents" are in the 1797 edition of John Nathan Hutchins's *United States Almanack*.

35. P. K. Whelpton, "Occupational Groups in the United States," *Journal of the American Statistical Association* 21 (September 1926): 340. See also Chapters 4–5, below.

36. *Niles Register* 15 (14 November 1818): 196; ibid. 31 (2 December 1826): 222; ibid. 31 (13 January 1827): 308; *Knickerbocker* 2 (August 1833): 160.

37. *Niles National Register* 58 (14 September 1839): 48.

38. *Niles Register* 19 (2 September 1820): 1; ibid. 39 (18 November 1830): 186; ibid. 74 (19 July 1848): 36–37.

39. Robert Gray Gunderson, *Log Cabin Campaign* (Lexington: University of Kentucky Press, 1957), p. 220; *Tippecanoe Almanac* (Philadelphia, 1841), p. 39.

40. Ibid., pp. 49–50; Charles Spelman Todd and Benjamin Drake, *Sketches of William Harrison* (Cincinnati: U. P. James, 1840), p. 165; Isaac Rand Jackson, *Life of Major General Harrison* (Philadelphia: Gregg & Elliott, 1840), p. 89; Samuel Jones Burr, *The Life and Times of William Henry Harrison* (New York: L. W. Ranson, 1840), p. 257. For a typical barb against Harrison, see U.S., Congress, House, *Congressional Globe,* 26th Cong., 1st sess., 1840, app., p. 240.

41. It is important to note that Harrison's death was attributed, not to the infirmities of age, but to "the vanity of man and the mutability of things temporal." See, for example, Horatio Potter, *Discourses on the Death of William Henry Harrison* (Albany: Hoffman, White and Visscher, 1840), p. 257.

42. Francis Newton Thorpe, *Federal and State Constitutions, Colonial Charters and Other Organic Laws, 1492–1908,* 7 vols. (Washington, D.C.: Government Printing Office, 1909), 3: 1906.

43. See ibid., 4: 2486, for New Hampshire; ibid., 1: 543, for Connecticut; ibid., 1: 107, for Alabama; ibid., 4: 2158, for Missouri; ibid., 3: 1727–28, for Maryland; and ibid., 5: 2647, for New York: For Maine, see Benjamin Perley Poore, *The Federal and State Constitutions,* 2 vols. (1924; reprint ed., New York: Burt Franklin, 1972), 1: 796.

44. John Adams to Thomas Jefferson, July 12, 1822, in *The Adams–Jefferson Letters,* ed. Lester J. Cappon, 2 vols. (Chapel Hill: Institute of Early American History and Culture, 1959), 2: 582.

45. Alexander Hamilton et al., *The Federalist Papers,* no. 79 (New York: New American Library Edition, 1961), pp. 474–75.

46. John Theodore Horton, *James Kent* (New York: D. Appleton-Century Co., 1939), pp. 249–50, 264–66. See also New York State, *Court of Chancery* 7 (1837): 346–47, for a bitter postscript written by Kent's clerk on the day the chancellor retired.

47. Thorpe, *Federal and State Constitutions,* 5: 2634. For Marshall's vitality, see "Chief Justice Marshall," *North American Review* 42 (January 1836): 236–37; and *Niles Register* 48 (25 July 1835): 369–70.

48. For farmers retiring, see Robert B. Thomas, *Farmer's Almanack* (December 1810), n.p. The Webster quotation comes from Wood, *Rising Glory,* p. 159.

49. *An American Dictionary of the English Language,* s.v. "retirement."

50. See the 1828 edition of Webster's *American Dictionary* for the definition of "superannuate"; cf. the definition of "green healthy old age" in James Morison, *Family Adviser,* 4th ed. (London: College of Health, 1833), p. 340. For eyewitness descriptions of Boone in old age, see *Niles Register* 15 (26 December 1818): 328, and ibid. 19 (1820): 152, 263. Daniel Bryan (*The Mountain Muse* [Harrisonburg, Va.: Davidson and Bourne, 1813], bk. 7, ll. 799–811) apotheosizes Boone in his old age. James Fenimore Cooper refers to Boone in *The Prairie* (1827; reprint ed., New York: Holt, Rinehart & Winston, 1965), p. 3. Cooper's novel, in fact, overflows with descriptions of advanced old age and reasons why Bumppo's experience and continued activities ensure him respect.

51. Hugh Henry Brackenridge, *Modern Chivalry,* ed. Lewis Leary, 2 vols. (1804; reprint ed., New Haven: College and University Press, 1965), vol. 1, bk. 1, ch. 2, p. 34. See also Thomas Jefferson to John Adams, 27 June 1822, in *Letters,* ed. Cappon, 2: 580.

52. "Solitude," *New England Almanack* (Isaac Bickerstaff, 1794); Morse, *Geography,* 2: 294; Henry Giles, *Christian Thoughts on Life* (Boston: Ticknor, Reed and Fields, 1850), p. 108; Thomas M'Kellar, "Life's Evening," *Graham's Magazine* 26 (November 1844): 202; *Godey's Lady's Book* 23 (December 1841): 262–63.

53. "Morison's *Life of Jeremiah Smith,*" *North American Review* 61 (July 1845): 108–12. See also Nathan Daboll, *New England Almanac* (1851), pp. 23–24; Thomas, *Farmer's Almanac* (1855), p. 36; ibid. (1862), p. 2; Sarah Josepha Hale, *American Sketches,* 2d ed. (Boston: Putnam & Hunt, 1830), p. 26; *Niles National Register* 57 (1 August 1839): 16; ibid. (7 December 1839): 239; *Littell's Living Age* 48 (February 1856): 576.

54. John Tasker Howard, *Stephen Foster* (New York: Thomas Y. Crowell, 1934), pp. 192–205; Clyde Griffen, "The Progressive Ethos," in *The Development of American Culture,* ed. Stanley Coben and Lorman Ratner (Englewood Cliffs: Prentice Hall, Inc., 1970) pp. 130–33; Ann Douglas, *The Feminization of American Culture* (New York: Alfred A. Knopf, 1977).

55. *Niles Register* 29 (1 October 1825): 70–71. See also ibid. 14 (28 February 1818): 15; ibid. 21 (15 September 1821): 34; *United States Magazine and Democratic Review,* 3 (September 1838): 26–28.

56. *Niles Weekly Register* 14 (11 July 1818): 329; ibid. 29 (19 November 1825): 177; ibid. 46 (2 August 1834): 384. On Charles Carroll, see *Niles Register* 34 (12 July 1838): 317 and ibid. 38 (19 June 1830): 395. See also Robert Middlekauff's suggestive essay, "The Ritualization of the American Revolution," in *Development of American Culture,* ed. Coben and Ratner, pp. 31–44, and Fred Somkin, *The Unquiet Eagle* (Ithaca: Cornell University Press, 1967), p. 175.

57. "An Old Lady's History," *Littell's Living Age* 20 (January–March 1849): 550; "An Old Man's Reminiscence," *Knickerbocker Monthly* 22 (October 1843): 298. See also Nathaniel S. Dodge, *Sketches of New England* (New York: E. French, 1842), p. 61.

58. John Greenleaf Whittier, *Legends of New England* (1831; reprint ed., Gainesville: Scholars' Facsimiles and Reprints, 1965), pp. 27–28, 66, 75, 117–18. See also John Brainard's poem, "Connecticut River," at the frontispiece.

59. See, for example, Nathaniel Hawthorne, *Grandfather's Chair* (1850; reprint ed., Boston: Houghton Mifflin, 1883), p. 25, and the review of Walter Scott's *Tales of a Grandfather* in *North American Review* 94 (January 1862), pp. 269–70. See also Singleton, "An Old Man's Records," *Knickerbocker* 6 (October 1835): 336; Rosa, "An Old Man's Musings," *Graham's Magazine* 47 (September 1855): 248–49.

60. "Shakespeare's Sixth Age," *Knickerbocker* 12 (August 1838): 113–18. See also "Old People," *Boston Weekly Magazine* 2 (26 October 1839): 60–61; "Comforts of Age," *Harper's Magazine* 9 (September 1854): 705; *North American Review* 79 (July 1854): 249–50.

61. Mathews, *Americanisms,* 2: 1793. See also B. A. Botkin, ed., *A Treasury of American Folklore* (New York: Crown Publishers, 1944), p. 286; *Encyclopedia Americana,* s.v. "Samuel Wilson."

CHAPTER 2

1. For medical observations, see Bartholomew Parr, *The London Medical Dictionary,* 2 vols. (1808; reprint ed., Philadelphia: Mitchell, Ames & White, 1819), 2:342; Benjamin Rush, "An Account of the State of the Mind and Body in Old Age," in *Medical Inquiries and Observations,* 4 vols. (1793; reprint ed., Philadelphia: Thomas Dobson, 1797), 2: 295–316; Anthony F. Willich, *Domestic Encyclopedia,* 2d American ed., 3 vols. (Philadelphia: Abraham Small, 1821), 2:5; Charles Alfred Lee, ed., *Copland's Dictionary of Practical Medicine,* 3 vols., rev. ed. (New York: Harper Bros., 1860), 1: 52–55; For similar popular views, see Ebenezer Gay, *The Old Man's Calendar* (Stockbridge: Loring Andrews, 1794), p. 2; William Mountford, *Euthanasy,* 2d ed. (Boston: W. Crosby and H. P. Nichols, 1850), p. 138; William Alexander, "Age," *Graham's Magazine* 41 (September 1852): 290.

2. Charles Caldwell, *Thoughts on the Effects of Age on the Human Constitution* (Louisville: John C. Noble, 1846), p. 25.

3. Ethel Shanas and Associates, *Old People in Three Industrial Societies* (New York: Atherton Press, 1968), p. 427.

4. David Hackett Fischer, *Growing Old in America* (New York: Oxford University Press, 1977), pp. 62–66; Lawrence Stone, "Walking over Grandma," *New York Review of Books,* 12 May, 1977, p. 10. John Demos, *The Little Commonwealth* (New York: Oxford University Press, 1970), pp. 75–76, shows colonial precedents for this practice.

5. On age-specific wealth patterns in antebellum America, see Lee Soltow, *Men and Wealth in the United States, 1850–1870* (New Haven: Yale University Press, 1975), pp. 72–73; idem, *Wealthholding in Wisconsin* (Madison: University of Wisconsin Press, 1971), pp. 8, 22, 47.

6. On Jefferson, see Fawn Brodie, *Thomas Jefferson* (New York: W. W. Norton, 1974), pp. 456–57. On Monroe, see *Niles Register* 35 (12 November 1838): 195. For more on perceptions of old-age dependency before 1860, see below, Chapter 4.

7. L. Maria Child, *The Mother's Book,* 6th ed. (New York: C. S. Francis & Co., 1844), pp. 115–16; C. C. Colton, "Old Age," *Knickerbocker* 10 (December 1837): 490; Albert Barnes, *Life at Three-Score: A Sermon,* 2d ed. (Philadelphia: Parry and McMillan, 1859), pp. 75–76. On the aged's sense of rejection, see John Galt, "The Old Man's Reverie," *Knickerbocker* 11 (March 1838): 247; E.C.E., "The Old Man's Lament," ibid. 9 (December 1836): 642; Oliver Wendell Holmes, "Lost Blossom," (1857–58) in *The Works of Oliver Wendell Holmes,* 12 vols. (Boston: Houghton Mifflin Co., 1892), 11: 412.

8. The word "fogy" originated in Scotland in the latter part of the eighteenth century to describe an invalid or garrison soldier. The word sometimes had age connotations in America before 1880 (when it first appeared in Webster's dictionary, and when the *O.E.D.* lists the first American reference). See, for instance, A. Wallace Hunter, "Old Abram," *Knickerbocker* 50 (September 1857): 292. Yet authors of an article in *U.S. Democratic Review* 30 (April 1852): 367–76, entitled "The Nomination—The 'Old Fogies' and the 'Fogy Conspiracy,'" claim not only to have coined the expression but to give it political overtones not associated with being old per se.

To be sure, one can find other disparaging observations between 1790 and 1860 about the elderly's old-fashioned mannerisms and outlook, particularly among those Transcendentalists who celebrated the innocent and/or unique experiences of youth. See Odell Shepard, *The Journals of Bronson Alcott*, 2 vols. (1938; reprint ed., Port Washington: Kennikat Press, 1966), 2: 411, and Henry David Thoreau, *Walden* (1854; reprint ed., New York: Holt, Rinehart and Winston, 1948), p. 6. But this theme is age-old, and such remarks should not be construed as novel comments on the liabilities of being old.

9. John Greenleaf Whittier, "Ichabod," in Burton Egbert Stevenson, *The Home Book of Verse*, 9th ed., 2 vols. (1912; reprint ed., New York: Henry Holt & Co., 1953), 2: 1837–38.

10. See, for example, "Old Batchelors," *Atkinson's Casket* 12 (August 1835): 462; Mary Boykin Chestnut, *A Diary From Dixie*, ed. Ben Ames Williams (Boston: Houghton Mifflin, 1949), p. 412.

11. Cortlandt Van Rensselaer, *Old Age: A Funeral Sermon* (Washington, D.C.: By the author, 1841), p. 67; see also John Waters, "Old Age," *Knickerbocker* 28 (October 1846): 294; "Fear of Age," ibid. 37 (June 1851): 63; C. H. Waterman, "The Death of the Aged," *Gentleman's Magazine* 3 (July 1838): 107; Lydia H. Sigourney, "Mourning for Age," *Godey's Lady's Book* (January 1844), p. 25.

12. Thomas Bernard, *The Comforts of Old Age*, 5th ed. (London: John Murray, 1820), pp. 4, 59.

13. *An American Dictionary of the English Language*, 1st ed., s.v. "senility."

14. Benjamin Rush, *Medical Inquiries and Observations, upon the Diseases of the Mind* (1812; reprint ed., New York: Hafner Publishing Co., 1962), pp. 55–58.

15. Willich, *Domestic Encyclopedia*, 2: 9.

16. Philip Freneau, *The Last Poems of Philip Freneau*, ed. Lewis Leary (New Brunswick: Rutgers University Press, 1945), p. 109. See also the frontispiece to the 1823 edition of Robert B. Thomas, *Farmer's Almanack*.

17. "On the Happy Temperament," *North American Review* 9 (June 1819): 210. See also William Godwin, *Enquiry concerning Political Justice and Its Influence on Morals and Happiness*, 2 vols. (1793; reprint ed., Toronto: University of Toronto Press, 1940), 2: 523.

18. "Review of *The Comforts of Age*," *Virginia Evangelical and Literary Magazine* 1 (June 1818): 271.

19. John Adams to Thomas Jefferson, May 6, 1816, in *Writings of Thomas Jefferson*, ed. Albert E. Bergh, 20 vols. (Washington, D.C.: Thomas Jefferson Memorial Association, 1903–7), 15: 14–15. See also Gay, *Old Man's Calendar*, p. 4; Job Orton, *Discourses to the Aged on Several Important Subjects* (Shrewsbury: J. Eddowes, 1771), pp. 206–20; James Fenimore Cooper, *The Prairie* (1827; reprint ed., New York: Holt, Rinehart & Winston, 1965), p. 130.

20. For examples, see the detailed descriptions in Isaac Hays, *American Cyclopedia of Practical Medicine and Surgery*, 2 vols. (Philadelphia: Carey, Lea and Blanchard, 1834), 1: 256–58; John Forbes, ed., *The Cyclopedia of Practical Medicine*, 4 vols. (Philadelphia: Lea and Blanchard, 1849), 1: 57–58; Richard Dennis Hoblyn, *Dictionary of Terms Used in Medicine and the Collateral Sciences*, 1st new American ed. (1846; reprint ed., Philadelphia: H. C. Lea, 1865), p. 94. See also Caleb Ticknor, *The Philosophy of Living* (New York: Harper and Bros., 1836), pp. 299–301; Caldwell, *Effects of Age*, pp. 10–15; Thomas Bailey, *Records of Longevity* (London: Darton and Co., 1859), p. 51.

21. Charles W. Baird, "To Live Too Long," *Graham's Magazine* 26 (February 1845): 91; Nathaniel Hawthorne, *The Dolliver Romance* (1864; reprint ed., Boston: Houghton Mifflin Co., 1883), pp. 28–33.

22. Ralph H. Gabriel, "Evangelical Religion and Popular Romanticism in Early Nineteenth Century America," *Church History* 19 (March 1950): 45; David Carew Huntington, *Art and the Excited Spirit* (Ann Arbor: University of Michigan Press, 1972), p. 1; John Higham, "Hanging Together," *Journal of American History* 61 (June 1974): 16–18; Sydney E. Ahlstrom, *A Religious History of the American People* (New Haven: Yale University Press, 1972), pts. 4, 5.

23. Some romantic writers, it should be noted, applied this line of reasoning not only to amplify the republican contention that older people were ideally qualified to put life into perspective, but also to justify their claim that the aged were *uniquely* qualified to serve as society's promoters of health, guardians of virtue, and veterans of productivity (roles described in Chapter 1, above). For a more systematic development of this point, see W. Andrew

Achenbaum, "Old Age in the United States, 1790 to Present" (Ph.D. diss., University of Michigan, 1976), ch. 2. For a discussion of other moral watchdogs in action, see David Brion Davis, ed., *Ante-Bellum Reform* (New York: Harper & Row, 1967), and Kathryn Kish Sklar, *Catharine Beecher* (New Haven: Yale University Press, 1973).

24. Van Rensselaer, *Old Age,* p. 5; H. W. Rockwell, "Grey Hairs," *Knickerbocker* 28 (October 1846): 333; "Address to Gray Hair," *Harper's Magazine* 3 (March 1851), p. 699; Cornelia M. Dowling, "Old!," *Godey's Lady's Book* 50 (April 1855): 348. Psychologists have found a somewhat similar situation in contemporary cross-cultural studies. See, for example, David Gutmann, "The Cross-Cultural Perspective: Notes toward a Comparative Psychology of Aging," in *Handbook of the Psychology of Aging,* ed. James E. Birren and K. Warner Schaie (New York: Van Nostrand Reinhold Co., 1977), pp. 315–16.

25. Albert Barnes, *The Peaceful Death of the Righteous* (Philadelphia: Henry B. Ashmead, 1858), p. 6.

26. "Mr. Cole's Pictures," *Knickerbocker* 16 (December 1840): 544. For more on Cole's painting, see Louis Noble, *Course of the Empire, Voyage of Life and Other Pictures of Thomas Cole, N.A.* New York: Cornish, Lamport & Co., 1853), pp. 282–83; Huntington, *Excited Spirit,* p. 19. For similar sentiments, see "Shakespeare's Seventh Age," *Knickerbocker* 12 (September 1838): 232–35; "A Review of the *Last Moments of Eminent Men,*" *North American Review* 38 (January 1834): 120, 132; Thomas H. Howard, "Age," *Knickerbocker* 42 (August 1853): 118–19.

27. For comparable sentiments in a variety of other media, see Pliny Earle, "Stanzas," *Knickerbocker* 16 (July 1840): 28; "Youth and Age," *Living Age* 49 (April–June, 1856): 100; Ahlstrom, *A Religious History,* pp. 587–89.

28. Mountford, *Euthanasy,* p. 349. See also John Bell, *On Regimen and Longevity* (Philadelphia: Hasnell & Johnson, 1842), p. 377; Orville Dewey, *The Problem of Human Destiny,* 2d ed. (New York: James Miller, 1854), pp. 121–22, 273. For a fuller development of the "romantic spiral" idea, see M. H. Abrams, *Natural Supernaturalism* (New York: W. W. Norton, 1973), pp. 183–190.

29. Ralph Waldo Emerson, "Old Age," *Atlantic Monthly* 9 (January 1862): 134–38.

30. Ibid., p. 135.

31. Ibid., p. 135–36.

CHAPTER 3

1. See, for example, Horace Bushnell, "How to Make a Right and Ripe Old Age," *Hours at Home* 4 (December 1866): 106–8; "Ideal of Old Age," *Living Age* 122 (17 March 1874): 704; Henry Wadsworth Longfellow, "Morituri Salutamus," in *Complete Poetic Works of Henry Wadsworth Longfellow,* Cambridge ed. (Boston: Houghton Mifflin Co., 1922), p. 314; "Fruitful Age," *Godey's Lady's Book* 41 (December 1875): 566–67; S. G. Lathrop, ed., *Fifty Years and Beyond; or, Gathered Gems for the Aged* (New York: F. H. Revell, 1881); Margaret E. White, *After Noontide* (1888; reprint ed., Boston: Houghton Mifflin, 1907), p. 33; "Can We Spare the Old Men?," *Independent* 55 (2 July 1903): 1580–82; J. Madison Taylor, "The Conservation of Energy in Those of Advancing Years," *Popular Science Monthly* 64 (February 1904): 349; "Some Grand Old Women," *World Today* 21 (July 1911): 886; and M. M. Pattison Muir, "Some Compensations of Age," *Living Age* 276 (22 March 1913): 740–43.

It is important to note that favorable estimates of the aged's place in society were not confined to middle-class, white, native-born writers. Religious bodies, such as the various branches of Judaism, and sects, such as the Quakers and Shakers, described the aged's status in positive terms because of their spiritual tenets. Several immigrant groups also maintained respect for the aged in the new land in accordance with cultural assumptions they had adhered to in the old world. See, for instance, Virginia Yans-McLaughlin, *Family and Community* (Ithaca: Cornell University Press, 1977), pp. 256–57.

2. W. H. DePuy, *Three Score Years and Beyond* (New York: Nelson and Phillips, 1873), pp. i–iii, 7; Nathan Allen, "The Law of Longevity," *Medical Record* 9 (1874): 108–11; Edward Henry Sieveking, *The Medical Adviser in Life Assurance* (Hartford: N. P. Fletcher,

1875), p. 97; George Murray Humphry, *Old Age: The Results of Information Received Respecting Nearly Nine Hundred Persons Who Had Attained the Age of Eighty Years, Including Seventy-four Centenarians* (Cambridge: Macmillan and Bowes, 1889), pp. 140–41; and John M. Keating, *How to Examine for Life Insurance* (Philadelphia: W. B. Saunders, 1891), pp. 177–78.

3. For more on this shift, see John Higham et al., *History* (Englewood Cliffs, N.J.: Prentice-Hall, Inc., 1965), pp. 92–95, and Stow Persons, *American Minds* (New York: Holt, Rinehart and Winston, 1958), pp. 201–3, 217–38.

4. Gert Brieger, ed., *Medical America in the Nineteenth Century* (Baltimore: The Johns Hopkins University Press, 1972), pp. 255, 278; Charles E. Rosenberg, *The Cholera Years* (Chicago: The University of Chicago Press, 1962), pp. 5, 228; Barbara G. Rosenkrantz, *Public Health and the State* (Cambridge, Mass.: Harvard University Press, 1972), pp. 5, 72–77, 107.

5. Charlton T. Lewis, "The Influence of Civilization on the Duration of Life," *Sanitarian* 5 (May 1877): 175, 197. See also "Longevity," *Science* 7 (29 January 1886): 109; "Do We Live Longer?" *Independent* 53 (28 March 1901): 741; "Longevity," *Johnson's Universal Encyclopedia*, 8 vols. (New York: A. J. Johnson, 1894), 5: 348; Langdon Kain, "Man's Span of Life," *North American Review* 166 (April 1898): 493.

6. This argument is consistent, I believe, with the finding that there was an increasing contemporaneous reliance on "professional" judgments pervading American culture itself. For fuller analyses of this point, see Charles E. Rosenberg, *No Other Gods* (Baltimore: The Johns Hopkins University Press, 1976), pp. 2–4; Burton Bledstein, *The Culture of Professionalism* (New York: W. W. Norton, 1976), pp. 80, 90, 99.

7. Nicholas Smith, *Masters of Old Age* (Milwaukee: The Young Churchman, 1905), pp. 1–2. See also "Of Growing Old," *Atlantic Monthly* 71 (March 1893): 305; Robson Roose, "The Art of Prolonging Life," *Popular Science Monthly* 35 (October 1889): 766–73; "When Does a Man Become Old?," *Current Literature* 32 (February 1902): 191; Henry M. Friedman, "Problems of Life," *Medical Record* 86 (7 November 1914): 796.

8. Lester Snow King, *Growth of Medical Thought* (Chicago: University of Chicago Press, 1963), p. 218; Thomas Bonner, *American Doctors and German Universities* (Lincoln, Neb.: University of Nebraska Press, 1963), p. 111. It is worth noting that the concept of disease specificity itself is quite old: it had been expressed in more general terms even before Morgagni of Padua demonstrated in 1761 that disease processes were often localized in organs. See Richard H. Shryock, *Medicine and Society in America, 1660–1860* (New York: New York University Press, 1960), pp. 63–64.

9. Jean-Martin Charcot, *Clinical Lectures on the Diseases of Old Age*, trans. Leigh Hunt (New York: William Wood, 1881), p. 24. For more on Charcot, see Joseph T. Freeman, "Medical Perspectives in Aging," *Gerontologist* 5 (March 1965), pt. 2, pp. 21–22; and M. D. Grmek, *On Ageing and Old Age* (Den Haag: Uitgeverig Dr. W. Junk, 1958), pp. 71–72, 78.

10. Charcot, *Clinical Lectures*, p. 26.

11. For instance, Karl Friedrich Constatt, working in an obscure German village, published *Die Krankheiten des hoheren Alters und ihre Heilung* in 1839. This compendium of diseases in old age rested, however, more on personal speculative philosophy than clinical observations. In addition, Maxime Durand-Fardel published a *Traité clinique des maladies des vieillards* (Paris: Bailliere, 1854), which some medical historians consider to be sounder than Charcot's work even though it did not enjoy the attention Charcot attracted. See Frederic D. Zeman, "Life's Later Years: XI," *Journal of Mt. Sinai Hospital* 13 (1946–47): 246–49 and idem, "Life's Later Years: XII," ibid. 16 (January–February 1950): 308–12.

12. There was at least one work, already published in English, that shared Charcot's assumption that subtle, latent changes in the aged organism modified ordinary diseases and produced peculiar symptoms. See John Gardner, *Longevity: The Means of Prolonging Life after Middle Age* (London: Henry S. King, 1874), pp. iii, 18–19, 28–35, 144, 157–58. Unlike Charcot, however, Gardner did not link the causes of old-age diseases to the concept of localized pathology.

13. The factors summarized here are developed more fully in Richard H. Shryock, *Medicine in America* (Baltimore: The Johns Hopkins University Press, 1966), pp. 22–30, 168–69; Bonner, *American Doctors*, pp. 29–39, 69, 109–11; Joseph F. Kett, *The Formation of the American Medical Profession* (New Haven: Yale University Press, 1968), pp. vii, 180.

14. See, for example, Samuel G. Dorr, "Care and Treatment of Old People," *Buffalo Medical Journal* 35 (1896): 145–48; George W. Post, *Cottage Physician* (Springfield, Mass.: King-Richardson, 1898), p. 585; Joseph G. Richardson, *Modern Family Physician and Home Guide* (Rochester: Rochester Book Company, 1889), pp. 1095–96; D. A. Sargent, "Exercise and Longevity," *North American Review* 164 (May 1897): 556–61; William G. Anderson, "How a Woman Renewed Her Strength," *Ladies Home Journal* 28 (January 1911): 12.

15. On home remedies, Post, *Cottage Physician,* pp. 585–86, is typical. See also J. Y. Dale, "Opium as a Hypnotic in Old Age," *University Medical Magazine* 6 (1894): 322–24.

16. Charles Sedgwick Minot, "Senility," in *Reference Handbook of Medical Science,* ed. Albert H. Buck, 7 vols. (New York: William Wood, 1885), 6: 388. See also Richard Quain, *A Dictionary of Medicine* (New York: D. Appelton & Co., 1883), p. 1416; George M. Gould, *Illustrated Dictionary of Medicine, Biology and Applied Science,* 5th ed. (Philadelphia: P. Blakiston & Co., 1903), p. 1315; Christian A. Herter, *Biological Aspects of Human Problems* (New York: Macmillan Co., 1911), pp. 112–19.

17. Zeman, "Life's Later Years: XII," pp. 65–66.

18. Newell Dunbar, ed., *Dr. Brown-Séquard's Own Account of the "Elixir of Life"* (Boston: J. G. Cupples Co., 1889), pp. 22–28. Brown-Séquard proposed, but never tested, that a mixture of crushed ovaries could be used to restore vitality to women.

19. Elie Metchnikoff, *Prolongation of Life* (New York: G. P. Putnam's Sons, 1908), pp. 36, 72, 161–81.

20. Idem, "Old Age," in *Smithsonian Institution Annual Report, 1903–4* (Washington, D.C.: Government Printing Office, 1905), p. 548. Metchnikoff was not the first scientist ever to classify old age as a disease; variations on this idea had been circulating since at least classical Rome. But the theory as Metchnikoff formulated it seemed particularly credible because it was consistent with other medical principles in vogue in late–nineteenth-century America. In that particular context, Metchnikoff's ideas were more widely discussed and accepted in both medical and nonprofessional circles than they might have been at an earlier point in time.

21. See, for example, Charles G. Stockton, "The Delay of Old Age and the Alleviation of Senility," *Journal of the American Medical Association* 45 (15 July 1905): 169; Arnold Lorand, *Old Age Deferred* (1910; reprint ed., Philadelphia: F. A. Davis, 1912), pp. 51, 90, 114; Marshall Langton Price. "Ancient and Modern Theories of Age," *Maryland Medical Journal* 49 (February 1906): 45–61; Elie Metchnikoff, *The Nature of Man* (New York: G. P. Putnam's, 1905), p. 261.

22. The quotation is from L. Menard, "Remedies for Old Age," *Scientific American Supplement,* no. 1756 (28 August 1909), p. 138.

23. Carl Snyder, "The Quest for Prolonged Youth," *Living Age* 251 (10 November 1906): 323. See also "Growing Old," *Godey's Lady's Book* 86 (February 1873): 147; *Encyclopedia Americana* (1904), s.v. "diseases of old age"; J. G. Bandaline, "The Physiology of Old Age," *Current Literature* 35 (September 1903): 344; Harriet Paine, *Old People* (Boston: Houghton Mifflin Co., 1910), pp. 171–72.

24. For more on this point, see John C. Green, *The Death of Adam* (Ames: Iowa State University Press, 1959), p. 335; David W. Marcell, *Progress and Pragmatism* (Westport: Greenwood Press, 1974), pp. 102, 115–16, 129, 143.

25. Francis Galton, *Hereditary Genius* (London: Henry King, 1869); idem, *Inquiries into the Human Faculty* (London: Macmillan Co., 1883); George M. Beard, *Legal Responsibilities in Old Age* (New York: Russells', 1874); idem, *American Nervousness* (New York: G. P. Putnam's Sons, 1881).

26. W. A. Newman Dorland, *The Age of Mental Virility* (New York: The Century Co., 1908), pp. 31, 70–71. See also B. W. Richardson, "Memory as a Test of Age," *Scientific American* 65 (10 October 1891): 224; Nathaniel Southgate Shaler, *The Individual: A Study of Life and Death* (New York: D. Appelton & Co., 1901), p. 275; Samuel Butler, *Life and Habits* (1877; reprint ed., London: A. C. Fifield, 1911), pp. 170, 295–99.

27. William James, *Principles of Psychology,* 2 vols. (New York: Henry Holt & Co., 1890), 2: 1910. See also "Young World," *Outlook* 105 (4 October 1913): 256.

28. *An American Dictionary of the English Language* (1880), s.v. "fogy."

29. Beard, *American Nervousness,* p. 250. See also J. T. Trowbridge, "Old Man Gram," *Harper's Magazine* 56 (January 1878): 225–28; "Restlessness in Age," *Living Age* 240 (9

January 1904): 124–25; Ada Cambridge, "The Retrospect," *Atlantic* 103 (January 1909): 133.

30. Kain, "Man's Span of Life," p. 472. See also "Age vs. Youth," *Scribner's Magazine* 40 (August 1906): 251. New words were coined to describe the aged's eccentricities. According to Harold Wentworth and Stuart Berg Flexner, *Dictionary of American Slang* (New York: Thomas Y. Crowell, 1967), the earliest use of "geezer" and "fuddy duddy" in America date around 1900.

31. John Harvey Kellogg, *Plain Facts about Sexual Life* (Battle Creek, Mich.: Office of the Health Reformer, 1877), p. 92. This "fact" also appeared in the 1881, 1889, and 1903 editions of this influential and popular guide.

32. Idem, *Plain Facts for Young and Old* (Burlington, Iowa: Segner and Condit, 1881), p. 123. See also Carroll Smith-Rosenberg, "Puberty to Menopause," in *Clio's Consciousness Raised*, ed. Mary Hartman and Lois Banner (New York: Harper Torchbooks, 1974), pp. 23–38.

33. Kellogg first diagnosed satyriasis in 1881. See also Colin A. Scott, "Old Age and Death," *American Journal of Psychology* 8 (October 1896): 120–21.

34. Metchnikoff, *Nature of Man*, p. 131. Interestingly, Metchnikoff does not cite statistics on women committing suicide. It is worth noting that Emile Durkheim's study of suicide (1897) stated that suicide "achieves its culminating point only at the final limits of human existence" (Emile Durkheim, *Suicide*, ed. George Simpson [New York: Free Press, 1968], pp. 101–3).

35. *New England Almanack* (January 1872), p. 22. See also "Old Age," *Living Age* 182 (31 August 1889): 531; "The Intellectual Effect of Old Age," ibid. 184 (25 January 1890): 250–51; "Centenarians," ibid. 221 (20 May 1899): 532.

36. Thomas C. Cochran, *American Business* (New York: Harper and Row, 1968), p. 51; Elisha P. Douglass, *Coming of Age of Business* (Chapel Hill: University of North Carolina Press, 1971), pp. 287–88; Melvyn Dubofsky, *Industrialism and the American Worker* (New York: Thomas Y. Crowell, 1975), pp. 1–29; Louis Galambos, "The Emerging Organizational Synthesis in Modern American History," *Business History Review* 44 (Autumn 1970): 288.

37. Robert Wiebe, *Search for Order* (New York: Hill and Wang, 1968), pp. 145–63; Glenn Porter, *Rise of Big Business* (New York: Thomas Y. Crowell, 1973), p. 21. On the efficiency craze, see Samuel Haber, *Efficiency and Uplift* (Chicago: The University of Chicago Press, 1964), and Daniel Nelson, *Managers and Workers* (Madison: University of Wisconsin Press, 1975), esp. ch. 4.

38. See, for example, Peter Finley Dunne, *Mr. Dooley's Opinions* (New York: R. H. Russell, 1901), p. 183.

39. "Independent Opinions," *Independent* 75 (28 August 1913): 504.

40. U.S., *Revised Statutes,* 2d ed., sec. 1443. U.S., *Statutes at Large,* vol. 39, sec. 579.

41. U.S., *Revised Statutes,* 2d ed., sec. 4756. See amendments in U.S., *Statutes at Large* vol. 23, sec. 305, and ibid., vol. 30, sec. 997.

42. U.S., *Revised Statutes,* 2d ed., Sect. 714.

43. Lee Welling Squier, *Old Age Dependency in the United States: A Complete Survey of the Pension Method* (New York: Macmillan Co., 1912), pp. 74–82, 110–20; Alden Hatch, *American Express* (Garden City: Doubleday & Co., 1950), p. 89. See also the forthcoming works by William Graebner and Carole Haber.

44. Murray Webb Latimer, *Industrial Pension Systems in the United States and Canada,* 2 vols. (New York: Industrial Relations Counselors, 1932), 1: 50.

45. F. Spencer Baldwin, "Retirement Systems for Municipal Employees," *Annals of the American Academy of Political and Social Science* 38 (1911): 6; Alcott W. Stockwell, "Problem of Superannuation in the Civil Service," *Putnam's Magazine* 7 (1909–10): 565–71. See also Gilman M. Ostrander, *American Civilization in the First Machine Age* (New York: Harper Torchbooks, 1972), p. 263.

46. Burton J. Hendrick, "The Superannuated Man," *McClure's Magazine* 32 (December 1908): 117.

47. See Webster, *American Dictionary,* s.v. "retirement," "superannuation"; and *Zell's Popular Encyclopedia* (Philadelphia: T. Ellwood Zell, 1871), p. 954.

48. Dorland, *Mental Virility*, pp. 3–4. See also "The Spectator," *Outlook* 67 (20 April 1901): 899; Emerson G. Taylor, "The Best Years," *Reader Magazine* 9 (December 1906): 67; E. P. Powell, "Passing of Old Age," *Independent* 77 (9 March 1914): 344.

49. See, for instance, Forbes Lindsay, "The Man of Fifty," *Harper's Weekly* 53 (16 October 1909): 15; John A. Fitch, "Old Age at Forty," *American Magazine* 71 (March 1911): 655–56; Edward T. Devine, *Misery and Its Causes* (New York: The Macmillan Co., 1909), pp. 124–25.

50. Hendrick, "Superannuated Man," p. 118. For comparable trends in management, see David Brody, *Steelworkers in America* (Cambridge, Mass.: Harvard University Press, 1960), pp. 25–26.

51. For material on civil service employees, see Franklin MacVeigh, "Civil Service Pensions, *Annals of the American Academy of Political and Social Science* 38 (1911): 4; and U.S., Congress, House, *Report on Retirement of Superannuated Civil Service Employees*, 62d Cong., 2d sess., 1912, H. Doc. 732. On other professionals, see "How to Grow Old," *Nation* 83 (1 November 1906): 365; Martha Bruère, "Growing Old Together," *Good Housekeeping* 58 (January 1914): 87; "Old Age and War," *Outlook* 108 (11 November 1914): 567.

52. Martha Bruère and Robert Bruère, "The Waste of Old Women," *Harper's Bazaar* 47 (March 1913): 115. See also "The Leisured Class," *Living Age* 250 (14 July 1906): 120; Richard Washburn Child, "What Shall We Do with the Old?," *Everybody's* 21 (September 1909): 356; and Margaret E. Sangster, "Another Talk with Old Ladies," *Ladies Home Journal* 17 (May 1900): 34.

53. N. E. Yorke-Davies, "Why Grow Old?," *Popular Science Monthly* 43 (June 1893): 230–31; An Elderly Woman, "The Land of Old Age," *Harper's Bazaar* 40 (August 1906): 675; "Work and Long Life," *Outlook* 104 (2 August 1913): 737; Amelia E. Barr, *Three Score and Ten* (New York: D. Appelton, 1915), pp. 241–43; Marcus M. Marks, "Retirement from Business," *Review of Reviews* 36 (November 1907): 557–58; John F.Cargill, "The Value of Old Age," *Popular Science Monthly* 67 (August 1905): 313.

54. Hendrick, "The Superannuated Man," p. 120.

55. John Fiske, *Man's Destiny Viewed in Light of His Origin* (London: Macmillan, 1884), pp. 25–30. See also Humphry, *Old Age,* pp. 10–11; Shaler, *Individual*, pp. 62–63; Herter, *Human Problems,* pp. 178–79; Charles Horton Cooley, *Social Process* (1918; reprint ed., Carbondale: Southern Illinois University Press, 1966), p. 56; Brooks Adams, *The Law of Civilization and Decay* (1896; reprint ed., New York: Alfred A. Knopf, 1943), p. 31. For more on the general point, see Frederic Cople Jaher, *Doubters and Dissenters* (New York: The Free Press, 1964), pp. 3–14, 20–27; and Marcell, *Progress and Pragmatism,* pp. 31–36.

56. Cooley, *Social Process,* p. 408. See also T. E. Young, *On Centenarians; and the Duration of the Human Race* (London: Charles and Edwin Layton, 1899), pp. 130–31; M. G. Watkins, "Old Age," *Living Age* 221 (5 October 1901): 59; Herbert Spencer, *The Principles of Biology,* rev. ed., 2 vols. (1899; reprint ed., New York: D. Appelton, 1904), 2: 413; James Mark Baldwin, *Individual and Society* (Boston: The Gorham Press, 1911), p. 156; "The Tragedy of Age," *Harper's Bazaar* 47 (May 1913): 222; *Independent* 75 (28 August 1913): 504.

57. Randolph S. Bourne, *Youth and Life* (1913; reprint ed., New York: Books for Libraries Press, Inc., 1967), pp. 12–14. Samuel Butler had anticipated Bourne's assertion in *Life and Habits* (London: Trübner & Co., 1877), p. 299. See also "Old Men, by One of Them," *Living Age* 192 (5 March 1892): 630; Washington Gladden, *Ruling Ideas of the Present Age* (Boston: Houghton Mifflin, 1895), pp. 9–10; Shaler, *Individual*, p. 262.

58. Dorland, *Mental Virility,* p. 24; Sangster, "Another Talk with Old Ladies," p. 34; James, *Principles of Psychology,* 2: 401; James Quayle Dealey, *The Family in Its Sociological Aspects* (Boston: Houghton Mifflin, 1912), p. 90.

59. G. Stanley Hall, *Adolescence,* 2 vols. (New York: D. Appelton & Co., 1905), 1: 50 and 2: 60. See also "A Secret of Youth," *Outlook* 86 (6 July 1907): 498; Jane Addams, *The Spirit of Youth and the City Streets* (New York: Macmillan, 1909), pp. 140–42; Edwin L. Sabin, "In Praise of Age," *Lippincott's Magazine* 89 (May 1912): 715.

60. Joseph F. Kett, *Rites of Passage* (New York: Basic Books, 1977), esp. chs. 5 and 8; John Higham, "The Reorientation of American Culture in the 1890s," in *Writing American History* (Bloomington: Indiana University Press, 1970), pp. 79–88; John Demos and Virginia Demos, "Concept of Adolescence in History," *Journal of Marriage and the Family* 31 (November 1969): 632–36.

61. "What Dr. Osler Really Said," *Scientific American* 92 (25 March 1905): 243; Edmund Osgood Brown, *De Senectute* (Chicago: The Lakeside Press, 1914), pp. 35–36; Beard, *Legal Responsibilities*, pp. 19–21; Andrew Lang, "In Love with Youth," *Living Age* 245 (6 May 1905): 381; "On Growing Old," *Living Age* 251 (24 November 1906): 464–65.

62. For hints aimed at women, see Martha Cutler, "How to Remain Young," *Harper's Bazaar* 43 (September 1909): 131; "A Word for the Modern Old Lady," *Atlantic Monthly* 100 (July 1907): 283–84; and "Eternal Youth," *Scribner's Magazine* 43 (March 1908): 378. For hints aimed at men, see Alvin Wood Chase, *Dr. Chase's Recipes* (Ann Arbor: A. W. Chase, 1866); advertisements in the *North American Review Advertiser* 156 (January–June 1893): 43, 52; and Sanford Bennett, *Old Age, Its Cause and Prevention: The Story of an Old Body and Face Made Young,* 2d ed. (New York: The Physical Culture Publishing Co., 1912), pp. 40–42.

63. "Young World," *Outlook* 105 (4 October 1913): 257. See also James Payn, "The Backwater of Life," *Living Age* 205 (1 June 1895): 572; G. S. Street, "The Persistence of Youth," *Living Age* 231 (30 November 1901): 569.

64. "On Death," *Hesperian* 1 (December 1895): 267; Joseph Jacobs, "The Death of Dying," *Fortnightly Review* 72 (August 1899): 264–66; Shaler, *Individual*, pp. 227–28, 239; Joslyn Gray, "Nox Dormienda," *Atlantic Monthly* 91 (January 1903): 103–6. For actuarial evidence presented at the time, see Karl Pearson, *The Chances of Death and Other Studies in Evolution,* 2 vols. (New York: Edward Arnold, 1897), 1: 1–41; John K. Gore, "On the Improvement in Longevity in the United States during the Nineteenth Century," *Proceedings of the Fourth International Congress of Actuaries* 1 (1904): 32–53.

65. See Newman Smyth, *The Place of Death in Evolution* (London: T. Fisher Unwin, 1897), pp. 173–74, on the social need for the elderly to die. On aged death, see Post, *Cottage Physician,* pp. 586–87. Works by August Weismann, collected in *Essays upon Heredity and Kindred Biological Problems* (1891; reprint ed., Oxford: Clarendon Press, 1899), were influential in shaping a new scientific conception of the biological process of death.

66. Scott, "Old Age and Death," pp. 91–92. See also Metchnikoff, *Nature of Man,* p. 131; Cambridge, "The Retrospect," pp. 131–32.

67. Williams James, *The Varieties of Religious Experience* (1901–2; reprint ed., New York: New American Library, 1958), p. 121. See also Shaler, *Individual*, p. 200; Scott, "Old Age and Death," p. 109; William Knight, "De Senectute," *Living Age* 250 (23 December 1905): 750. 753.

68. B. A. Crankenthorpe, "The Plaint of the Old," *Living Age* 200 (10 March 1894): 606. See also Margaret Deland, "The Wickedness of Growing Old," *Harper's Bazaar* 39 (February 1905): 101; and Elderly Woman, "The Land of Old Age," in three parts in *Harper's Bazaar* 40 (August, September, and December, 1906): 675, 777, 1149–50.

CHAPTER 4

1. Gaius Marcus Brumbaugh, *Maryland Records: Colonial, Revolutionary, County and Church* (Baltimore: Williams & Wilkins, 1928); Robert V. Wells, *The Population of the British Colonies in North America before 1776* (Princeton: Princeton University Press, 1975), pp. 72–73; David Hackett Fischer, *Growing Old in America* (New York: Oxford University Press, 1977), p. 222.

2. See tables 5.1 and 5.2 below.

3. Ibid.

4. Ibid.

5. John Higham, *Send These to Me* (New York: Atheneum, 1975), p. 13. See also John Higham, *Strangers in the Land* (New York: Atheneum, 1971) for a full discussion of the nativist ideology. I shall return to this point elsewhere in the text.

6. Although demographers use several formulas to calculate growth rates, I have chosen the one I find most appropriate in describing the nature of growth as a continuous process. See George N. Barclay, *Techniques of Population Analysis* (New York: John Wiley & Sons, Inc., 1958), pp. 31–32. For the exact figures, see W. Andrew Achenbaum, "Old Age in the United States, 1790 to Present," (Ph.D. diss., University of Michigan, 1976), pp. 202, 540.

7. For the regional breakdown by sex and place of birth, see Achenbaum, "Old Age," pp. 538–39.

8. Note that the growth rate of each group quickened somewhat between 1900 and 1910. This may merit further investigation (especially the increase in New England's foreign-born population) but its transience casts significant doubt on its long-range importance in shaping negative perceptions of older persons.

9. The following observations are based on analyses of data found in the 1865–95 Rhode Island censuses, the 1855, 1875, and 1895 New York censuses, and the 1895 Michigan census as well as urban-rural statistics in the 1910–40 federal censuses. For more information, see Achenbaum, "Old Age," pp. 542–45. For the sake of consistency, I used the Bureau of Census definition of an urban area as any incorporated place having a population over 2,500 people.

10. See Appendix technical note B for a discussion of some deficiencies and limitations in census data on occupational status.

11. Cited in Jon Hendricks and C. Davis Hendricks, *Aging in Mass Society* (Cambridge, Mass.: Winthrop Publishers Inc., 1977), pp. 176–77.

12. Consult Victor S. Clark, *History of Manufacturers in the United States,* 3 vols. (1929; reprint ed., New York: Peter Smith, 1948), vol. 2: 1860–1893 and vol. 3: 1893–1928, for a detailed survey of the transformation in manufacturing during the period.

13. P. K. Whelpton, "Occupational Groups in the United States," *Journal of the American Statistical Association* 21 (September 1926): 339–40.

14. See Appendix technical note C for a detailed explanation of how the estimate was derived. For the 1890 baseline, see Gertrude Bancroft, *The American Labor Force* (New York: John Wiley & Sons, Inc., 1958), p. 207.

15. Existing published data preclude discussion of trends for blacks. I computed the percent of white males from data in the U.S. Bureau of the Census, *Eleventh Census of the United States: 1890* (Washington, D.C.: Government Printing Office, 1890), vol. 1, pt. 2, pp. 373–407. See also John D. Durand, *The Labor Force in the United States* (1948; reprint ed., New York: John Wiley & Sons, Inc., 1968), p. 210.

16. In 1840, roughly 48% of all men employed in the state were farmers; another 35.3% were engaged in manufacturing and trades. By 1885, only 13.7% of all working men were in agricultural pursuits; the percentage of men employed in manufacturing and trade has risen to 66.8%.

To make the estimates, I used data in the U.S., Bureau of the Census, *Sixth Census of the United States: 1840* (Washington, D.C.: T. Allen, 1841), p. 475, and Secretary of the Commonwealth of Massachusetts, *Census of Massachusetts: 1885. Population and Social Statistics* (Boston: Wright and Porter, 1887), pt. 2, p. 628.

17. On the basis of presently available evidence, this hypothesis can be neither confirmed nor rejected for nineteenth-century America. Peter N. Stearns, however, attests to the phenomenon in France in *Old Age in European Society* (New York: Holmes & Meier, 1976), p. 53. Tamara K. Hareven cites twentieth-century evidence to document changes in employment opportunities over an individual's life cycle in "The Last Stage: Historical Adulthood and Old Age," *Daedalus* 105 (Fall 1976): 20. Forthcoming work by Professors Hareven and Howard Chudacoff, using the life cycle and family cycle approach, should elucidate the matter.

18. Evidence based on data cited in Harvey C. Lehman, *Age and Achievement* (Princeton: Princeton University Press, 1953), p. 286.

19. Nelson W. Polsby et al., "The Growth of the Seniority System in the U.S. House of Representatives," *American Political Science Review* 63 (September 1969): 798–807; Allen G. Bogue et al., "Members of the House of Representatives and the Processes of Modernization," *Journal of American History* 63 (September 1976): 275–302.

20. S. G. Lathrop, ed., *Fifty Years and Beyond; or, Gathered Gems for the Aged* (New York: F. H. Revell, 1881), p. 27. For other representative examples, see "Shakespeare's Seventh Age," *Knickerbocker* 12 (September 1838): 236; John Blassingame, *Slave Community* (New York: Oxford University Press, 1972), p. 171; Sarah Josepha Hale, *Traits of American Life* (Philadelphia: E. L. Carey and A. Hart, 1835), pp. 255–56; Catherine E. Beecher and Harriet Beecher Stowe, *An American Woman's Home: or, Principles of Domestic Science* (New York: J. B. Ford, 1869), pp. 18, 303–6; and Frederick J. Hoffman, "The

Problem of Poverty and Pensions in Old Age," *American Journal of Sociology* 14 (July 1908): 193.

21. This information was derived by using the references in table 103, "Civil Liability of the Child for Support of Relatives," in Chester Garfield Vernier, *American Family Laws*, 5 vols. (Stanford: Stanford University Press, 1931–38), 4: 96–105. I determined when the statute cited for each state was enacted by going backward through the statutes and codes until I found the earliest reference.

22. James Schouler, *A Treatise on the Law of Domestic Relations* (Boston: Little, Brown & Co., 1870), pp. 344–45, 363–65; *Lawyer Reporter Annual* 4 (1906): 1159; *American State Reports* 117 (1908): 128–30; Vernier, *American Family Laws,* 4: 106–8.

23. Sharon R. Custard found comparable household patterns in an unpublished case study of approximately four hundred men and women in Warwick County, (southern) Indiana, in 1880. Research in progress using the 1900 federal census manuscript by Michel Dahlin, Mark Friedberger, Richard Jensen, and Daniel Scott Smith, at The Newberry Library in Chicago should clarify the issue considerably.

24. This definition of an "almshouse" comes from Anthony F. Willich, *Domestic Encyclopedia*, 2d American ed., 3 vols. (Philadelphia: Abraham Small, 1821), 1: 38. For more on the persistence of bidding out the poor, see Robert H. Bremner, *From the Depths* (New York: New York University Press, 1956), p. 47, and Sarah Orne Jewett, "Town Poor," in *The Country of the Pointed Firs and Other Stories* (Garden City: Doubleday & Co., Anchor edition, 1956), p. 278.

25. See an 1824 report compiled by John N. Yates, which is found in New York State Board of Charities, *Annual Report for 1900* (Albany: J. B. Lyon, 1901), pp. 1010, 1104. See also Thomas R. Hazard, *Commissioner on Condition of the Poor and Insane* (Providence: John Knowles, 1851), p. 90, and Raymond A. Mohl, *Poverty in New York* (New York: Oxford University Press, 1971), pp. 92–94.

26. Homer Folks, "Disease and Dependence," *Charities* 11 (3 October 1903): 298. See also Alexander Johnson, *The Almshouse: Construction and Management* (New York: Charities Publication Committee, 1911), p. 66.

27. Quoted in James Leiby, *Charity and Correction in New Jersey* (New Brunswick: Rutgers University Press, 1976), pp. 70–71. See also Jane Addams, *Twenty Years at Hull House* (1910; reprint ed., New York: Signet Classic, 1961), pp. 118–19; and Will Carleton, "Over the Hill to the Poor-House," *Harper's Weekly* 15 (17 June 1871): 545. In 1873, Carleton published "Over the Hill *from* the Poor-House" (*Farm Ballads* [New York: Harper and Brother, 1873], pp. 59–62), in which a long-lost son retrieves his mother and buys a new homestead for himself and his aged kin.

28. Gary B. Nash, "Poverty and Poor Relief in Pre-Revolutionary Philadelphia," in *Colonial America,* ed. Stanley N. Katz, 2d ed. (Boston: Little, Brown, 1976), pp. 375–401; Mohl, *Poverty,* pp. 28, 137, 149; and Michael Zimmerman, "Old-Age Poverty in Preindustrial New York City," in *Growing Old in America,* ed. Beth Hess (New Brunswick: Transactions Press, 1976), p. 88.

29. U.S., Bureau of Labor Statistics, *Care of Aged Persons in the United States,* Bulletin no. 489 (Washington, D.C.: Government Printing Office, 1929), pp. 131, 176, 193; Louise S. Dorr, "An Old Lady's Story," *Godey's Lady's Book* 84 (January 1872): 77; "Old People's Homes Maintained by Nationality Groups," *Monthly Labor Review* 28 (April 1929): 691–94. See also Carole Haber, "The Old Folks at Home," *Pennsylvania Magazine of History and Biography* 101 (April 1977): 240–57, and Lilith R. Kunkel's forthcoming dissertation on old-age homes in Wisconsin.

30. U.S., Bureau of Labor Statistics, *Care of Aged Persons,* Bulletin no. 489, pp. 296–98; Hace Sole Tishler, *Self Reliance and Social Security, 1870–1917* (Port Washington: Kennikat Press, 1971), p. 23.

31. Lee Welling Squier, *Old Age Dependency in the United States: A Complete Survey of the Pension Method* (New York: Macmillan Press, 1912), pp. 187–92; Sarah K. Bolton, "Helping People in Their Homes," *Chautauquan* 61 (February 1911): 391–94.

32. Murray Webb Latimer, *Trade Union Pension Systems and Other Total Disability Benefits in the United States and Canada* (New York: Industrial Relations Counselors,

1932), pp. 8, 13–26; Squier, *Old Age Dependency,* pp. 56–64; David Brody, *Steelworkers in America* (Cambridge, Mass.: Harvard University Press, 1960), pp. 93, 101–2.

33. Some companies underwrote the entire cost of the program; others required employees to contribute a certain percentage of their salaries. Eligibility varied, though most companies did set age and service criteria: retirement age ranged from fifty-five to seventy years old; workers generally had to be employed continuously for twenty to thirty-five years to receive benefits. Some firms insisted on mandatory retirement; a few made retirement voluntary before seventy; still other established specific rules for mandatory and voluntary retirement. See Squier, *Old Age Dependency*, chs. 3–4; Albert DeRoode, "Pensions as Wages," *American Economic Review* 3 (June 1913): 290–95. See also William Graebner's forthcoming monograph on the evolution of retirement policies.

34. Squier, *Old Age Dependency*, pp. 266–68.

35. Another reason that unions did so little for the elderly is that their organizations attracted younger men interested in more immediate concerns such as increasing membership, raising wages, and shortening work schedules. See American Federation of Labor, *Proceedings of the 23d Convention* (Bloomington: Pantagraph Printing, 1903), p. 115; Squier, *Old Age Dependency,* p. 64; Otis L. Graham, Jr., *The Great Campaigns* (Englewood Cliffs, N.J.: Prentice-Hall, 1971), p. 159.

36. Squier, *Old Age Dependency,* pp. 139–228. On state military pensions, see Robert W. Kelso, *Poverty* (New York: Longmans, Green & Co., 1929), p. 293, and Elizabeth Wisner, *Social Welfare in the South* (Baton Rouge: Louisiana State University Press, 1970), pp. 51–52.

37. Ethel E. McClure, *More Than a Roof* (St. Paul: Minnesota Historical Society, 1968), pp. 74–75. On California, see Martha A. Chickering, "State Aid to the Aged, California, 1883–1895," *Social Service Review* 12 (March 1938): 45–49; on Massachusetts, see Alton A. Linford, *Old-Age Assistance in Massachusetts* (Chicago: The University of Chicago Press, 1949), pp. 5–41.

38. Thomas Paine, *Agrarian Justice* (Philadelphia: R. Fowle, 1797); Alexander H. Everett, *New Ideas on Population* (Boston: Oliver Everett, 1823).

39. William Henry Glasson, *History of Military Pension Legislation in the United States* (New York: Columbia University Press, 1900), pp. 33–36; U.S., Bureau of Labor Statistics, *Care of Aged Persons*, Bulletin no. 489, pp. 17, 65. See also Judith G. Cetina's dissertation on the early history of veterans' homes, "A History of Veterans' Homes in the United States, 1811–1930" (Case Western Reserve University, 1977).

40. Glasson, *Military Pension Legislation,* pp. 37–38, 49–52. *Niles Register* 25 (27 December 1823): 262, gives a state-by-state breakdown of pensioners; the 1840 figure is calculated with data in the U.S., Bureau of the Census, *Sixth Census,* p. 475. Incidentally, although Niles criticized those who speculated with pension monies, he frequently urged that more liberal benefits be awarded.

41. Squier, *Old Age Dependency,* pp. 229–30; William Henry Glasson, *Federal Military Pensions in the United States* (New York: Oxford University Press, 1918), pp. 233–35, 258–61.

42. U.S., Congress, House, *Congressional Record,* 62d Cong., 1st sess., 1911, 47:3699. For more on the American effort, see Edward Everett Hale, "Old Age Pensions," *Charities and the Commons* 18 (1 June 1907): 276; Tishler, *Self Reliance,* p. 89; and "Pensions, Old Age," *American Labor Legislation Review* 1 (September 1911): 121. For more on European developments, see Edith Sellers, "The Nations and Their Aged Poor," *American Monthly Review of Reviews* 18 (July 1898): 97–98; Barbara N. Armstrong, *Insuring the Essentials* (New York: The Macmillan Co., 1932), pp. 399–401; and Hugh Heclo, *Modern Social Politics in Britain and Sweden* (New Haven: Yale University Press, 1974), pp. 156, 162, 195.

43. Bremner, *From the Depths,* pp. 123–25, 201; Kelso, *Poverty,* pp. 38–54; Roy Lubove, *The Professional Altruist* (Cambridge, Mass.: Harvard University Press, 1965), pp. 2–21, 52; Clarke A. Chambers, *Paul U. Kellogg and the Survey* (Minneapolis: University of Minnesota Press, 1971), pp. 6, 10, 24, 30, 49, 52–53.

44. Alice Willard Solenberger, *One Thousand Homeless Men: A Study of Original Records* (New York: Charities Publication Committee, 1911), pp. 112–13. See also Henry R. Seager, "Old Age Pensions," *Charities and Commons* 21 (3 October 1908): 11–12; and

Edward T. Devine, *Misery and Its Causes* (New York: The Macmillan Co., 1909), pp. 48, 227–29. An exception to this viewpoint was Robert Hunter, *Poverty* (New York: The Macmillan Co., 1904), pp. 56–58. Hunter was probably the earliest American writer to cite the impact of the new social order on old-age dependency. Yet it is important to note that he offers little proof of his claim. Neither does he explain how and why industrialization per se adversely affected the old.

45. William Dwight Porter Bliss, "Old Age Pensions," *The Encyclopedia of Social Reform* (New York: Funk and Wagnalls, 1897), pp. 952–54. Interestingly, Bliss did not refer to the United States at all in a 1908 revision of this article. See also Amos G. Warner, *American Charities* (New York: Thomas Y. Crowell, 1894), pp. 34–39; Devine, *Misery,* pp. 225–29.

CHAPTER 5

1. This interpretation is based on United Nations, *The Aging of Populations and Its Economic and Social Implications,* Population Studies no. 25 (New York: United Nations, 1956), pp. 1–2, 22, 43; John Grauman, "Comment on Notestein's 'Mortality, Fertility and the Size-Age Distribution,' " in *The Commission on Population Growth and the American Future,* ed. Charles Westoff and Robert Parke (Washington, D.C.: Government Printing Office, 1972), 1:275–78; and Edward Rossett, *Aging Process of the Population* (New York: The Macmillan Co., 1964), pp. 178, 335.

2. U.S., Bureau of the Census, "Some Demographic Aspects of Aging in the United States," in *Current Population Reports,* series P–23, no. 43 (Washington, D.C.: Government Printing Office, 1973), pp. 4–6.

3. From data reported in James Schulz, *The Economics of Aging* (Belmont, Ca.: Wadsworth Publishing Co., Inc., 1976), p. 35.

4. U.S., Bureau of the Census, "Aspects of Aging," p. 7.

5. Ibid., pp. 5, 7

6. Reynolds Farley, "Mortality and Fertility among Blacks in the United States," in *Commission on Population Growth,* ed. Westoff and Parke, 1: 115–17; idem, *Growth of the Black Population* (Chicago: Markham Publishing, 1970), pp. 7–14; Bernard Okun, *Trends in Birth Rates in the United States since 1870* (Baltimore: The Johns Hopkins University Press, 1968), pp. 14–16.

7. The conclusions in this paragraph are based on analyses in Richard Easterlin, "American Population," in *American Economic Growth,* ed. Lance Davis et al. (New York: Harper & Row, 1972), pp. 128–30; Donald J. Bogue, *The Population of the United States* (Glencoe: The Free Press, 1959), pp. 110–15; and Wilson H. Grabill et al., *The Fertility of American Women* (New York: John Wiley and Sons, Inc., 1958), pp. 51, 382.

8. U.S., Bureau of the Census, *Historical Statistics of the United States* (Washington, D.C.: Government Printing Office, 1976), pt. 1, p. 26.

9. Idem, "Aspects of Aging," pp. 13–14.

10. Stephen M. Golant, "Residential Concentrations of the Future Elderly," *Gerontologist* 15, no. 1, pt. 2 (February 1975): 17; see also table 4.6, above. For age segregation in the suburbs in the 1950s, see William Whyte, *The Organization Man* (Garden City: Doubleday, 1956), p. 351–55.

11. W. Andrew Achenbaum, "Old Age in the United States, 1790 to Present" (Ph.D. diss., University of Michigan, 1976), pp. 551–52, 560–64.

12. U.S., Bureau of the Census, "Farm Population," in *Current Population Reports,* series P–27, no. 43 (Washington, D.C.: Government Printing Office, 1972), pp. 1–2; idem, *Historical Statistics,* pt. 1, p. 465; Achenbaum, "Old Age," pp. 565–66.

13. E. Grant Youmans, ed., *Older Rural Americans: A Sociological Perspective* (Lexington: University of Kentucky Press, 1967), pp. 27–35; Joseph T. Drake, *The Aged in American Society* (New York: Ronald Press, 1958), pp. 13–15, 24–27; T. Lynn Smith, "The Aged in Rural Society," in *The Aged and Society,* ed. Milton Derber (New York: Industrial Relations Research Association, 1950), pp. 45–49; and Pitirim A. Sorokin et al., *A Systematic Source Book in Rural Sociology,* 2 vols. (Minneapolis: University of Minnesota Press, 1930), 1: 537.

14. U.S., Bureau of the Census, *Women at Work* (Washington, D.C.: Government Printing Office, 1907), pp. 125–26; Ronald L. Mighell, *American Agriculture* (New York: John Wiley and Sons, Inc., 1958), p. 151.

15. John L. Shover, *First Majority—Last Minority* (DeKalb: Northern Illinois University Press, 1976), esp. chs. 1–2; H. Dewey Anderson and Percy C. Davidson, *Occupational Trends in the United States* (Stanford: Stanford University Press, 1940), pp. 16–21, 74–75.

16. U.S., Bureau of the Census, *Historical Statistics,* pt. 1, pp. 132, 139. While fundamental changes in the occupational structure as well as the manner in which the census classifies data preclude a more detailed and systematic discussion, the major tendencies are unmistakable.

17. For an analysis of the significance of white-collar jobs in changing women's labor status, see Gertrude Bancroft, *The American Labor Force* (New York: John Wiley & Sons, Inc., 1958), pp. 35–39. The data on which this argument is based come from table 5.4; U.S., Bureau of the Census, *Historical Statistics,* pt. 1, p. 140; and Anderson and Davidson, *Occupational Trends,* p. 19.

18. Henry D. Sheldon, *The Older Population of the United States* (New York: John Wiley & Sons, Inc., 1958), p. 173; William G. Bowen and T. Aldrich Finegan, *The Economics of Labor Force Participation* (Princeton: Princeton University Press, 1969), pp. 353–55.

19. Using 1958 and 1966 data, Bowen and Finegan (ibid., pp. 367, 374) argue that the incidence of chronic disability among elderly men rose. Yet comparable census data, gathered in 1970, show a reduction. See U.S., Department of Health, Education and Welfare, *Limitations of Activity Due to Chronic Conditions, United States, 1970,* Vital and Health Statistics, series 10, no. 80 (Washington, D.C.: Government Printing Office, April 1973), tables 1, 3, 4, B.

20. Clarence D. Long, *The Labor Force under Changing Conditions of Income and Employment* (Princeton: Princeton University Press, 1958), pp. 13, 159–61; Bowen and Finegan, *Economics of Labor Force,* pp. 373–74. Note that Long's analysis further undercuts a hypothesis left unresolved in the previous chapter: if he is correct, then the shift of the elderly population from a rural to an urban setting was *not* a crucial factor affecting shifting ideas about the elderly's worth.

21. For a representative argument, see Wilbert E. Moore, "The Aged in Industrial Society," in *The Aged and Society,* ed. Derber, p. 32.

22. Bowen and Finegan, *Economics of Labor Force,* p. 374; Long, *Labor Force,* pp. 172–73; Sheldon, *Older Population,* pp. 55–56; Peter M. Blau and Otis Dudley Duncan, *The American Occupational Structure* (New York: John Wiley and Sons, Inc., 1967), pp. 428–29.

23. Harold L. Sheppard, "Work and Retirement," in *Handbook of Aging and the Social Sciences,* ed. Robert H. Binstock and Ethel Shanas (New York: Van Nostrand Reinhold, 1976); Bowen and Finegan, *Economics of Labor Force,* pp. 274–75, 374; Long, *Labor Force,* pp. 14, 174–77.

24. Cited in Schulz, *Economics of Aging,* p. 42. The figures do not add up to 100% because older people often have several income sources.

25. Matilda White Riley and Associates, *Aging and Society,* 3 vols. (New York: Russell Sage Foundation, 1968–72), 1: 80; Schulz, *Economics of Aging,* p. 60; Bowen and Finegan, *Economics of Labor Force,* pp. 282, 355, 373–75.

CHAPTER 6

1. Richard Le Gallienne, "The Art of Not Growing Old," *Harper's Magazine* 142 (April 1921): 655.

2. Harry L. Hollingworth, *Mental Growth and Decline: A Survey of Developmental Psychology* (New York: D. Appleton & Co., 1927), p. 308. See also Johnson Brigham, *Youth of Old Age* (Boston: Marshall Jones Co., 1934), p. 6; Virginia Terhune Van de Water, "Our Modern Old People," *Scribner's Monthly* 75 (May 1924): 558; Della T. Lutes, "Why I Don't Tell My Age," *Forum* 97 (April 1937): 248.

3. Stanley M. Rinehart, "How Old Are You?," *Saturday Evening Post* 193 (3 July 1920): 20; Walter B. Pitkin, *Life Begins at Forty* (New York: McGraw-Hill Book Co., 1932), pp. 25–26; "Old Age," *Encyclopedia of Social Sciences*, 15 vols. (New York: Macmillan Co., 1937), 11: 452; Frank Bruno, *Trends in Social Work* (New York: Columbia University Press, 1957), p. 247.

4. Edward L. Thorndike, Elsie O. Bregman, J. Warren Tilton, and Ella Woodyard, *Adult Learning* (New York: The Macmillan Co., 1928), p. 131.

5. Hollingworth, *Mental Growth*, pp. 310–11; Thorndike et al., *Adult Learning*, pp. 1, 131. Not everyone agreed. A research project conducted by Dr. Irving Lorge in the 1930s indicated that older people earned lower test scores because time limitations in the testing situation biased the scores downward. Hence Lorge argued that older people did not necessarily decline mentally, but they did respond more slowly. See Irving Lorge, "Never Too Old to Learn," *Vital Speeches* 3 (1 April 1937): 364. It is important to note, however, that the hypothesis that learning capacity declined with age was not seriously questioned before World War II and was not severely undermined until recent times.

6. Richard King, "Watching the World Go By," *Forum* 70 (December 1923): 2254–55; Corra Harris, "When the Tide Turns," *Saturday Evening Post* 198 (7 November 1925): 188; Samuel Crowther, "When Is a Man Old?," *Ladies Home Journal* 46 (July 1929): 25; "In the Driftway," *Nation* 139 (14 November 1934): 564.

7. For professional studies, see Lillien Martin and Clare De Gruchy, *Salvaging Old Age* (New York: The Macmillan Co., 1930), pp. 20–22, 44–45, 78–80; Hollingworth, *Mental Growth*, pp. 318–22; G. Stanley Hall, *Senescence: The Last Half of Life* (New York: D. Appelton & Co., 1922), pp. 8, 25–27, 100. Hall and Martin also wrote for popular journals. See, for example, "Old Age," *Atlantic* 127 (January 1921): 29–30, and Lillien J. Martin, "Old Age—Life's Harvest Time," *Ladies Home Journal* 48 (October 1931): 112. See also "What Makes a Woman Old," *Good Housekeeping* 78 (January 1924): 23, 186, and Lee Wilson Dodd, "The Sixth Decade," *Forum* 86 (October 1931): 228.

8. George Lawton, "The Study of Senescence: Psychiatric and Sociological Aspects," *American Journal of Sociology* 44 (September 1938): 280; "Old Age," *Encyclopedia of Social Sciences*, 11: 453; Hollingworth, *Mental Growth*, p. 320. For the relationship between fear of aging and the fear of death, see Hall, *Senescence*, pp. 145–47, 356–57, 438, 514–15; "Do You Dread Getting Old?" *American Magazine* 86 (October 1918): 27; Robert McKenna, *Adventure of Life* (New York: The Macmillan Co., 1919), pp. 223–24; Sarah Comstock, "The Peppermint Years," *Harper's Magazine* 159 (July 1929): 186–87.

9. Gelett Burgess, "Accent on Youth," *Reader's Digest* 30 (May 1937): 8.

10. Havelock Ellis, *Psychology of Sex,* 2d ed. (1933; reprint ed., New York: Emerson Books, 1954), pp. 27, 210–11, 320–21. See also Daniel J. Mc Carthy, "When Nature Throws Us Over," *Literary Digest* 102 (7 September 1929): 65; Hall, *Senescence,* pp. 376–77; Serge Voronoff, *Sources of Life* (Boston: Houghton Mifflin, 1943), pp. 38, 58–60.

11. Alfred C. Kinsey et al., *Sexual Behavior in the Human Male* (Philadelphia: W. B. Saunders Co., 1948), pp. 226–38. Kinsey began his research in 1939, building on other twentieth-century researchers' data.

12. Lutes, "My Age," p. 248.

13. Corra Harris, "The Borrowed Timers," *Ladies Home Journal* 43 (September 1926): 35. See also idem, "The Prosody of Old Age," *Saturday Evening Post* 198 (8 May 1926): 149; Josephine Lawrence, *Years Are So Long* (New York: Frederick A. Stokes, 1934), p. 39; "A Modest Proposal," *Nation* 140 (10 April 1935): 405.

14. Albert W. Atwood, "The Financial Problem of Old Age," *Saturday Evening Post* 199 (26 March 1927): 12; "Banishing the Poorhouse, *"Literary Digest* 102 (17 August 1929): 23; Louis I. Dublin, "The Job and the Life Span," *Harper's Monthly* 160 (January 1930): 247; Warren S. Thompson and P. K. Whelpton, "A Nation of Elders in the Making," *American Mercury* 19 (April 1930): 394–95; President's Research Committee, *Recent Social Trends,* 2 vols. (New York: McGraw-Hill Co., 1933), 1: 658; "Old Age," *Encyclopedia of Social Sciences,* 11: 454–55; "Attack on Old Age Problems Launched by Health Service," *Science Newsletter* 38 (7 December 1940): 356.

15. Marie L. Dallach, "Old Age, American Style," *New Outlook* 162 (October 1933): 50. See also "Youth Is Always Right," *Nation* 114 (15 March 1922): 307–8; Will Payne,

"Chloroform at Sixty," *Saturday Evening Post* 199 (2 April 1927): 113; Ralph Linton, "Age and Sex Categories," *American Sociological Review* 7 (August 1942): 592–93, 597, 601. Talcott Parsons, "Age and Sex in the Social Structure of the United States," ibid., pp. 615–21.

16. Robert S. Lynd and Helen M. Lynd, *Middletown* (1929; reprint ed., New York: Harcourt, Brace & World, 1956), p. 35; "Old Age Security," *Saturday Evening Post* 201 (25 May 1929): 32; Thompson and Whelpton, "Nation of Elders," pp. 392–93; Arthur S. Y. Chen, "Social Significance of Old Age," *Sociology and Social Research* 23 (July–August 1939): 519–27; Paul Henry Landis, *Rural Life in Process* (New York: McGraw-Hill, 1940), p. 48–51.

17. U.S., Social Security Board, *Economic Insecurity in Old Age* (Washington, D.C.: Government Printing Office, 1937), pp. 28–29, 108; Solomon Barkin, *The Older Worker in Industry* (Albany: J. B. Lyon, 1933), pp. 45–46, 225–28; Channing Pollock, "Death Begins at Forty," *Forum* 98 (November 1937): 213–16; E. B. Mittelman, "Displacement of Workers, 45–64 Years of Age," *American Economic Review* 26 (March 1936): 82–83; Jesse K. Sprague, "How Old Is Old?," *Saturday Evening Post* 210 (22 January 1938): 25.

18. E. L. Thorndike and Ella Woodyard, "The Relation of Earning Power to Age on Professional Workers under Conditions of Nearly Free Competition," *Journal of American Statistical Association* 21 (September 1926): 293–306; Boyden Sparkes, "Rip Van Winkle Wants a Job," *Saturday Evening Post* 201 (27 October 1928): 29; Lynd and Lynd, *Middletown*, p. 35; Barkin, *Older Worker*, p. 341.

19. Johanna Lobsenz, *The Older Woman in Industry* (New York: Scribner's Sons, 1929), pp. vii–viii, 23, 89–95, 102, 166–67; Sophonista Breckinridge, *Women in the Twentieth Century* (New York: McGraw-Hill, 1933), p. 277.

20. Hall, *Senescence*, p. 24; Robert W. McKenna, *Adventure of Death* (London: John Murray, 1916), p. 13; Lawrence, *Years Are So Long*, p. 106; Herbert J. Samuels, "Granite Benchers," *Overland Magazine* 88 (July 1930): 207; Pitkin, *Life Begins at Forty*, pp. 156–57; Eleanor Roosevelt, "Too Old for the Job," *Woman's Home Companion* 61 (February 1934): 4.

21. J. R. Sprague, "The Dangerous Age," *Saturday Evening Post* 194 (20 August 1921): 6; Abraham Epstein, "Facing Old Age," *Commonweal* 11 (11 December 1929): 163; Barkin, *Older Worker*, pp. 286, 316; "The Full Years," *Collier's* 95 (16 February 1935): 58; E. V. Cowdry, "Woods Hole Conference on the Problem of Aging," *Science* 86 (23 July 1937): 76; I. M. Rubinow, *The Quest for Security* (New York: Henry Holt & Co., 1934), pp. 222–23.

22. *Recent Social Trends,* 1: 811. See also Gorton James, "The Problem of the Old Man," *Survey* 46 (15 September 1921): 673–74; Abraham Epstein, "Old Age Security–A National Issue," *The World Tomorrow* 12 (October 1929): 418–20; Barbara N. Armstrong, *Insuring the Essentials* (New York: The Macmillan Co., 1932), pp. 386–87; Dwight L. Palmer and John A. Brownell, "Influence of Age on Employment Oppportunities," *Monthly Labor Review* 48 (April 1939): 780. For more on institutional changes after World War I, see Daniel Nelson, *Managers and Workers* (Madison: University of Wisconsin Press, 1975), pp. 151–56.

23. Epstein, "Facing Old Age," p. 163. For a sample of how this assumption pervades many different types of work, see Mabel Louise Nassau, *Old Age Poverty in Greenwich Village* (New York: Fleming F. Revell, 1915), p. 49; Pennsylvania Commission on Old Age Pensions, *Report* (Harrisburg: J. L. L. Kuhn, 1919), p. 212; Abbott Payson Usher, "Justice and Poverty," *American Journal of Sociology* 26 (May 1921): 702–3; Gifford Pinchot, "Old Age Assistance in Pennsylvania: Righting the Neglects of Yesterday," *American Labor Legislation Review* 14 (February 1924): 290–91; Louise A. Schlicting, "Causes of Old Age Dependency," in *Aged Clients of Boston Social Agencies*, ed. Lucille Eaves (Boston: Women's Educational and Industrial Union, 1925), pp. 53–56; Gladys Fisher, "Three Score and Ten in 1931," *Survey* 66 (15 August 1931): 464; Abraham Epstein, *Insecurity*, 3d ed. rev. (1933; reprint ed., New York: Harrison Smith & Robert Haas, 1936), p. 506; U.S., Social Security Board, *Economic Insecurity in Old Age*, p. 2. See also Clarke Chambers, *Seedtime of Reform* (Minneapolis: University of Minnesota Press, 1963), pp. 155–56.

24. Robert W. Kelso, *Poverty* (New York: Longmans, Green & Co., 1929), p. 156.

25. W. D. Howells, "Eighty Years and After," *Harper's Magazine* 140 (December 1919): 27; Edna Ferber, "Old Man Minick" (1922), in *One Basket* (New York: Dell

NOTES TO PAGES 116–19

Publishing, 1964), pp. 110–27; Corra Harris, "Fortune Telling for Old People," *Saturday Evening Post* 43 (May 1926): 198; Lynd and Lynd, *Middletown,* p. 110; "Old Age Intestate," *Harper's Monthly* 162 (May 1931): 712–14; "I Am the Mother-in-Law in the Home," *Reader's Digest* 31 (November 1937): 11–14; Lyman P. Powell, *The Second Seventy* (Philadelphia: Macrae Smith Co., 1937), p. 148.

26. U.S., Social Security Board, *Economic Insecurity in Old Age,* pp. 18–19, 154–55. For the situation in the 1930s, see Chapter 7, below.

27. Lynd and Lynd, *Middletown,* pp. 98–99; John M. Gries and James Ford, eds., *President's Conference on Housing,* vol. 7: Farm and Village Housing (Washington, D.C.: National Capital Press, 1932), pp. 7–10; *Recent Social Trends,* 1: 667. The relationship between domestic architecture and intergenerational networks merits attention.

28. Harry C. Evans, *The American Poorfarm and Its Inmates* (Mooseheart, Ill.: Fraternal Congresses and Loyal Order of the Moose, 1926), p. 5. See also "Banishing the Poorhouse," *Literary Digest* 102 (17 August 1929): 23; Carlton J. H. Hayes, "America and the Aged," *Commonweal* 11 (18 December 1929): 187; "Old Age Pensions," ibid. 17 (1 February 1933): 367. For a portrait of well-managed almshouses, see Francis Bardwell, *The Adventure of Old Age* (Boston: Houghton Mifflin Co., 1926), pp. 11–12, and idem., "Almshouse Boarders," *Survey* 55 (15 March 1926): 687.

29. Barkin, *Older Worker,* pp. 65–70; Robert F. Hoxie, *Scientific Management and Labor* (1915; reprint ed.,New York: Augustus Kelly, 1966), pp. v, 97–98; Ida M. Tarbell, "The Golden Rule in Business," *American Magazine* 80 (August 1915): 70–72.

30. Le Gallienne, "Art of Not Growing Old," p. 658; A. Lapthorn Smith, *How to Be Useful and Happy from Sixty to Ninety* (London: The Bodley Head, 1922), p. 57; Francis G. Peabody, "On Keeping Young," *Atlantic Monthly* 145 (June 1930): 824; Elaine V. Emans, "Plan for the Years," *Good Housekeeping* 100 (January 1935): 15; Ralph Barton Perry, *Plea for an Age Movement* (New York: Vanguard Press, 1942), pp. 16–17.

31. Smith, *How to Be Useful,* p. 15; Ruth F. Wadsworth, "Let's Stay Young Together," *Collier's* 83 (13 April 1929): 22, 61; Eudora Ramsay Richardson, "Old Men," *North American Review* 234 (October 1932): 313–14; Powell, *Second Seventy,* pp. 11–12; "Life Begins at Eighty!," *American Mercury* 48 (October 1939): 216–23; Walter B. Pitkin, "Before I'm Eighty . . .," *Reader's Digest* 37 (December 1940): 81.

32. [Attributed to G. Stanley Hall], "Old Age," *Atlantic* 127 (January 1921): 29–30; Hall, *Senescence,* pp. v, ix, 133, 405–7. See also William Lyon Phelps, *Happiness* (New York: E. P. Dutton & Co., 1927), p. 40; Gerald W. Johnson, "What an Old Girl Should Know," *Harper's Magazine* 168 (April 1934): 608; Quintus Quiz, "The Opsi-Math," *Christian Century* 42 (6 November 1935): 402.

33. Martin, "Old Age," p. 112; Marie L. Dallach, "Fearing Old Age," *Commonweal* 15 (23 December 1931): 205; Lillien J. Martin, *A Handbook for Old Age Counsellors* (San Francisco: Geertz Printing Company, 1944), p. 3. On the need for the old to help themselves, see David Marshall Ramsay, "An Old Man Answers His Daughter,"*North American Review* ·235 (February 1933): 177. For information on local clubs operated for and by senior citizens, see John Anson Ford, "Borrowers of Time," *American Magazine* 75 (February 1913): 32; Harris, "Borrowed Timers," p. 209; W. A. Mc Keever, "Live-A-Century School," *Reader's Digest* 28 (June 1936): 16. "Work and Play for Those over 70," *Literary Digest* 122 (26 September 1936): 18.

34. Genevieve Grandcourt, "Eternal Youth as Scientific Theory," *Scientific American* 121 (15 November 1919): 482; Serge Voronoff, *Life* (New York: E. P. Dutton Co., 1920), pp. 63, 113–18, 151–53; idem, *Sources of Life,* p. 89; Paul Kammerer, *Rejuvenation and the Prolongation of Human Efficiency* (New York: Boni & Liveright, 1923), pp. 48–49, 69–71; Jerome Lackenbruch, "The Fight to Conquer Old Age," *Scientific American* 128 (January 1923): 22; "Can Old Age Be Deferred?," ibid. 133 (October 1925): 226.

35. "The Salt of Old Age," *Literary Digest* 106 (20 September 1930): 26; Henry S. Simms and Abraham Stolman, "Changes in Human Tissue Electrolytes in Senescence," *Science* 86 (17 September 1937): 270; Henry Rubin, "Youth by Radiation," *Forum* 72 (November 1924), pp. 653–55.

36. Charles Sedgwick Minot, *The Problem of Age, Growth and Death* (New York: G. P. Putnam's Sons, 1908), pp. 249. Minot actually discarded his previous assumption that old age

was a pathological disorder in light of his subsequent research. See also Charles Manning Child, *Senescence and Rejuvenescence* (Chicago: The University of Chicago Press, 1915), pp. 58, 271, 301, 309, 459, 465.

37. I. L. Nascher, *Geriatrics* (Philadelphia: P. Blakiston's Son & Co., 1914), pp. 2, 14–18, 69, 283. Idem, "Longevity and Rejuvenescence," *New York Medical Journal* 89 (17 April 1909): 796; idem, "Old Age," in *Reference Handbook of the Medical Sciences,* ed. Thomas Lohr Stedman, 3d ed., 8 vols. (New York: Harper Bros., 1913), 6: 846, 860–61.

38. I. L. Nascher, "A History of Geriatrics," *Medical Review of Reviews* 32 (June 1926): 283; Barclay Moon Newman, "Geriatrics," *Scientific American* 163 (October 1940): 190.

39. On the relation of theories in cytology to old age, see Hall, *Senescence,* pp. 204–5; Humphry Davy Rolleston, *Some Medical Aspects of Old Age* (London: Macmillan & Co., 1922), pp. 86–89; Morris Fishbein, "The Years of Man," *Outlook* 152 (28 August 1929): 699. On pertinent developments in endocrinology, see Louis Berman, *The Glands Regulating Personality* (New York: The Macmillan Co., 1921), pp. 224, 256–57; Gregorio Marañón, *The Climacteric* (St. Louis: C. V. Mosby, 1929), pp. 349–50; Raymond Pearl, *The Biology of Death* (Philadelphia: J. B. Lippincott, 1922), p. 75. On new currents in pathology, see Rolleston, *Medical Aspects of Old Age,* pp. 135–36; Aldred Scott Warthin, *Old Age, The Major Involution* (New York: Paul B. Holber, Inc., 1929), pp. 70–75, 159; and William M. Malisoff, *The Span of Life* (Philadelphia: J. B. Lippincott, 1937), pp. 181–82.

40. George W. Gray, "The Mystery of Aging," *Harper's Magazine* 182 (February 1941): 283. For examples of other scientists grappling with this problem, see Rolleston, *Medical Aspects of Old Age,* pp. 66–68, 82–91; and Newman, "Geriatrics," pp. 190–91.

41. U.S., Bureau of Labor Statistics, *Care of Aged Persons in the United States,* Bulletin no. 489 (Washington, D.C.: Government Printing Office, October 1929), pp. 12–15; Frederick Mackenzie, "Old Age Insurance Legislation Now up to the States," *American Labor Legislation Review* 10 (December 1920): 254–55; Edward T. Devine, *The Normal Life,* 2d ed. rev. (New York: The Macmillan Co., 1924), pp. 178–79.

42. Statistics come from U.S., Bureau of Labor Statistics, *Care of Aged Persons,* pp. 2–3, 86–87, and M. B. Folsom, "Old Age on the Balance Sheet," *Atlantic Monthly* 164 (September 1929): 406. For corporate old-age workshops, see "Industrial Pensioners," *Scientific American* 150 (March 1934): 121.

43. For three encyclopedic, contemporary assessments of the rationale behind industrial pension systems, see Luther Conant, Jr., *A Critical Analysis of Industrial Pension Systems* (New York: The Macmillan Co., 1922); National Industrial Conference Board, *Industrial Pensions in the United States* (New York: National Industrial Conference Board, Inc., 1925); and Arthur David Cloud, *Pensions in Modern Industry* (Chicago: Hawkins and Loomis, 1930). See also Stuart Brandes, *American Welfare Capitalism* (Chicago: University of Chicago Press, 1975), pp. 102–10.

44. James J. Walsh, "The Care of Children and the Aged," *Catholic World* 104 (October 1916): 59; Usher, "Justice and Poverty," pp. 701–2; Homer Folks, "Home Life for the Aged," *Survey* 53 (15 October 1924): 71; *Recent Social Trends,* 1: 673; Ruth Manson Belcher and Mabel P. Taylor, "Economic Resources and Living Conditions of the Aged Poor in Boston," in *Aged Clients,* ed. Eaves, pp. 80–94. To determine the changing status of state laws affecting parent-child relationships, I pursued references in Chester G. Vernier, *American Family Laws,* 5 vols. (Stanford University Press, 1936), 4: 96–109.

45. U.S., Bureau of Labor Statistics, *Care of Aged Persons,* pp. 3–4. See also Philip Klein et al., *A Social Study of Pittsburgh* (New York: Columbia University Press, 1938), pp. 575–81; Ethel E. McClure, *More Than a Roof* (St. Paul: Minnesota Historical Society, 1968), pp. 234–36.

46. Quoted in Alton A. Linford, *Old-Age Assistance in Massachusetts* (Chicago: The University of Chicago Press, 1949), pp. 60–65.

47. "Old Age Pensions and Relief," *Monthly Labor Review* 26 (June 1928): 93–94; Rubinow, *Quest for Security,* pp. 242–26; Epstein, *Insecurity,* p. 500. See also Louis Leotta, "Abraham Epstein and the Movement for Old Age Security," *Labor History* 16 (Summer 1975): 359–66.

48. "Public Pensions for Aged Dependents," *Monthly Labor Review* 22 (June 1926): 1811; *Recent Social Trends,* 2: 1230–31, 1444; Pinchot, "Old Age Assistance in Pennsylvania," p. 291; "Pennsylvania Acts," *Survey* 50 (15 July 1923): 448.

49. Belle Flegelman, "If You Grow Old in Montana," *Survey* 50 (15 May 1923): 239–40; "Official Report Tells Why Old Age Pensions Are Needed," *American Labor Legislation Review* 15 (1925): 265; U.S., Bureau of Labor Statistics, *Public Old-Age Pensions and Insurance in the United States and Foreign Countries,* Bulletin no. 561 (Washington, D.C.: Government Printing Office, 1932), p. 5. For the Pennsylvania Supreme Court decision, see Busser vs. Snyder, *Atlantic Review* 128 (1925): 80–86. See also Helen I. Clarke, *Social Legislation* (New York: D. Appelton-Century Co., 1940), p. 496, and Irving Bernstein, *The Lean Years* (1960; reprint ed. Boston: Houghton Mifflin Co., 1972), pp. 237–38.

50. Roy Lubove, *The Struggle for Social Security, 1900–1935* (Cambridge, Mass.: Harvard University Press, 1968), pp. 136–38; "Why Governor Blaine Signed the Old Age Pension Bill," *American Labor Legislation Review* 15 (September 1925): 264; "Prepare Now for Pensions," ibid. 19 (December 1929): 358; U.S., Bureau of Labor Statistics, *Public Old-Age Pensions,* pp. 11–12; "Old Age Pensions," *Encyclopedia of Social Sciences,* 11:460.

51. For Dublin's estimate, see Louis I. Dublin, "Public Pensions for Aged Dependents," *Monthly Labor Review* 22 (June 1926): 1177; National Civic Federation, *Extent of Old Age Dependency* (New York: National Civic Federation, 1928), pp. 1–5, 11–16, 153–54; "Extent of Old Age Dependency," *Monthly Labor Review* 26 (May 1928): 960–61. For less sanguine critiques, see again the references at note 47.

52. Lubove, *Struggle for Social Security;* Alfred D. Chandler and Louis Galambos, "The Development of Large-Scale Organizations in Modern America," *Journal of Economic History* 30 (March 1970): 216.

53. U.S., Bureau of Labor Statistics, *Care of Aged Persons,* pp. 2–3.

CHAPTER 7

1. Murray Rothbard, *America's Great Depression* (1963; reprint ed., Los Angeles: Nash Publishing, 1972), p. 1. The statistics come from Edwin C. Rozwenc, *The Making of American Society,* 2 vols. (Boston: Allyn & Bacon, 1973), 2: 333, and U.S., Congress, House, *The Economic Security Act: Hearings on H.R. 4120,* 73d Cong., 2d sess., 1935, p. 19.

2. The data are taken from Paul H. Douglas, *Social Security in the United States* (New York: McGraw-Hill Co., 1936), p. 6.

3. On the inadequacy of savings, see Sonia Kay and Irma Rittenhouse, "Why Are the Aged Poor?," *Survey* 75 (15 September 1930): 486; I. M. Rubinow, *The Quest for Security* (New York: Henry Holt & Co., 1934), p. 250. On pensions, see John J. Corson and John W. McConnell, *Economic Needs of Older People* (New York: Twentieth Century Fund, 1956), p. 285; Murray Webb Latimer, *Industrial Pension Systems in the United States and Canada,* 2 vols. (New York: Industrial Relations Counselors, 1932), 2: 893, 902, 922, 931, 946–47; idem, *Trade Union Pension Systems and Other Total Disability Benefits in the United States and Canada* (New York: Industrial Relations Counselors, 1932), p. 36; "Old Age Pensions," *Encyclopedia of Social Sciences,* 15 vols. (New York: Macmillan Co., 1937), 11: 456–57.

4. U.S., Congress, House, *Economic Security Act,* pp. 38–39. See also U.S., Social Security Board, *Economic Insecurity in Old Age* (Washington, D.C.: Government Printing Office, 1937), p. 37; Frank G. Dickinson, "New Class War," *Saturday Evening Post* 210 (7 August 1937): 23, 81. Although Willa Cather's "Old Mrs. Harris," in *Obscure Destinies* (New York: A. A. Knopf, 1932), pp. 96–136, does not refer explicitly to the Depression, her themes are clearly consonant with the times.

5. Douglas, *Social Security,* pp. 6–7. See also Marie L. Dallach, "Old Age, American Style," *New Outlook* 162 (October 1933): 50; Twentieth Century Fund, Inc., *More Security for Old Age* (New York: Twentieth Century Fund, Inc., 1937), pp. 3, 9; " 'Youth' and 'Age' May Be Future Political Parties," *Science News Letter* 35 (10 June 1939): 360; Marian Castle, "Our New Old," *Harper's Magazine* 174 (February 1937): 326.

6. For a detailed analysis of Sinclair and Townsend's schemes, see Jackson K. Putnam, *Old-Age Politics in California* (Stanford: Stanford University Press, 1970), esp. chs. 3–4.

7. Daniel Nelson, *Unemployment Insurance* (Madison: University of Wisconsin Press, 1969), pp. 26–27, 152.

8. Wilbur J. Cohen, "Attitude of Organized Groups toward Social Insurance," in *Readings in Social Security,* ed. William Haber and Wilbur Cohen, 1st ed. (Englewood Cliffs, N.J.: Prentice-Hall, 1948), p. 130. See also Robert H. Bremner, *From the Depths* (New York: New York University Press, 1956), pp. 244–45; Nelson, *Unemployment Insurance,* p. 67; Richard S. Kirkendall, "The Great Depression: Another Watershed in American History?," in *Change and Continuity in Twentieth-Century America,* ed. John Braeman, Robert H. Bremner, and Everett Walters (New York: Harper & Row, 1966), p. 162.

9. For a more elaborate development of this point, see ibid., pp. 147–51; William E. Leuchtenberg, "The New Deal and the Analogue of War," in *Change and Continuity,* ed. Braeman, Bremner, and Walters, pp. 87–88; Bremner, *From the Depths,* p. 261; Otis L. Graham, Jr., *The Great Campaigns* (Englewood Cliffs, N.J.: Prentice-Hall, 1971), p. 133; Sidney Fine, *Laissez-Faire and the General Welfare State* (Ann Arbor: University of Michigan Press, 1956), pp. 373–78, 397; Henry Steele Commager, *The American Mind* (New Haven: Yale University Press, 1950), pp. 210–20, 337–38, 355–58; Barry Karl, *Executive Reorganization and Reform in the New Deal* (Cambridge, Mass.: Harvard University Press, 1963), pp. viii, 259.

10. For a fuller discussion, see Roy Lubove, *The Struggle for Social Security, 1900–1935* (Cambridge, Mass.: Harvard University Press, 1968), p. 137; Douglas, *Social Security,* pp. 9–26; Louis Leotta, "Abraham Epstein and the Movement for Old Age Security," *Labor History* 16 (Summer 1975): 372–73.

11. Franklin Delano Roosevelt, "Review of Legislative Accomplishments of the Administration and Congress," in U.S., Congress, House, 73d Cong., 2d sess., H. Doc. 397, 1934, p. 4.

12. U.S., Congress, House, *Hearings on Economic Security Act,* p. 38. The interpretation set forth in this section, I must acknowledge, builds on the work of many other people. Good introductory analyses of the Social Security Act appear in Arthur M. Schlesinger, Jr., *The Coming of the New Deal* (Boston: Houghton Mifflin, 1958), pp. 301–15, and William E. Leuchtenberg, *Franklin D. Roosevelt and the New Deal* (New York: Harper & Row, 1963), pp. 130–33. For a comprehensive study of the actual steps leading to the passage of the act and the early days of the program, see Charles McKinley and Robert W. Frase, *Launching Social Security* (Madison: University of Wisconsin Press, 1970), and Douglas, *Social Security.* Memoirs are helpful; see, in particular, Arthur J. Altmeyer, *The Formative Years of Social Security* (Madison: University of Wisconsin Press, 1966), and Edwin E. Witte, *The Development of the Social Security Act* (Madison: University of Wisconsin Press, 1963). For cogent analyses of the philosophical origins of the act's provisions, see Lubove, *Struggle for Social Security,* and J. Douglas Brown, *An American Philosophy of Social Security* (Princeton: Princeton University Press, 1972), esp. pp. 3–25.

13. See, for example, Walter S. Gifford, "Are Old Age Pensions Un-American?," *Survey* 63 (15 March 1930): 700. This article first appeared in the February 1930 issue of *Atlantic Monthly.*

14. Richard L. Neuberger and Kelley Loe, *An Army of the Aged* (Caldwell, Idaho: Caxton Printers, 1936), pp. 50–52, 203–6; Corson and McConnell, *Economic Needs,* pp. 117–18; Putnam, *Old-Age Politics,* pp. 56–57.

15. Lubove, *Struggle for Social Security,* pp. 42–43, 142–43, 173–74.

16. U.S., Congress, Senate, *The Economic Security Act: Hearings on S. 1130,* 74th Cong., 1st sess. 1935, pp. 82–85.

17. Douglas, *Social Security,* pp. 113–14, 176–82; Altmeyer, *Formative Years,* p. 20; U.S., Social Security Board, *Social Security in America* (Washington, D.C.: Government Printing Office, 1937), p. 178.

18. Title I, *Social Security Act,* 49 Stat. 620 (1935), ch. 531. See also Arthur P. Miles, *Introduction to Public Welfare* (Boston: D. C. Heath, 1949), pp. 237–38.

19. U.S., Social Security Board, *Social Security in America,* pp. 161–71; New York state, *New York Laws,* 159th sess., 1936, ch. 693.

20. For the original wording of Title I, see U.S., Social Security Board, *Social Security Bill, Summary of Provisions, Comparison of Text of Original Bill, and Ways and Means Redraft, Compilation of Proposed Amendments, etc., for Committee on Finance* (Washington,

D.C.: Government Printing Office, 1935), p. 7. For Witte's defense, see U.S., Congress, Senate, *Economic Security Act*, p. 70. In point of fact, these laws provided no such precedent: the phrasing "compatible with decency and health" did not appear in either Massachusetts or New York statutes before 1935. For more on this, see W. Andrew Achenbaum, "Old Age in the United States, 1790 to Present" (Ph.D. diss., University of Michigan, 1976), p. 436.

21. U.S., Congress, Senate, *Economic Security Act*, pp. 70–71, 517, 917.

22. For provisions, see Title II, *Social Security Act*, 49 Stat. 620, ch. 531.

23. See, for instance, the remarks by Henry Morganthau, Jr., the secretary of the Treasury, in U.S., Congress, House, *The Economic Security Act*, pp. 901–2.

24. Douglas, *Social Security*, pp. 30–31; W. S. Woytinsky, *Labor in the United States, Basic Statistics for Social Security* (Washington, D.C.: Social Science Research Council, 1938), pp. 3–4, 26.

25. Frank Bane, "The Social Security Act Expands," *Social Service Review* 13 (December 1939): 608–9; William Haber and Wilbur J. Cohen, eds., *Social Security: Programs, Problems and Policies* (Homewood, Ill.: Richard D. Irwin, Inc., 1960), pp. 81, 87.

26. The distinction between "social adequacy" and "individual equity" was, and remains, crucial in all discussions of Social Security. See an important essay written in the 1930s by Richard Hohaus, "Equity, Adequacy and Related Factors in Social Security," in *Social Security*, ed. Haber and Cohen. For more recent analyses, see Joseph A. Pechman, Henry J. Aaron, and Michael K. Taussig, *Social Security: Perspectives for Reform* (Washington, D.C.: Brookings Institution, 1968), p. 33, and Michael Taussig, "The Social Security Retirement Program and Welfare Reform," in *Integrating Income Maintenance Programs*, ed. Irene Lurie (New York: Academic Press, 1975), pp. 212–13.

27. For an excellent discussion of the issues, see Wilbur J. Cohen, *Retirement Policies under Social Security* (Berkeley and Los Angeles: University of California Press, 1957), pp. 1–4, 25, 69–71. On the 1935 measures, see U.S., Social Security Board, *Comparison of Bills*, pp. 15, 20, 29; Murray Webb Latimer, "Notes on Retirement," Wilbur Cohen Papers, Ann Arbor, p. 8. On the 1939 amendments, see U.S., Congress, House, *Compilation of the Social Security Laws*, Document no. 312, 2 vols., 89th Cong., 1st sess., 1965, 2: 474; U.S., Congress, House, Committee on Ways and Means, *Hearings Relating to the Social Security Act Amendments of 1939*, 3 vols., 76th Cong., 1st sess., 1939, 1: 899, 3: 1158, 1192.

28. Frances Fox Piven and Richard A. Cloward, *Regulating the Poor* (New York: Vintage Books, 1971), pp. 100–104; Putnam, *Old-Age Politics*, pp. 89–115.

29. Rozwenc, *Making of American Society*, 2: 362; Robert S. Lynd and Helen M. Lynd, *Middletown in Transition* (New York: Harcourt, Brace & Co., 1937), pp. 128–129, 246.

30. See the essays by Eveline Burns and Abraham Epstein in American Association for Social Security, *Social Security in the United States* (New York: American Association for Social Security, 1936); Eveline Burns, *Toward Social Security* (New York: McGraw-Hill, 1936), pp. 53, 122; Abraham Epstein, *Insecurity*, 3d ed. rev. (1933; reprint ed., New York: Harrison Smith & Robert Haas, 1936), pp. v–vii, 759–84; Rubinow, *Quest for Security*, p. 523. See also Daniel S. Sanders, *The Impact of Reform Movements on Social Policy Change* (Fair Lawn, N.J.: R. E. Burdick, Inc., 1973), pp. 70–79, 145–48; Nelson, *Unemployment Insurance*, p. 215.

31. George H. Gallup, *The Gallup Poll: Public Opinion, 1935–1971*, 3 vols. (New York: Random House, 1972), 1: 9, 76.

32. Quoted in Michael E. Schiltz, *Public Attitudes toward Social Security, 1935–1965* (Washington, D.C.: Government Printing Office, 1970), p. 34. Schiltz's analysis of popular attitudes during the 1930s merits close reading.

33. U.S., Congress, Senate, *Constitutionality of the Social Security Act,* Document no. 74, 75th Cong., 1st sess., 1937, pp. 32–35.

34. Title VII, *Social Security Act,* sect. 702.

35. U.S., Social Security Board, *Economic Insecurity,* pp. 12–13. See also "Old Age Pensions," Encyclopedia of Social Sciences, 11: 456.

36. These statistics were calculated on the basis of data in U.S., Social Security Board, *Economic Insecurity,* pp. 4–5. For a more comprehensive analysis, see Achenbaum, "Old Age," app. 4, table J.

37. Ibid., p. 7.

38. Roy Helton, "Old People: A Rising National Problem," *Harper's Monthly* 179 (October 1939): 459.

39. Nathan W. Shock, *Trends in Gerontology,* 2d ed. (Stanford: Stanford University Press, 1957), pp. 50–51; A. I. Lansing, ed., *Cowdry's Problems of Aging,* 3d ed. (1939; reprint ed., Baltimore: Williams and Wilkins Co., 1952), pp. ix–xi; and Alfred H. Lawton, "The Historical Developments in the Biological Aspects of Aging and the Aged," *Gerontologist* 5, pt. 2 (March 1965): 29.

40. Edward J. Stieglitz, "Problems of Aging," *Science* 92 (29 November 1940): 506. See also William Malisoff, *The Span of Life* (Philadelphia: J. B. Lippincott, 1937), pp. 285, 290; George Lawton, "The Study of Senescence: Psychiatric and Sociological Aspects," *American Journal of Sociology* 44 (September 1938): 280–81.

CHAPTER 8

1. "Social Security—Forty Years Later," *Social Security Bulletin* (August 1975), p. 1; U.S., Department of Health, Education and Welfare, "History of Program Provisions of Old–Age, Survivors, Disability, and Health Insurance and of the Supplemental Security Income for the Aged, Blind and Disabled, 1935–1974, and Automatic Increases under the Social Security Programs Effective 1975," Publication no. 76–11703 (Washington, D.C.: Government Printing Office, 1976), p. 3.

2. Wilbur J. Cohen, "The Social Security Act—1935–1975: Forty Years of Progress," *Public Welfare* (Fall 1975), p. 6; "Social Security—Forty Years Later," p. 1; Edna C. Wentworth and Dena K. Motley, *Resources after Retirement,* Social Security Research Report no. 34 (Washington, D.C.: Government Printing Office, 1970), p. 8; Henry Owen and Charles L. Schultze, eds., *Setting National Priorities* (Washington, D.C.: Brookings Institution, 1976), p. 509.

3. White House Conference on Aging, *Toward a National Policy on Aging,* final report, 2 vols. (Washington, D.C.: Government Printing Office, 1971), 1: 46–59; Robert N. Butler, *Why Survive?: Being Old in America* (New York: Harper & Row, 1975), pp. 204, 329–32.

4. Robert N. Butler, "Mission of the National Institute on Aging," *Journal of the American Geriatric Society* 25 (March 1977): 97.

5. The phrase comes from Michael Harrington, *The Other America* (Baltimore: Penguin Books, 1962), p. 117. See also Harold L. Wilensky and Charles Lebeaux, *Industrial Society and Social Welfare* (New York: Russell Sage, 1958); John Kenneth Galbraith, *The Affluent Society* (1958; reprint ed., New York: New American Library, 1970), pp. 100–115; Mollie Orshansky, "Counting the Poor: Another Look at the Poverty Profile," *Social Security Bulletin* 28 (Summer 1965): 3–29; Sar A. Levitan, *The Great Society's Poor Law* (Baltimore: The Johns Hopkins University Press, 1969), pp. 309–13; Herman P. Miller, "Recent Trends in Family Income," in *Issues in Social Inequality,* ed. Gerald Thielbar and Saul Feldman (Boston: Little, Brown & Co., 1972), pp. 375–81.

6. This interpretation is based on my reading of Robert Lampman, "What Does It Do for the Poor?" *Public Interest,* no. 34 (Winter 1974), p. 74; James L. Sundquist, ed., *On Fighting Poverty* (New York: Basic Books, 1969), pp. 6–8, 34–36; Daniel P. Moynihan, ed., *On Understanding Poverty* (New York: Basic Books, 1968), pp. 19, 68.

7. Michael E. Schiltz, *Public Attitudes toward Social Security, 1935–65* (Washington, D.C.: Government Printing Office, 1970), pp. 124–29; Richard Harris, *A Sacred Trust* (New York: New American Library, 1966); J. Douglas Brown, *An American Philosophy of Social Security* (Princeton: Princeton University Press, 1972), chs. 14–15; Theodore Marmor, *The Politics of Medicare,* rev. ed. (Chicago: Aldine Publishing Co., 1973); Karen Davis, *National Health Insurance* (Washington, D.C.: The Brookings Institution, 1975).

8. Older Americans Act of 1965, 42 U.S.C., ch. 3001. See also Butler, *Why Survive?,* pp. 125–30, 153, 329, and William Oriol and David Affeldt, "Federal Directions for the Aged," *Social Policy* 7 (November/December 1976): 76.

9. "Social Security—Forty Years Later," p. 4.

10. Alvin Schorr, *Explorations in Social Policy* (New York: Basic Books, 1968), p. 299; Wilbur Cohen and Milton Friedman, *Social Security: Universal or Selective?* (Washington,

D.C.: American Enterprise Institute, 1972), ch. 1. For somewhat more critical evaluations, see Nathan Glazer, "The Limits of Social Policy," *Commentary* 52 (September 1971): 54, 57; Frederick Doolittle et al., "The Mirage of Welfare Reform," *Public Interest,* no. 47 (Spring 1977), p. 63.

11. Henry Pratt, *The Gray Lobby* (Chicago: The University of Chicago Press, 1977); Nathan W. Shock, *Trends in Gerontology,* 2d ed. (Stanford: Stanford University Press, 1957), p. 89; Butler, *Why Survive?,* pp. 335–43, 435.

12. Nathan W. Shock, *Trends in Gerontology* (Stanford: Stanford University Press, 1951), p. 86. In the 1950s, Shock compiled the first exhaustive bibliography on research in gerontology and geriatrics. It remains an invaluable source, in part because Shock continues to update it in bibliographic sections in the *Journal of Gerontology.* The best current reference on "the state of the field" is the three-volume *Handbook on Aging* (New York: Van Nostrand Reinhold, 1976–77) cited throughout the chapter.

13. Paul R. Harbrecht, *Pension Funds and Economic Power* (New York: The Twentieth Century Fund, 1959), pp. 5–11; "Pensions: What to Do about the Old Folks," *Newsweek* 35 (20 March 1950): 58, 63; Peter F. Drucker, "Pension Fund 'Socialism,' " *Public Interest,* no. 42 (Winter 1976), p. 5.

14. Peter F. Drucker, *The Unseen Revolution* (New York: Harper & Row, 1976), ch. 1. The statistics come from data in Shock, *Trends,* 2d. ed., p. 40; Margaret S. Gordon, "The Older Worker and Retirement Policies," *Monthly Labor Review* 83 (June 1960): 578; U.S., Bureau of the Census, *Historical Statistics of the United States* (Washington, D.C.: Government Printing Office, 1957), p. 73; ibid., *The Statistical Abstract of the United States,* 96th ed. (New York: Grosset & Dunlap, 1976), p. 293. The commercial edition of this volume is called *The U.S. Fact Book,* and will be cited as such henceforth.

15. U.S., Congress, Senate, *The Economic Security Act: Hearings on S. 1130,* 74th Cong., 1st sess., 1935, pp. 179, 989, 1238, 1269; Wilbur J. Cohen, *Retirement Policies under Social Security* (Berkeley: University of California Press, 1957), pp. 3, 17–21; Murray Webb Latimer, "Notes on Retirement Age," Wilbur Cohen Papers, Ann Arbor, pp. 3–5.

16. The 1951 data cited in this paragraph come from Peter O. Steiner and Robert Dorfman, *The Economic Status of the Aged* (Berkeley: University of California Press, 1957), p. 110; the 1967 data from Butler, *Why Survive?,* p. 24; and the 1968 statistics from Lenore Epstein Bixby et al., *Demographic and Economic Characteristics of the Aged,* Social Security Administration Research Report no. 45 (Washington, D.C.: Government Printing Office, 1975), p. 139. British surveys reveal comparable trends; see Peter Townsend and Dorothy Wedderburn, *The Aged in the Welfare State* (London: G. Bell and Sons, Ltd., 1965), pp. 77, 104, 109.

17. Bixby et al., *Demographic and Economic Characteristics,* p. 138; Wilbur J. Cohen, "Income Maintenance for the Aged," in *Social Contributions by the Aging,* ed. Clark Tibbitts (Philadelphia: The Annals of the American Academy of Political and Social Science, 1952), p. 154.

18. Statistics come from *U.S. Fact Book,* p. 403. See also James Schulz et al., *Providing Adequate Retirement Income* (Hanover: University of New England Press, 1974), pp. 10–16; Owen and Schultze, *Setting Priorities,* p. 523; Robert D. Plotnick and Felicity Skidmore, *Progress against Poverty* (New York: Academic Press, 1975), pp. 73–74.

19. Steiner and Dorfman, *Economic Status of the Aged,* pp. 110–13; James N. Morgan et al., *Income and Welfare in the United States* (New York: McGraw-Hill, 1962), p. 194; Janet A. Fisher, "Measuring the Adequacy of Retirement Incomes," in *Aging and the Economy,* ed. Harold Orbach and Clark Tibbitts (Ann Arbor: University of Michigan Press, 1963), p. 107; Wentworth and Motley, *Resources after Retirement,* p. 10; Peter Henle, "Recent Trends in Retirement Benefits Related to Earnings," *Monthly Labor Review* 95 (January 1972): 15–29; Schulz et al., *Retirement Income,* p. 43; Bixby et al., *Demographic and Economic Characteristics,* pp. 75–79, 139.

20. *U.S. Fact Book,* pp. 401, 403. Comparable trends have persisted since the 1950s, when such data were first collected on the aged. See James Schulz, *Economics of Aging* (Belmont: Wadsworth Publishing, 1976), ch. 2.

21. U.S., Social Security Board, *Social Security in America* (Washington, D.C.: Government Printing Office, 1937), p. 189; Ethel E. McClure, *More Than a Roof* (St. Paul: Minnesota Historical Society, 1968), pp. 169, 234–39.

22. "Nursing Homes Offer an Investment Lure," *Business Week* (23 July 1966), p. 113. An analogous argument about the indirect effects of old-age legislation on the housing industry and other commercial enterprises might also be made. See, for instance, "How the Old Age Market Looks," ibid. (13 February 1960), p. 72, and "Retirement City—Haven or Ghetto?," ibid. (11 April 1964), p. 128–30.

23. Butler, *Why Survive?*, pp. 261–67, 286–87. See also Richard A. Garvin and Robert E. Burger, *Where They Go to Die* (New York: Delacorte Press, 1968), and Claire Townsend, *Old Age: The Last Segregation* (New York: Bantam Books, 1971).

24. Philip Klein et al., *A Social Study of Pittsburgh* (New York: Columbia University Press, 1938), p. 610; Ethel J. Hart, "The Responsibility of Relatives under State Old-Age Assistance Laws," *Social Service Review* 16 (March 1941): 24.

25. Robert M. Dinkel, "Attitudes of Children toward Supporting Aged Parents," *American Sociological Review* 9 (August 1944): 375–79; Karl R. Stolz, *Making the Most of the Rest of Life* (New York: Abingdon-Cokesbury Press, 1941), p. 110.

26. Although income is an important factor determining living arrangements among the elderly, it obviously is not the only factor. Advancing age and the death of a spouse cause changes in residential patterns in ways that had obtained prior to 1935. Furthermore, it is probable that increased adult longevity and long-term changes in the elderly male–female ratio have been more responsible than the existence of old-age assistance and insurance benefits for the rising likelihood that older women will be found living alone. (Indeed, only twenty percent of all older people were living alone in 1940, compared to fifty percent in 1970.) For more thorough analyses of changes in living patterns during the past forty years, see Matilda White Riley et al., *Aging and Society*, 3 vols. (New York: Russell Sage, 1968–72), 1: 168; Hugh Clark and Paul Glick, *Marriage and Divorce* (Cambridge, Mass.: Harvard University Press, 1970), p. 155; Paul Glick, "A Demographer Looks at American Families," *Journal of Marriage and the Family* 37 (February 1975): 24; A. Chevan and J. H. Korson, "The Widowed Who Live Alone: An Examination of Social and Demographic Factors," *Social Forces* 57 (1972): 45–53; James N. Morgan et al., *Five Thousand American Families*, 4 vols. to date (Ann Arbor: Institute of Social Research, 1974–), 4: 158–71.

27. For a more comprehensive discussion of these issues, see the important essays by Margaret Keeney Rosenheim, Max Rheinstein, and Juanita Kreps in *Social Structure and the Family*, ed. Ethel Shanas and Gordon F. Streib (Englewood Cliffs, N.J.: Prentice-Hall, 1965); Morgan et al. *Income and Welfare*, pp. 158–60, 177; Schorr, *Social Policy*, pp. 94, 110–12; and Ethel Shanas and Marvin B. Sussman, eds., *Family, Bureaucracy and the Elderly* (Durham: Duke University Press, 1977).

28. Ethel Shanas and Associates, *Old People in Three Industrial Societies* (New York: Atherton Press, 1968), pp. 426–27; Butler, *Why Survive?*, p. 267.

29. See, for instance, James Birren et al., *Human Aging*, 2 vols. (Washington, D.C.: National Institute of Mental Health, 1971); Caleb Finch and Leonard Hayflick, eds., *Handbook of the Biology of Aging* (New York: Van Nostrand Reinhold, 1977); and Erdman Palmore, ed., *Normal Aging* (Durham: Duke University Press, 1974).

30. Data come from Jon Hendricks and C. Davis Hendricks, *Aging in Mass Society* (Cambridge, Mass.: Winthrop Publishing, 1977), p. 177. For summaries of the "state of the field" in efforts to formulate satisfactory physiological theories of old age and aging at various points in time between 1940 and the present, see A. I. Lansing, "General Physiology," in *Cowdry's Problems of Aging*, ed. A. I. Lansing, 3d ed. (1939; reprint ed. Baltimore: Williams and Wilkins, 1952), pp. 4–17; Alex Comfort, *The Biology of Senescence* (New York: Rinehart, 1956); Eugene A. Confrey and Marcus S. Goldstein, "The Health Status of Aging People," in *Handbook of Social Gerontology*, ed. Clark Tibbitts (Chicago: The University of Chicago Press, 1960), pp. 165–72; Howard J. Curtis, "Biological Mechanisms Underlying the Aging Process," *Science* 141 (22 August 1963): 686–94; and Douglas C. Kimmel, *Adulthood and Aging* (New York: John Wiley and Sons, Inc., 1974), pp. 344–56.

31. A. T. Welford, *Skill and Age* (London: Oxford University Press, 1951), p. 147. Others have amplified Welford's findings over time. See, for example, Shock, *Trends in Gerontology*, 2d ed., p. 27; and the essays by Walter W. Survillo and Jack Szafran in *Human Aging and Behavior*, ed. George Telland (New York: Academic Press, 1968).

32. Among the earliest reports in this vein were Jerome A. Mark, "Comparative Job Performance by Age," *Monthly Labor Review* 80 (December 1957): 1467–51; Shock,

Trends in Gerontology, 2d ed., pp. 25–26; Welford, *Skill and Age*, pp. 148–49; Alastair Heron and Sheila M. Chown, "Expectations of Supervisors concerning Older Workers," in *Processes of Aging*, ed. Richard H. Williams et al., 2 vols. (New York: Atherton Press, 1963), 1: 282–83.

33. James E. Birren, Klaus F. Riegel, and Donald F. Morrison, "Intellectual Capacities, Aging and Man's Environment," in *Processes of Aging*, ed. Williams, 1: 37–38. Birren's pathbreaking work has been known for nearly three decades. For an early reporting, see "Why We Grow Old," *Newsweek* 36 (2 October 1950): 42, 44. See also Kimmel, *Adulthood and Aging*, pp. 376, 381; Hendricks and Hendricks, *Aging*, pp. 140–44.

34. Harvey C. Lehman, *Age and Achievement* (Princeton: Princeton University Press, 1953), pp. 17, 33; Butler, *Why Survive?*, pp. 77–79.

35. Two of the earliest proponents of this viewpoint were Erik K. Erikson, *Childhood and Society*, 2d ed. (1950; reprint ed., New York: W. W. Norton, 1963), pp. 268–74; and David Riesman, "Some Clinical and Cultural Aspects of Aging," *American Journal of Sociology* 59 (January 1954): 379. For more recent discussions, see Bernice L. Neugarten, ed., *Middle Age and Aging* (Chicago: The University of Chicago Press, 1968); Jack Botwinick, *Aging and Behavior* (New York: Springer Publishing Co., 1973), p. 92; George L. Maddox and Elizabeth B. Douglass, "Aging and Individual Differences: A Longitudinal Analysis of Social, Psychological and Physiological Indicators," *Journal of Gerontology* 29 (September 1974): 555–65; and James Birren and K. Warner Schaie, eds., *Handbook of the Psychology of Aging* (New York: Van Nostrand Reinhold, 1977).

36. Irving Rosow, *Social Integration of the Aged* (New York: Free Press, 1967), pp. 10–13; Margaret Clark and Barbara Anderson, *Culture and Aging* (Springfield, Ill.: Charles C. Thomas, 1967), pp. 176–77, 390; Gordon F. Streib and Clement J. Schneider, *Retirement in American Society* (Ithaca: Cornell University Press, 1971), p. 181.

37. William Masters and Virginia Johnson, *Human Sexual Response* (Boston: Little, Brown, 1966), pp. 238–41, 263; Botwinick, *Aging and Behavior*, pp. 46–48; Riley and Associates, *Aging and Society*, 1: 262; I. Rubin, *Sexual Life after Sixty* (New York: Basic Books, 1976).

38. Evelyn Mills Duval, "Aging Family Members' Roles and Relationships," in White House Conference on Aging, *National Policy on Aging*, 1: 209–10; "Louis Harris Survey for NCOA Assesses Myths and Realities of Life for Older Americans," *Perspectives on Aging* 4 (March/April 1975): 19.

39. For a classic study of retirement in the 1950s, see Eugene A. Friedmann and Robert J. Havighurst, *The Meaning of Work and Retirement* (Chicago: The University of Chicago Press, 1954), pp. 1–4, 181–85, 190–94. For more recent appraisals, see George L. Maddox, "Retirement as a Social Event in the United States," in *Aging and Social Policy*, ed. John C. McKinney and Frank T. deVyver (New York: Appelton-Century-Crofts, 1966), pp. 119, 132; and Harold L. Sheppard, "Work and Retirement," in *Handbook of Aging and the Social Sciences*, ed. Robert H. Binstock and Ethel Shanas (New York: Van Nostrand Reinhold, 1976).

40. R. J. Havighurst, "Flexibility in Retirement," *American Journal of Sociology* 59 (1959): 309; Streib and Schneider, *Retirement*, pp. 165–66; Binstock and Shanas, eds., *Handbook of Aging*, esp. pts. 3, 4; Bert Kruger Smith, *Aging in America* (Boston: Beacon Press, 1973).

41. For proposals to reform Social Security and other income programs, see Joseph A. Pechman, Henry J. Aaron, and Michael K. Taussig, *Social Security: Perspectives for Reform* (Washington, D.C.: Brookings Institution, 1968); Martin Feldstein, "Toward a Reform of Social Security," *Public Interest*, no. 40 (Summer 1975), pp. 80–81; Schulz, *Economics of Aging*, pp. 96–107, 146–51. See also Milton Friedman, *Capitalism and Freedom* (Chicago: University of Chicago Press, 1962); D. P. Moynihan, *The Politics of a Guaranteed Income* (New York: Random House, 1973); and Glazer, "Social Policy," pp.54–57.

42. Plotnick and Skidmore, *Progress against Poverty*, pp. xi, 32–37, 180; Schulz, *Economics of Aging*, pp. 25–30; Morgan et al., *Five Thousand Families*, 4: 336; Morton Paglin, "The Measurement and Trend of Inequality: A Basic Revision," *American Economic Review* 65 (September 1975): 598–609.

43. Irene Lurie, ed., *Integrating Income Maintenance Programs* (New York: Academic Press, 1975), pp. 10–15.

44. Owen and Schultze, *Setting Priorities*, pp. 555–58; James Q. Wilson and Patricia Rachel, "Can Government Regulate Itself?," *Public Interest*, no. 46 (Winter 1977), p. 4; Robert Binstock and Martin Levin, "The Political Dilemmas of Intervention Politics," in *Handbook of Aging*, ed. Binstock and Shanas, pp. 511–35.

45. Sundquist, ed., *Fighting Poverty*, pp. 219–20; Marmor, *Politics of Medicare*, p. 90; Glazer, "Social Policy," pp. 53–54.

46. For a fuller development of this point, see Lampman, "What Does It Do for the Poor?," and Gilbert Y. Steiner, "Reform Follows Reality," *Public Interest*, no. 34 (Winter 1974).

47. See, for instance, Sar A. Levitan et al., *Still a Dream* (Cambridge, Mass.: Harvard University Press, 1975), pp. 37, 216–21, 237; Hendricks and Hendricks, *Aging*, pp. 349–79; Moynihan, *Understanding Poverty*; Institute of Gerontology, *Minority Aged in America* (Ann Arbor: Institute of Gerontology, 1975).

48. Tish Sommers, "Social Security: A Feminist Critique," in Institute of Gerontology, *The Economics of Aging* (Ann Arbor: Institute of Gerontology, 1976), pp. 57–71; Dalmer Hoskins and Lenore E. Bixby, *Women and Social Security*, Social Security Administration Report no. 42 (Washington, D.C.: Government Printing Office, 1973), pp. 90–94; Institute of Gerontology, *No Longer Young* (Ann Arbor: Institute of Gerontology, 1975).

49. Juanita M. Kreps, *Lifetime Allocation of Work and Income* (Durham, N.C.: Duke University Press, 1971), pp. 145, 153–54; Juanita M. Kreps, ed., *Employment, Income and Retirement Problems of the Aged* (Durham: Duke University Press, 1963), p. 207.

50. Schulz et al., *Retirement Income*, pp. 60–64. For a clear discussion of the assumptions made in calculating social security costs and benefits, see R. J. Myers, *Social Insurance and Allied Government Programs* (Homewood: Richard D. Irwin, Inc., 1965).

51. Owen and Schultze, *Setting Priorities*, pp. 1, 13; John Rawls, *Toward a Theory of Justice* (Cambridge, Mass.: Harvard University Press, 1971), pp. 250–60; Duncan Mac Rae, Jr., *The Social Function of Social Science* (New Haven: Yale University Press, 1976), pp. 278, 306; Otis L. Graham, Jr., *Toward a Planned Society* (New York: Oxford University Press, 1976), esp. ch. 6.

52. Elias S. Cohen, "Toward a Social Policy on Aging," *Gerontologist* 10 (Winter 1970), pt. 2, p. 20. For the results of two initial forays in this area, see Bernice L. Neugarten and Robert J. Havighurst, eds., *Social Policy, Social Ethics and the Aging Society* (Washington, D.C.: Government Printing Office, 1977), and the forthcoming proceedings of a two-year "Human Values and Aging" project, directed by David D. Van Tassel. At the Institute of Gerontology in Ann Arbor, John Tropman, Terrence Tice, and I are currently studying the relationship between changing social values and old-age policies in recent American history.

53. Butler, *Why Survive?*, p. 12.

54. Louis Harris and Associates, Inc., *The Myth and Reality of Aging in America* (Washington, D.C.: The National Council on the Aging, 1975), pp. 30–33, 46, 174, 204.

55. Ibid., pp. 193, 196. See also Beth B. Hess, "Stereotypes of the Aged," *Journal of Communication* 24 (1974): 76–85; Adella J. Harris and Jonathan F. Feinberg, "Television and Aging," *Gerontologist* 17 (October 1977): 464–69.

56. For example, Elaine Cumming and William E. Henry argued, in *Growing Old* (New York: Basic Books, 1961), p. 14, that "aging is an inevitable, mutual withdrawal or disengagement, resulting in decreased interaction between the aging person and others in the social systems he belongs to." Although most elderly people do withdraw from previous activities to some degree, Cumming and Henry's formulation provoked heated controversy because it described modal tendencies as if they were innate and universal and because it played down important mediating circumstances and variations in the disengagement process. Indeed, the original tenets have been radically transformed as a result of subsequent research. Scholars now play closer attention to the problems of measuring social, psychological, and normative engagement and cross-sectional differences in race, sex, occupation, and location. The lesson is clear: gerontologists must exercise great care to ensure that their research does not compound problems of shaping programs for a population with diverse and fluid interests and needs. See Arlie Russell Hochschild, "Disengagement Theory: A Critique and Proposal," *American Sociological Review* 40 (October 1975): 553–69.

57. William E. Oriol, "Social Policy Priorities; Age vs. Youth; The Federal Government," *Gerontologist* 10 (Autumn 1970): 207–8; Amitai Etzioni, "Old People and Public Policy," *Social Policy* 7 (November/December 1976): 21; Paul J. Nathanson, "Age Discrimination in Employment," *Humanist* 37 (September/October 1977): 9.

CONCLUSION

1. In building models based on "modernization theory," readers should consider the suggestions offered in Raymond Grew, "Modernization and Its Discontents," *American Behavioral Scientist* 21 (November/December 1977): 289–312; and W. Andrew Achenbaum and Peter N. Stearns, "Old Age and Modernization," *Gerontologist* 18 (June 1978): 307–13.

APPENDIX: TECHNICAL NOTE B

1. U.S., Bureau of the Census, *Eleventh Census of the United States: 1890*, 25 vols. (Washington, D.C.: Government Printing Office, 1895–99), vol. 1, *Population*, pt. 2, p. cxxii. See also U.S., Bureau of the Census, *Ninth Census of the United States: 1870. Statistics of Population*, 2 parts (Washington, D.C.: Government Printing Office, 1871), pt. 1, pp. 660–63; U.S., *Senate Miscellaneous Documents*, no. 26, 45th Cong., 3d sess., 1878, pp. 11–12, 15; U.S., Bureau of the Census, *Twelfth Census of the United States: 1900*, 10 vols. (Washington, D.C.: Government Printing Office, 1904), *Special Reports: Occupations*, pp. xxiii, cxvii.

2. Carroll D. Wright, *History and Growth of the U.S. Census* (Washington, D.C.: Government Printing Office, 1900), pp. 154–55, 157, 166, 171.

3. Ibid., p. 178.

4. John B. Sharpless and Ray M. Shortridge, "The Methodological Implications of Enumeration Bias in Census Manuscripts," *Journal of Urban History* 1 (August 1975): 409–39.

5. R. J. Meyers, "Errors and Bias in the Reporting of Ages in Census Data," *Transactions of the Actuarial Society of America* 14 (1940): 395–415.

6. Edwin G. Nourse, *America's Capacity to Produce* (Washington, D.C.: The Brookings Institution, 1934), pp. 496–98.

7. For a more detailed analysis of the implications of this change for studying the aged's work patterns in historical perspective, see Louis J. Ducoff and Margaret Jarman Hagood, *Labor Force Definition and Measurement*, Social Science Research Council Bulletin 56 (New York: Social Science Research Council, 1947); John D. Durand, *The Labor Force in the United States* (1948; reprint ed., New York: John Wiley & Sons, Inc. 1968), pp. 12–13, 197–200.

Selected Bibliography

Books

Altmeyer, Arthur J. *The Formative Years of Social Security*. Madison: University of Wisconsin Press, 1966.

American Association for Social Security. *Social Security in the United States*. New York: American Association for Social Security, 1936.

Armstrong, Barbara N. *Insuring the Essentials*. New York: The Macmillan Co., 1932.

Bailey, Thomas. *Records of Longevity: With an Introductory Discourse on Vital Statistics*. London: Darton and Co., 1859.

Barkin, Solomon. *The Older Worker in Industry*. Albany: J. B. Lyon, 1933.

Barnes, The Rev'd. Albert. *Life at Three-Score: A Sermon*. 2d ed. Philadelphia: Parry and McMillan, 1859.

Barton, William. *Observations on the Progress of Population and the Probabilities of Duration of Human Life in the United States of America*. Philadelphia: Aitken, 1791.

Beard, George M. *American Nervousness*. New York: G. P. Putnam's Sons, 1881.

———. *Legal Responsibility in Old Age*. New York: Russells', 1874.

Beecher, Catherine E., and Stowe, Harriet Beecher. *The American Woman's Home: or, Principles of Domestic Science*. New York: J. B. Ford, 1869.

Bell, John, M.D. *On Regimen and Longevity*. Philadelphia: Hasnell and Johnson, 1842.

Bennett, Sanford. *Old Age, Its Causes and Prevention: The Story of an Old Body and Face Made Young*. New York: The Physical Culture Publishing Co., 1912.

Bernard, Thomas. *The Comforts of Old Age*. 5th ed. London: John Murray, 1820.

Binstock, Robert, and Shanas, Ethel, eds. *Handbook of Aging and the Social Sciences*. New York: Van Nostrand Reinhold, 1976.

Birren, James, and Schaie, K. Warner, eds. *Handbook of the Psychology of Aging*. New York: Van Nostrand Reinhold, 1977.

Bourne, Randolph S. *Youth and Life*. 1913. Reprint. New York: Books for Libraries Press, Inc., 1967.

Bowen, William G., and Finegan, T. Aldrich. *The Economics of Labor Force Participation*. Princeton: Princeton University Press, 1969.

Brackenridge, Henry Marie. *A Eulogy, On The Lives and Characters of John Adams and Thomas Jefferson*. Pensacola, Fla.: W. Hasell Hunt, 1826.

Brown, Edmund Osgood. *De Senectute*. Chicago: The Lakeside Press, 1914.

Brown, J. Douglas. *An American Philosophy of Social Security*. Princeton: Princeton University Press, 1972.

Burns, Eveline M. *The American Social Security System*. Boston: Houghton-Mifflin, 1949.

Butler, Robert N., M.D. *Why Survive?: Being Old in America*. New York: Harper & Row, 1975.

Caldwell, Charles, M.D. *Thoughts on the Effects of Age on the Human Constitution*. Louisville: John C. Noble, 1846.

Cappon, Lester J., ed. *The Adams-Jefferson Letters*. 2 vols. Chapel Hill: Institute of Early American History and Culture, 1959.

Carlisle, Anthony. *An Essay on the Disorders of Old Age, and on the Means for Prolonging Human Life*. London: Longman, 1817.

Charcot, J. M. , M.D. *Clinical Lectures on the Diseases of Old Age*. Translated by Leigh Hunt. New York: William Wood, 1881.

Child, Charles Manning. *Senescence and Rejuvenescence*. Chicago: The University of Chicago Press, 1915.

Child, L. Maria. *Looking toward Sunset*. Boston: Ticknor and Fields, 1866.

Cohen, Wilbur J. *Retirement Policies under Social Security*. Berkeley and Los Angeles: University of California Press, 1957.

Comfort, Alex. *The Biology of Senescence*. New York: Rinehart, 1956.

Cooper, James Fenimore. *The Prairie*. 1827. Reprint. New York: Holt, Rinehart & Winston, 1965.

Cowdry, Edmund Vincent. *Problems of Aging: Biological and Medical Aspects*. 3d ed. Baltimore: Williams and Wilkins Co., 1952.

Cumming, Elaine, and Henry, William E. *Growing Old*. New York: Basic Books, 1961.

de Beauvoir, Simone. *The Coming of Age*. New York: Putnam's Sons, 1972.

Depew, Chauncey Mitchell. *My Memories of Eighty Years*. 1921. Reprint. New York: Charles Scribner's Sons, 1924.

DePuy, W. H., D.D. *Three Score Years and Beyond*. New York: Nelson and Phillips, 1873.

Derber, Milton, ed. *The Aged and Society*. New York: Industrial Relations Research Association, 1950.

Devine, Edward T. *Misery and Its Causes*. New York: The Macmillan Co., 1909.

Dorland, W. A. Newman. *The Age of Mental Virility*. New York: The Century Co., 1908.

Douglas, Paul H. *Social Security in the United States*. New York: McGraw-Hill Book Co., 1936.

Eaves, Lucille, ed. *Aged Clients of Boston Social Agencies*. Boston: Women's Educational and Industrial Union, 1925.

Epstein, Abraham. *The Challenge of the Aged*. New York: Vanguard Press, 1928.

Evans, Harry C. *The American Poorfarm and Its Inmates*. Mooseheart, Ill.: Fraternal Congresses and Loyal Order of the Moose, 1926.

Finch, Caleb, and Hayflick, Leonard, eds. *Handbook of the Biology of Aging*. New York: Van Nostrand Reinhold, 1977.

Gallup, George H. *The Gallup Poll: Public Opinion, 1935–1971*. 3 vols. New York: Random House, 1972.

Gardner, John, M.D. *Longevity: The Means of Prolonging Life after Middle Age*. London: Henry S. King, 1874.

Gay, Ebenezer. *The Old Man's Calendar*. Stockbridge: Loring Andrews, 1794.

Glasson, William H. *Federal Military Pensions in the United States*. New York: Oxford University Press, 1918.

Gruman, Gerald J., M.D. *A History of Ideas about the Prolongation of Life: The Evolution of Prolongevity Hypotheses to 1800*. Philadelphia: The American Philosophical Society, 1966.

Haber, William, and Cohen, Wilbur J., eds. *Social Security: Programs, Problems and Policies*. Homewood, Ill.: Richard D. Irwin, Inc., 1960.

Hall, G. Stanley. *Senescence: The Last Half of Life*. New York: D. Appelton & Co., 1922.

Harrington, Michael. *The Other America*. Baltimore: Penguin Books, 1962.

Harris, Louis, and Associates. *The Myth and Reality of Aging in America*. Washington, D.C.: The National Council on the Aging, 1975.

Hollingworth, Harry L. *Mental Growth and Decline: A Survey of Developmental Psychology*. New York: D. Appleton & Co., 1927.

Hufeland, Christopher Wilhelm. *The Art of Prolonging Life*. 1797. Reprint. New York: Thomas O'Kane, 1873.

Humphry, George Murray. *Old Age: The Results of Information Received Respecting Nearly Nine Hundred Persons Who Had Attained the Age of Eighty Years, Including Seventy-Four Centenarians*. Cambridge: Macmillan and Bowes, 1889.

Institute of Gerontology. *Minority Aged in America*. Ann Arbor: Institute of Gerontology, 1975.

Jewett, Sarah Orne. *The Country of the Pointed Firs and Other Stories*. Garden City: Doubleday & Co., Anchor edition, 1956.

Johnson, Alexander. *The Almshouse: Construction and Management*. New York: Charities Publication Committee, 1911.

Kellogg, John Harvey, M.D. *Plain Facts for Old and Young*. Burlington, Iowa: Segner & Condit, 1881.

Kreps, Juanita M., ed. *Lifetime Allocation of Work and Income: Essays in the Economics of Aging*. Durham, N.C.: Duke University Press, 1971.

Lathrop, Reverend S. G. *Fifty Years and Beyond; or, Gathered Gems for the Aged*. New York: F. H. Revell, 1881.

Latimer, Murray Webb. *Industrial Pension Systems in the United States and Canada*. 2 vols. New York: Industrial Relations Counselors, 1932.

Lehman, Harvey C. *Age and Achievement*. Princeton: Princeton University Press, 1953.

Linford, Alton A. *Old-Age Assistance in Massachusetts*. Chicago: The University of Chicago Press, 1949.

Lobsenz, Johanna. *The Older Woman in Industry*. New York: Scribner's Sons, 1929.

Lorand, Arnold, M.D. *Old Age Deferred*. 1910. Reprint. Philadelphia: F. A. Davis, 1912.

Lubove, Roy. *The Struggle for Social Security, 1900–1935*. Cambridge, Mass.: Harvard University Press, 1968.

McKinney, John C., and deVyver, Frank T., eds. *Aging and Social Policy*. New York: Appelton-Century-Crofts, 1966.

Marmor, Theodore. *The Politics of Medicare*. Revised edition. Chicago: Aldine Publishing Co., 1973.

Martin, Lillien J., and De Gruchy, Clare. *Salvaging Old Age*. New York: The Macmillan Co., 1930.

Metchnikoff, Elie. *The Prolongation of Life*. New York: G. P. Putnam's Sons, 1908.

Minot, Charles S. *The Problem of Age, Growth and Death: A Study of Cytomorphosis*. New York: G. P. Putnam's Sons, 1908.

Nascher, I. L., M.D. *Geriatrics*. Philadelphia: P. Blakiston's Son & Co., 1914.

Nassau, Mabel Louise. *Old Age Poverty in Greenwich Village*. New York: Fleming H. Revell Co., 1915.

National Civic Federation. *Extent of Old Age Dependency*. New York: National Civic Federation, 1928.

Neugarten, Bernice L., ed. *Middle Age and Aging*. Chicago: The University of Chicago Press, 1968.

Neugarten, Bernice, and Havighurst, Robert, eds. *Social Policy, Social Ethics and the Aging Society*. Washington, D.C.: Government Printing Office, 1977.

Pearson, Karl. *The Chances of Death and Other Studies in Evolution*. 2 vols. New York: Edward Arnold, 1897.

Pechman, Joseph A.; Aaron, Henry J.; and Taussig, Michael K. *Social Security: Perspectives for Reform*. Washington, D.C.: Brookings Institution, 1968.

Pitkin, Walter B. *Life Begins at Forty*. New York: McGraw-Hill Book Co., 1932.

Pratt, Henry. *The Gray Lobby*. Chicago: The University of Chicago Press, 1977.

Putnam, Jackson K. *Old-Age Politics in California*. Stanford: Stanford University Press, 1970.

Riley, Matilda White, and Associates. *Aging and Society*. 3 vols. New York: Russell Sage Foundation, 1969–1972.

Rush, Benjamin, M.D. *Medical Inquiries and Observations, upon the Diseases of the Mind*. 1812. Reprint. New York: Hafner Publishing Co., 1962.

Sayle, Charles. *The Ages of Man*. London: John Murray, 1916.

Schiltz, Michael E. *Public Attitudes toward Social Security, 1935–1965*. Washton, D.C.: Government Printing Office, 1970.

Shaler, Nathaniel Southgate. *The Individual: A Study of Life and Death*. New York: D. Appelton & Co., 1901.

Shanas, Ethel, and Associates. *Old People in Three Industrial Societies*. New York: Atherton, 1968.

Sheldon, Henry D. *The Older Population of the United States*. New York: John Wiley and Sons, Inc., 1958.

Shock, Nathan W. *Trends in Gerontology*. Stanford: Stanford University Press, 1951.

Sieveking, Edward Henry. *The Medical Adviser in Life Assurance*. Hartford: N. P. Fletcher, 1875.

Solenberger, Alice Willard. *One Thousand Homeless Men: A Study of Original Records*. New York: Charities Publication Committee, 1911.

Squier, Lee Welling. *Old Age Dependency in the United States: A Complete Survey of the Pension Method*. New York: Macmillan Co., 1912.

Stearns, Peter N. *Old Age in European Society*. New York: Holmes & Meier, 1976.

Thoms, William J. *Human Longevity: Its Facts and Its Fictions.* New York: Scribner, Welford & Armstrong, 1873.

Thorndike, Edmund L.; Bregman, Elsie O.; Tilton, J. Warren; and Woodyard, Ella. *Adult Learning.* New York: The Macmillan Co., 1928.

Tibbitts, Clark, ed. *Handbook of Social Gerontology.* Chicago: The University of Chicago Press, 1960.

United Nations. *The Aging of Populations and Its Economic and Social Implications.* New York: United Nations, 1956.

Van Rensselaer, Reverend Cortlandt. *Old Age, A Funeral Sermon.* Washington: By the Author, 1841.

Welford, A. T. *Aging and Human Skill.* London: Oxford University Press, 1958.

White House Conference on Aging. *Toward a National Policy on Aging.* Final Report. 2 vols. Washington, D.C.: Government Printing Office, 1971.

Youmans, E. Grant, ed. *Older Rural Americans: A Sociological Perspective.* Lexington: University of Kentucky Press, 1967.

Periodicals

Years surveyed are indicated in parentheses.

Aging, Washington, D.C. (1957–76)

American Journal of Psychology, Urbana, Illinois (1887–1940)

American Journal of Sociology, Chicago (1895–1940)

American Magazine, New York (1876–1940)

American Labor Legislation Review, New York (1911–42)

Atlantic Monthly, Boston (1857–1940)

Boston Weekly Magazine, Boston (1802–41). Several magazines by this title were published independently between 1802 and 1841.

Brother Jonathan, New York (1842–43)

Burton's Gentleman's Magazine, Philadelphia (1837–40)

Catholic World, New York (1865–1940)

Charities [and the Commons], New York (1897–1909)

Commonweal, New York (1924–40)

Current Literature, New York (1888–1912)

Current Opinion, New York (1912–25)

Everybody's, New York (1899–1929)

Forum [and Century], New York (1886–1940)

Gerontologist, Washington, D.C. (1961–77)

Godey's Lady's Book, Philadelphia (1830–98)

Good Housekeeping, New York (1885–1940)

Graham's, Philadelphia (1826–58). Once known as *Atkinson's Casket.*

Harper's Bazaar, New York (1867–1940)

Harper's Magazine, New York (1850–1940)

Harper's Weekly, New York (1857–1916)

Hesperian, San Francisco. Several magazines were published independently under this title (intermittently) from 1838 to 1927.

Hours at Home, New York (1865–70)

Independent, New York & Boston (1848–1928)

International Journal of Aging & Human Development, Farmingdale; New York (ca. 1969–76)

Journal of Gerontology, Washington, D.C. (1946–77)

Knickerbocker, New York (1833–65)

Ladies' Home Journal, Philadelphia (1883–1940)

Lippincott's, Philadelphia (1868–1916)

Literary Digest, New York (1890–1938)

Littell's Living Age, Boston (1844–1941)

McClure's Magazine, New York (1893–1929)

Monthly Labor Review, Washington, D.C. (1915–76)

Munsey's Magazine, New York (1889–1929)

Nation, New York (1865–1940)

Nature, Washington, D.C. (1923–40)

Niles' [Weekly] Register, Philadelphia (1811–49)

North American Review, Boston & New York (1815–1940)

[New] Outlook, New York (1870–1935)

Overland Magazine, San Francisco (1868–1935)

Perspective on Aging, Washington, D.C. (1972–76)

Popular Science Monthly, New York (1872–1940)

Public Interest, New York (1965–77)

Putnam's, New York (1853–1910)

Reader's Digest, Pleasantville, New York (1922–40)

Sanitarian, New York (1873–1904)

Saturday Evening Post, Philadelphia (1821–1940)

Science Newsletter, Washington, D.C. (1921–40)

Scientific American [and supplements], New York (1876–1940)

Scribner's, New York (1887–1939)

U.S. Magazine and Democratic Review, Washington, D.C., & New York (1837–59)

Virginia Evangelical and Literary Magazine, Richmond, Virginia (1818–28)

Woman's Home Companion, Springfield, Ohio (1873–1940)

World Tomorrow, New York (1918–34)

Dictionaries, Encyclopedias, Almanacs, and Other Compendia

Because words such as "senility" and "retirement" have meant different things at different times, dating changes in dictionary definitions help to reveal broader, long-term changes in prevailing perceptions of old age. I have traced the meanings of various words in (successive) editions of twenty different popular and scientific dictionaries. Especially helpful were the particular revisions made over time in *An American Dictionary of the English Language* (originally compiled by Noah Webster) and *A Dictionary of Medical Science*. Dictionaries that did not have revised editions also provided valuable clues. Needless to say, I relied heavily on information in historical dictionaries, including the *Oxford English Dictionary*; Mitford M. Mathews, *A Dictionary of Americanisms on Historical Principles* (Chicago: The University of Chicago Press, 1951); and Eric Partridge, *A Dictionary of Slang and Unconventional English*, 6th ed. (New York: The Macmillan Company, 1967).

In addition, I systematically searched for pertinent material (under references such as "age," "longevity," "old age," "pensions," "retirement," and "senility") in all of the American- and/or British-published encyclopedias in the University of Michigan library system. Many contained no listings for any of my "key" words, a fact that is significant in its own right. Some apparently pirated articles from their rivals. Nevertheless, analyzing data in successive editions of the eighteen encyclopedias listed in my dissertation proved enormously helpful. I highly recommend that researchers use the *Encyclopedia Americana, Encyclopaedia Brittanica, The Encyclopedia of Social Sciences*, and *The New American Cyclopedia*.

I also utilized a fine collection of American almanacs housed in the William L. Clements Library on the Ann Arbor campus. The Clements Library has almanacs for selected years from many small communities settled east of the Mississippi. Perhaps more important, however, are the two series that enjoyed a remarkable longevity: Nathan Daboll and David Daboll's *The New England Almanack and Farmer's Friend* (1833–1900) and Robert Thomas's *The Farmer's Almanack* (1800–1923).

Finally, four different types of compendia deserve brief mention because of their importance to researchers in this field. The 1897 and 1908 editions of William Dwight Porter Bliss's *Encyclopedia of Social Reform* (New York: Funk and Wagnalls) offer a useful summary of the wide-ranging reform impulse at the beginning of the century. Chester Vernier's *American Family Laws*, 5 vols. (Stanford: Stanford University Press, 1931–38) facilitated the author's initial forays into law stacks in search for changes in family laws affecting the elderly. Victor Sheldon Clark's *History of Manufacturers in the United States*, 3 vols. (1929; reprint ed., New York, Peter Smith, 1948) provides an industry-by-industry analysis of the technological innovations adopted during the nineteenth century, which helps to explain changes in older men's occupational status. Finally, scholars will find the three-volume collection, *The Gallup Poll: Public Opinion, 1935–1971* (New York: Random House, 1972), useful in studying public attitudes in recent decades.

Government Publications

The decennial federal census provides an extraordinary wealth of information about the state of the nation in general and the status of elderly Americans in particular. To be sure, I sometimes combed volumes of tables that *almost* answered a seemingly simple question only to realize that someone had published the wrong data. Other problems with this source have already been noted. Nevertheless, with patience and persistence I found that the 1880, 1900, 1920, 1930, 1940, and 1970 censuses in particular yielded many details about the aged's demographic and socio-economic characteristics at a given point in time. Researchers should also canvass the seemingly infinite number of special reports published by the census bureau. State censuses—especially those published by Iowa, Massachusetts, Michigan, New York, Pennsylvania, and Rhode Island—are indispensable. And, when appropriate, researchers should utilize the manuscript reports on which these censuses are based.

  Series published by other federal and state government agencies should be mentioned briefly. For instance, researchers interested in public service retirement systems, institutions caring for the elderly, or public old-age relief and insurance programs before Social Security, should consult the U.S. Bureau of Labor Statistics bulletin, nos. 447, 489, and 561, respectively. In studying the relatively recent past, the first-rate studies and reports conducted by several branches of the Department of Health, Education, and Welfare (especially the Social Security Administration and the National Institute on Aging) merit careful reading.

  Those who attempt to reconstruct the evolution of old-age policies will quickly find themselves overwhelmed by the amount of data that should—much less could—be digested. The classic bibliographic aids for penetrating this nation's legal thicket proved enormously helpful. I strongly recommend consulting Benjamin Poore's *The Federal and State Constitutions,* 2d ed., 2 vols. (New York: Burt Franklin, 1972) and Francis Newton Thorpe, ed., *The Federal and State Constitutions, Colonial Charters and Other Organic Laws, 1492–1908,* 7 vols. (Washington, D.C.: Government Printing Office, 1909), which expedite efforts to study the extent of old-age discrimination/entitlement in these specific statutes. And while the time and energy spent reading committee reports and congressional hearings is rarely plea-sant, these sources are readily accessible and incredibly insightful.

An Agenda for Future Research

  Although the first published monographs on the history of old age have uncovered important continuities and changes in the meanings and experiences of being old by analyzing a variety of sources and studying trends over a relatively lengthy period of time, readers should note that there is a lot of room in this new area of research for a great deal more historical work. Some current controversies will have to be resolved, a few should be dismissed as spurious, and still others need to be redefined in light of new evidence and more sophisticated conceptual frameworks. Indeed, my own research in the field thus far suggests many key topics and issues that deserve intensive and extensive examination in the future.

  For example, we need to learn far more than we currently know about the actual socioeconomic characteristics and behavioral patterns of older Americans between the Revolutionary and Civil wars. (Undoubtedly, much of this information will emerge from careful case studies of local communities.) Furthermore, we ought to retrace the historic record of groups within the population over sixty-five years old.

Because the particular opportunities and problems of men and women in past times diverged in many important respects, it is necessary to investigate more systematically any long-term variations in the circumstances and conceptions of aged men and older women. More attention must be paid to the ways that major developments in the history of the elderly foreign-born depart from those of the native-born. Age-specific regional, ecological, class, and occupational differences merit fuller consideration. In light of current national problems and priorities, it is clearly imperative that we carefully assess the extent to which the situation of older blacks and other minority-group members has differed from the modal conditions of the aged white population in the past. Above all, we must sharpen the distinctions we already make between the history of age and the history of aging; as we continue to engage in longitudinal analyses of particular stages of life, we also should investigate the distinctive life-course experiences of those who age(d) at different points in time and in divergent societal surroundings.

Considering items on the "new social history" agenda leads, in turn, to suggesting topics that might interest cultural and intellectual historians. As I hope this present work illustrates, a rigorously eclectic approach to the subject matter is in fact vital: we cannot simply study the actual behavior of historical men and women from womb to tomb; we also need to understand how definitions of the life cycle as well as the special assets and liabilities attributed to each stage of human existence have evolved over time, and then attempt to synthesize the patterns we detect. Much remains to be done before we can piece together the whole puzzle. For example, cross-sectional and longitudinal comparisons are needed of the way the old were depicted in various media. We know very little about the portrayal of the aged in American literature, music, and folklore, and even less about the images of old age in painting, sculpture, graphics, movies, radio, and television. Scholars certainly should consider utilizing autobiographies, diaries, letters, oral histories, and other archival materials in exploring the range of attitudes about being old expressed by men and women in their later years. Furthermore, definitive research into the lives of gerontology's heretofore "unsung heroes" has not yet been done. Full-length biographies of J. M. Charcot, Lillien Martin, I. L. Nascher, Mabel Louise Nassau, Walter Pitkin, I. M. Rubinow, and Lee Welling Squier are certainly needed. Penetrating investigations of the ideas about old age set forth by eminent biological scientists such as Benjamin Rush, John Harvey Kellogg, and Elie Metchnikoff, by social scientists such as Eveline Burns, Abraham Epstein, and G. Stanley Hall, and by astute commentators such as L. Maria Child, Ralph Waldo Emerson, and William James (to mention just a few) would be helpful.

Finally, prospective investigators will find that other students in the field have only started to blaze the whole frontier of social-welfare or "public" history as it broadly relates to the aged. As family historians among other social scientists begin to publish first-rate studies of the psychological, economic, and structural features of multigenerational relationships in the past, their research generates new questions. It is now apparent that careful analyses of long-term shifts in child-parent laws and inheritance patterns as well as imaginative probes into the ways that domestic architecture literally may have shaped family life should be attempted. Other issues must be pursued. For example, we should learn as much as possible about the evolution and effectiveness of earlier veterans programs before the remaining survivors of

World War II become eligible for and/or demand additional benefits. Indeed, historians have much to do right now in elucidating the intricate development and future direction of policies affecting the aged. They must ensure that the architects of the original Social Security Act and other old-age proposals as well as the pioneers in gerontological and geriatric research tape their oral histories before they die. They should join with other applied social scientists in assessing the cumulative impact of the vast institutional network that has profoundly affected the recent history of old age. They should also prepare to engage in comparative international research so that the historical record of old age in the United States can be placed in the broadest context possible.

Index

Adams, Henry, 10
Adams, John: on coping with pain, 32–33; on retirement, 21
Adams, John Quincy, 20
Administration on Aging, 146
Adolescence: first perceived as a stage of life, 1; ideas about, before 1914, 51–53
Aged
—as counselors: on agriculture, 19, 96, 98; in contemporary society, 171; on education, 18; in the future, 167–68; to grandchildren, 23, 156; on health matters, 15–16; in industry, 48, 121; on morality, 17–18; role of, diminishes, 40, 45; about ultimate meanings of life, 27, 37, 118
—as a heterogeneous group, 2–3
—as volunteers, 156
Aged, differences among
—by place of birth: in current participation in federal programs, 160; in nineteenth-century demographic trends, 61–62; in occupational status, 96–97; in twentieth-century demographic trends, 91–93. See also Immigrants, aged
—by race: in current income, 150–51; difficulties in determining, 180; in nineteenth-century demographic trends, 61–62; in occupational status, 96–97; in twentieth-century demographic trends, 91–92. See also Blacks, aged; Indians; Minority aged; Spanish-speaking elderly
—by region: demographic, 62–64, 93; occupational, 72–73
—by sex: in current situations, 158, 160; in demographic characteristics, 61, 91–92; in household status, 76–80, 152; in income, 150–51; in occupational status, 66, 96, 102. See also Widowhood; Women, aged
Age-dependency ratios, changes in, 94–95. See also Dependency, extent of, in old age
Age Discrimination in Employment Act of 1967, 149, 163–64

Age-discrimination practices in the marketplace: in antebellum society, 20–21; contemporary, 163–64; in the late nineteenth century, 50–51; in the twentieth century, 114–16
Aged's worth, conceptions of: basis for, in general, 5; between 1790 and 1860, 9–11, 24–25, 27–28; between 1865 and 1914, 39–40, 53–54, 194 n. 1; between 1914 and 1940, 109–10; current, 153–54, 162–63; "republican," 28, 31–33; "romantic," 28, 33–36; summarized, 170–71
Age heaping, 180
Ageism, 162–63
Aging as an age-old phenomenon, 1
Aging of the population structure: actual extent of, 58–64, 90–94; feared in early twentieth century, 114; impact of, on pensions today, 161; influence of, on occupational structure, 103. See also Demographic patterns
Agriculture: aged play key role in, 19, 96; and blacks, 159; covered by Social Security, 144; data problems of, 180–81; as employment in old age, 68, 72–73, 95–98, 105; importance of, in society, 19, 98; as means of preventing old-age dependency, 29, 98
Alabama, 21, 134
Alaska, 136
Alcott, Bronson, 193 n. 8
Almshouse: characteristics of inmates of, 81, 116–17; as dreaded institutional support, 29, 80, 116–17; method rejected, 151; need for alternative to, recognized, 82, 121–22
American Association for Old Age Security, 122, 130
American Association for Social Security, 130
American Association of Labor Legislation, 122, 132
American Colonization Society, 24

American Express Company, 49
American Federation of Labor: endorses state-funded insurance, 130; opposes old-age pensions, 83. *See also* Unions
American Geriatrics Society, 147
American Medical Association, 147
American Psychological Association, 147–48
American Revolution. *See* Revolutionary War and the aged
Andrews, John B., 132
Aristotle, 4
Arizona, 83, 135
Arkansas, 134
Asian-American elderly, 160
Attitudes toward old age, distinguished from perceptions, 187 n. 9. *See also* Aged's worth, conceptions of; Old age, relationship between "rhetoric" and "reality" of

Bailey, Thomas, 15
Bailey, William, 119
Baldwin, F. Spencer, 49–50
Baltimore and Ohio Railroad, 24; establishes retirement policy, 49
Barton, William, 12
Beard, George M., 46–47
Belknap, Jeremy, 13
Bell, John, 13–14
Bickerstaff, Isaac, 23
Big-business organizations: impact of, on nineteenth-century ideas about the aged, 47–51; and Social Security, 137; twentieth-century innovations of, 115, 148, 206 n. 22
Blacks, aged: antebellum, and poverty, 29; current situation of, 159–60; and farming, 96; need for further study of, 227; organize, 147; population statistics of, 61–62, 92. *See also* Aged, differences among, by race; Slavery and the aged
Blair, Frank, 20
Boone, Daniel, 22, 191 n. 50
Bowen, William T., 103–5
Brackenridge, Henry Hugh, 22
Brandeis, Louis, 130
Brissot de Warville, J. P., 12
Bristed, John, 12–13
Brown-Séquard, Charles E., 44, 119
Buffalo, New York, 76–77
Bumppo, Natty, 22
Bureaucracy: principles and practices of, pervade society, 48, 74, 115; ready to serve the aged, 138
Burns, Eveline, 138, 227
Butler, Robert N., 162
Byrd, Henry, 134–35

Caldwell, Charles: on racial variations in longevity, 14; on relation between longevity and virtue, 15–16
California: 1883 old-age law of, 83; political lobbies in, 129, 138; Social Security benefits in, 135
Cardozo, Benjamin, 139
Carnegie Foundation for Advancement of Teaching, 82
Carroll, Charles, 24
Cather, Willa, 209 n. 4
Census data, deficiencies in, 179–81
Charcot, Jean-Martin, 227; influence of, 43–44; work of, 42–43, 120
Child, Charles Manning, 119
Child, L. Maria, 30, 227
Chronological age: moral relevance of, 163–64; significance of, in general, 2, 114; significance of age 65 to, 2, 149
Cicero, 4; read in antebellum period, 36
Civil Service employees: eligible for Social Security, 144; protected by federal retirement laws, 121; viewed as inefficient in later years, 50
Clerical jobs, aged in, 102
Cole, Thomas R., 26, 35
Colonial era: general conditions of the aged in, 4–5, 187 n. 7; guides to further study of, 176; old-age dependency in, 75–76, 192 n. 4
Colorado, 76, 122
Committee on Economic Security, 131–32; establishes age 65 as criterion for benefits, 149; prepares Social Security options, 134–35
Commons, John R., 130, 132
Condorcet, Antoine-Nicholas de, 13
Connecticut, 21, 121, 134
Connery, William, Jr., 131
Convalescent homes, 151. *See also* Rest homes
Cooper, James Fenimore, 191 n. 50
Cornaro, Luigi, 15
Cumming, Elaine, 216 n. 56
Currier and Ives, 23, 28

Darwinism, impact of, on ideas about older people, 39–40
Death and dying: affect the image of old age, 4; antebellum views of, 30, 35; attitudes toward, between 1865 and 1914, 52–53; attitudes toward, between 1914 and 1940, 112
Delbet, Pierre, 119
De Leon, Ponce, 52
Demographic patterns: and calculating growth rates, 199 n. 6; in the future, 161; in the

nineteenth century, 58–66; in the twentieth century, 90–95. *See also* Aging of the population structure; Mortality patterns, impact of, on relative numbers of old people; Rural-urban shift

Denmark, 84

Dependency, extent of, in old age: during the Depression, 128–29, 132; as determined by the Social Security Board, 140; early twentieth century estimates of, 122–23; since 1935, 143. *See also* Age-dependency ratios, changes in; Poverty, extent of, in old age

Dependency, perceptions of, in old age: antebellum, 29; before the Depression, 116, 122–23, 127–28; during the Depression, 129–32; before 1914, 75–86; after Social Security, 139–40, 163. *See also* Old age, perceptions of

Depression, the, impact of, 127–28; on the aged, 128–31, 143, 209 n. 3

Dill, Clarence, 130–31

Disability, extent of, in old age: in antebellum society, 28–29; current, 154, 204 n. 19; impact of, on employment, 67; minimalization of, 19, 117; in "second childhood," 3; social usefulness of, 27; studied between 1914 and 1940, 110. *See also* Health status of aged

Discrimination against elderly: current, 163–64; economic, 50, 114–15; informal, 30. *See also* Age-discrimination practices in the marketplace

Disengagement Theory, 216 n. 56

District of Columbia, 134

Dodge, Nathaniel, 24

Domestic service: in 1890, 68, 70–71; under Social Security, 144, 159

Dorland, W. A. Newman, 46

Dublin, Louis I., 123

Eastman Kodak, 121

Eaves, Lucille, 206 n. 23

Economic independence, ways of maintaining: before Social Security, 29, 67, 127–28; since Social Security, 137, 144, 148–50, 213 n. 16

Education: capacity for, in later years, 154–55; comparative disadvantage of the aged in, 105; influence of, on employment prospects, 104–5; opportunities for, in later years, 117–18, 148

Efficiency: current views of the aged and, 154; importance of, in general, 47–48; presumed lacking in old age, 49–51, 114–15

Elizabethan Poor Law of 1601, 76

Ellis, Havelock, 112

Ely, Richard, 130

Emerson, Ralph Waldo, 36–37, 227

Employment patterns in old age: in ancillary industrial tasks, 48; antebellum, 19–20, 22, 29; in contemporary era, 149; data problems in studying, 181; during the Depression, 129; over life cycle, 200 n. 17; during World War I, 117. *See also* Discrimination against elderly; Occupational status of the aged; Retirement

Energy crisis, 167–68

Enlightenment, views of, on the aged, 10

Epstein, Abraham, 227; as critic, 138; as government official, 122; ideas of, 123, 133, 137; as lobbyist, 122–23, 130

Everett, Alexander, 83

Family relationships: between 1914 and 1940, 116–17, 121; in the nineteenth century, 23, 76–79; under Social Security, 136. *See also* Parent-child relationships

"Father Simkins," 19

Federal government, responsibility of, for the aged, 144–45; criticized, 157–58; expanded after 1935, 143–46, 151; before 1914, 48–49, 83–85; precedents for, 130; in principle, 141; under Title I of Social Security, 135; under Title II of Social Security, 136

Federal Paper 79, 21

Federal Security Agency, 144

Ferris, Elmer E., 118

Fertility rates, impact of, on the aged, 89–90, 92–93, 95

Finegan, T. Aldrich, 103–5

Florida, 93

"Fogy": ageist connotations of, accentuated, 46; antebellum meanings of, 30, 192 n. 8; earlier meanings of, questioned, 155–56

Folks, Homer, 201 n. 26

Ford Foundation, 147

Foster, Stephen, 23

France, 132

Fraternal Congress and Loyal Order of the Moose, 116

Fraternal Order of Eagles, 122

Freneau, Philip, 32

"Fuddy duddy," 197 n. 30

Fuller, Ida M., 126

Future concerns and the aged, 160–62, 167–68, 171

Galbraith, John Kenneth, 145

Gallup surveys, 138–39

Galton, Francis, 46

"Geezer," 197 n. 30

General Electric, 121

Georgia, 135

Geriatrics, intellectual and institutional foundations for, 119–20

Germany, 84, 132

Gerontological Society, 147

Gerontologists: biases of, in research, 163; recent findings of, 153–57

Gerontology Research Center, 145

Godwin, William, 13

"Grand Climacteric," 2

Gray Panthers, 142, 147

Great Britain, 84, 132

"Green old age," 3

Guaranteed income, 136, 146. *See also* Social Security Act

Hall, G. Stanley, 227; on adolescence, 52; on senescence, 118

Hall, William H., 13

Hamilton, Alexander, 21

Harrington, Michael, 145

Harris, Corra, 113

Harris, Louis, 162–63

Harrison, William Henry, 20, 190 n. 41

Hawaii, 136

Hawthorne, Nathaniel,·24

Health insurance, 146, 159–60

Health status of the aged: current, 154; differences in, 3, 110; overall impact of, on occupational status, 67, 103–4. *See also* Disability, extent of, in old age

Henry, William E., 216 n. 56

History, uses of, in studying old age: in the future, 226–28; in general, 5–6, 165; in humanistic inquiries, 169–71; in policy analyses, 168–69; in social science research, 165–68

Hollingworth, Harry L., 111

Housing for the elderly: current developments in, 214 n. 22; and relation between house size and intergenerational ties, 116

Humanistic perspectives in gerontology: in general, 6; need for, 161–62

Human life span, 2

Hursley, Victor, 45

Ideas about old age. *See* Images of old age; Aged's worth, conceptions of

Illinois, 134

Images of old age: between 1790 and 1860, 9; between 1865 and 1914, 39; between 1914 and 1940, 109; current, 143, 162–63; and self-image, 51, 118–19, 163; sentimental, 23, 28, 170; significance of, 163. *See also* Aged's worth, conceptions of

Immigrants, aged: in the nineteenth century, 62, 194 n. 1; relative numbers of, affected by law, 90, 93. *See also* Aged, differences among by place of birth

Income, sources of, in old age: current, 105, 149–50; in the nineteenth century, 82–84. *See also* Employment patterns in old age; Pensions; Retirement

Incrementalism: in creating current old-age policies, 145–46; criticized, 157; in the future, 169; in general, 146

Independence, need for, in old age, 116, 155

Indiana, 76

Indians: experiences of, with federal programs, 160; treatment of elders by, 18

Individual Retirement Accounts, 148

Industrialization, impact of: on the elderly's occupational status in the nineteenth century, 68–74, 166; on perceptions of the aged, 47–51, 115; in the twentieth century, 98, 104. *See also* Technology

Institute of Gerontology, 178, 216 n. 52

Intelligence in old age: current views of, 3, 154–55; early twentieth century perspectives on, 111, 205 n. 5; nineteenth-century views of, 46

Intergenerational economic transfers, 149, 152, 160–61. *See also* Parent-child relationships in old age

IQ tests, 154. *See also* Intelligence in old age; Mental decline in old age

James, William, 227; on death and the aged, 53; on fogyism, 46

Jefferson, Thomas: brush of, with poverty, 29; on retirement, 191 n. 51

Kansas, 135

Kellogg, John Harvey, 47, 227

Kelso, Robert, 116

Kent, James, 21–22, 191 n. 46

Kentucky, 76, 123

Keynesian economics, 137

Kinsey, Alfred C., 112–13

Kuhn, Maggie, 142

Labor and aged. *See* Unions

Language, as symbols of ideas about old age, 178, 187 n. 4, 190 n. 30, 192 n. 8, 225

Lehman, Harvey, 155

Leisure in old age: current, 156, 167; before Social Security, 117–18, 121

Levitan, Sar, 159–60
Lewis, David J., 131
Life expectancy: at birth, 2, 89; and changing meaning of death, 53; in later life, 2, 60–61, 91; perceived as improving, 41
Life extension, 2, 168
Life insurance annuities, 82
Literature: consolatory, the aged in, 32, 35–36; elderly as narrators in, 24; general characterization of old age in, 4, 227
—aged in anecdotes, 23–24
Local community, responsibility of, for the aged, 75, 80
Loneliness in old age, 30, 53, 156
Long, Clarence D., 104
Longevity: aged as symbols of, 11–12; extreme incidence of, 60; factors affecting, 12–13; in the future, 168; historical ideas about, 188 n. 12; variations in, 14
Lorand, Arnold, 45
Lorge, Irving, 205 n. 5

McKeever, William, 118
Macy, Josiah, Jr., Foundation, 140–41
Maine, 21, 121
Malthus, Thomas Robert, 13
Marshall, John, 22
Martin, Lillien J., 118, 227
Maryland, 21
Massachusetts: appoints Commission on Old Age Pensions, 83; cited as precedent in Social Security draft, 134; colonial laws of, concerning old-age dependency, 76; establishes retirement for civil servants, 121; household status in, 76, 78–79; occupational status in, in nineteenth century, 72; passes old-age pension law, 123; sets tenure limits for justices, 20–21; unemployment in, in 1934, 128
Media and the aged, 163
Medicaid, 146, 151, 159–60
Medical views of senescence: antebellum, 14–16, 28; biases in, 110–11, 153; after Civil War, 40–46; and dying, 53; between 1914 and 1940, 110–11, 119–20, 208 n. 39; and prescriptions for the aged, 15, 43–44, 196 n. 15; republican definitions of, 31; romantic etiologies of, 33; since World War II, 147–48, 153–54, 214 n. 30
Medicare, 146, 151, 159–60
Men, aged: discriminated against in marketplace, 114–15; efforts of, at staying young, 199 n. 62; and politics, 20–21, 74–75; and sex, 47, 112; at work, 67, 69–74, 98–101. See also Aged, differences among, by sex

Mental decline in old age: elaborated upon, between 1914 and 1940, 111; explained, between 1865 and 1914, 46–47; extent of, challenged in recent era, 154–55; noted in antebellum times, 28–29. See also Senility
Metchnikoff, Elie, 227; on aged suicide, 47; on preventing old age, 44–45, 119
Michigan, urbanization in, 63, 65
"Middletown," 138
Migration patterns, impact of: on the aged's occupational status, 104; on relative size of elderly population, 90, 92–93. See also Rural-urban shift
Military service and aged: before Civil War, 20; under Social Security, 144. See also Veterans benefits
—retirement enacted, 48–49
Minority aged, 151, 160. See also Blacks, aged
Minot, Charles Sedgwick, 43, 119, 207 n. 36
Mississippi, 135
Missouri, 21, 134
Mobility in old age. See also Economic independence, ways of maintaining; Occupational status of the aged
—geographic, 93
—occupational, 68, 95–103; as perceived in the nineteenth century, 49–50; as perceived in the twentieth century, 114–15
—social, 74; as perceived in the nineteenth century, 50–51; as perceived in the twentieth century, 115–16
Moderation, need for, in life, 16
Modernization, impact of, on the aged: dependents, 115–16; farmers, 98; in general, 5, 166–68; in nineteenth century, 89–90
Modernization models, 165–66, 217 n. 1
Monroe, James, 29
Montana, 122
More, Hannah, 24
Mortality patterns, impact of, on relative numbers of old people, 2, 90, 92
Municipal retirement pension plans, 83, 121

Nascher, I. L., 119–20, 227
Nassau, Mabel Louise, 206 n. 23, 227
National Advisory Committee on Gerontology, 141
National Association of Manufacturers, 138
National Association of Retired Federal Employees, 147
National Caucus on the Black Aged, 147
National Civic Federation, 123
National Conference on Aging, 144
National Council of Senior Citizens, 147

National Council on the Aging, 147
National Endowment for the Humanities, 178
National Home for Disabled Volunteer Soldiers, 84
National Institute of Health, 141
National Institute on Aging, 145, 162
National Labor Relations Board, 148
National Research Council, 141
National Retired Teachers Association/ American Association of Retired Persons, 147
Nevada, 122, 135
New Hampshire, 21
New Jersey, 80, 121
New York: becomes urban state, 63, 65; changes laws to conform to Social Security guidelines, 134; inaugurates civil-service retirement plan, 121; passes old-age pension legislation, 123; sets age limit for judges, 21–22
New York Geriatrics Society, 120
New York Old Age Security Commission, 129
New Zealand, 84
Niles, Hezekiah: on remarkable longevity, 121; on service in Congress, 20
North Carolina, 135
Nursing homes, 151

Occupational status of the aged: actual, before 1914, 66–75; actual, in the twentieth century, 95–105; data problems in studying, 179–81, 217 n. 7; estimates of, before 1890, 183–84; and health factors, 154; as key predictor of economic security, 150; as perceived in the antebellum era, 19–24; as perceived before 1914, 48–51; and women's working history, 160
Ohio, 76
Oklahoma, 134
Old age: association of, with death, 30; chronological boundaries of, 2; fear of, 162; invidious comparisons between young and old affect, 4, 52, 193 n. 8; persistence of ambivalent, mixed, and conflicting feelings about aging and, 3–4; physical manifestations of, 2, 9, 178; possible debility in, 30; risk of deprivation in, 30; threat of dependency in, 30, 75. See also Images of old age
—as "national problem": antecedents for view of, 203 n. 44; current views on, 157–64; opinion of, arises between 1914 and 1940, 109–10, 113–17, 206 n. 23; opinion of, discounted, 123–24; summarized, 124–25, 171

—pathological manifestations of: American case studies of, reported, 28, 44, 112, 154; classified as disease, 44–45, 196 n. 20; described, 43–45, 119–20; existing models for interpreting, 195 nn. 8, 11, 12
—physiological characteristics of: descriptions of, before the Civil War, 28–29; early twentieth century views of, 110–13, 119–20; and "normal aging," 153–54; variations in, 2–3. See also Disability, extent of; Health status of the aged
—psychological traits of: current, 155–56; descriptions of, before the Civil War, 29–30, 34; descriptions of, between 1865 and 1914, 46–47, 53; descriptions of, between 1914 and 1940, 111–12
—relationship between "rhetoric" and "reality" of, 57–58, 167; current, 157, 162–63; in demographic terms, 59–63; in the nineteenth century, 86; in occupational terms, 74–75; summarized, 5, 170–71; in the twentieth century, 105–6, 124. See also Aged's worth, conceptions of
—social scientific views of: biases in, 153, 163; current, 3, 153–57; in the Depression, 130; increase in number since 1935, 147–48; between 1914 and 1940, 113–17
Old-age associations, 118–19, 147, 207 n. 33
Old-Age Center, 118
Old-age homes: between 1914 and 1940, 121–22, 128; in the nineteenth century, 82; today, 151. See also Nursing homes
Old-age movements: anticipated, 114; current, 147; obstacles to, 123–24; origins of, 118–19
Old Age Reserve Act, 135–36
Older Americans Act, 146
"Old Folks at Home" (1851), 23
Orshansky, Mollie, 157–58
"Over the Hill to the Poorhouse," 80

Paine, Thomas, 83
Parent-child relationships in old age: before the Civil War, 23, 29–30; during the Depression, 129; generally affect the image of old age, 3–4; legal responsibilities entailed in, 76, 121; between 1914 and 1940, 116; since Social Security, 152, 156; under Title II, 136. See also Family relationships; Intergenerational economic transfers
Paris School of Medicine, 14, 41–42
Parran, Thomas, 141
Pennsylvania, 121; old-age pension law of, 122

Pensions: coverage of, extended between 1914 and 1929, 121, 128; current significance of, 105, 149–50; disrupted by the Depression, 129; earliest, in private sector, 49, 82–83, 202 n. 33; earliest, in public sector, 48–49; new pressure for, at state level, 122, 128; reinstituted in private sector, 148. See also Big-business organizations; Federal government, responsibility of, for the aged; Retirement; Social Security Act; State government, responsibility of, for the aged; Unions; Veterans benefits

Philanthropic bequests to the aged, 82

Physical rejuvenation schemes, 52, 119

Physicians and sanitary reformers, roles of, compared to the aged, 15, 40, 45, 195 n. 6. See also Medical views of senescence; Sectarian physicians and the aged

Pinchot, Gifford, 122

Pitkin, Walter, 118, 227

Pohl's Spermine Preparation, 44

Policy decisions affecting the aged. See Social policies affecting the aged

Politics, the aged in: as lobbyists, 128, 132, 138, 147; at local level, 19, 156; at national level, 20, 74–75; at state level, 20–21. See also Old-age movements; Townsend, Francis E.

Poorhouse, See Almshouse

"Postindustrial" era, 167–68

Poverty, extent of, in old age: in antebellum society, 29, 33–34; during the Depression, 129; between 1914 and 1940, 115–16; "relative poverty," 145; and suicide, 47; since World War II, 143, 150–51, 157–58. See also Dependency, extent of, in old age

Poverty index, 157–58

Powell, Lyman Pierson, 118

Power of the aged: in antebellum society, 11, 17, 24; after the Civil War, 74–75; feared, 114. See also Politics, the aged in

Professionals, aged: in the nineteenth century, 50, 68, 70–71; in the twentieth century, 98–101

"Progress," individual and societal, contrasted, 51–52

Racism: as cause of current inequities, 159–60, 162; and negative attitudes toward the aged, 61–62

Railroad Retirement Act, 133

Realism, impact of, on the aged, 30–40, 57–58

Religion: and elderly's role in society, 17–18, 32, 34; need for, in old age, 117

Residence patterns among the aged: and aging in place, 93–94; impact of the law on, 152, 214 n. 26. See also Rural-urban shift

Respect for old age, 10–11. See also Veneration of the aged

Rest homes, 151. See also Nursing homes

Retirement: alternatives to, before Social Security, 117–18, 121; antecedents for, 19, 21–22, 191 n. 51; current impact of, on income, 105, 149–50; defined, 22, 50; on the farm, 96, 98; mandatory, initial instances of, 48–51; options under original Social Security Act, 137; reactions to, today, 156. See also Occupational status of aged; Pensions

Revolutionary War and the aged, 10–11, 23, 191 n. 56

Rhode Island: becomes urban, 63, 65; passes old-age assistance law, 134

Rogers, John, 23

Roosevelt, Franklin Delano, 131, 139

Rose, Benjamin, 82

Rubinow, I. M., 227; advocates federal support for needy, 133; disappointed with Social Security, 138; estimates extent of old-age poverty, 123

Rural-urban shift: actual impact of, on occupational status of the aged, 104, 204 n. 20; in the nineteenth century, 63, 65; presumed impact of, on occupational status, 114; in the twentieth century, 65, 93

Rush, Benjamin, 227; on environment and longevity, 13; on intelligence and longevity, 14; on madness, 31; on moral faculties in old age, 16–17

Sectarian physicians and the aged, 14–15, 43

Self-help literature for the elderly, 15, 117–18, 199 n. 62

Senate Special Committee on Aging, 146

"Senex," 17

Senility: antebellum definitions of, 31; case studies of, 44, 112; endocrinologists study, 120; Nascher redefines, 119; post–Civil War opinions on, 43

Seniority system, 74–75

Sentimentalism. See Images of old age

Sex and the aged, 47, 112–13, 156

Sexism, 160, 162

Sheldon, Henry D., 103

Shock, Nathan W., 213 n. 12

Shoemaker, Abraham, 16

Sinclair, Upton, 129

Slavery and the aged, 18, 29, 190 n. 32. See also Blacks, aged

Smith, Jedediah, 23
Social policies affecting the aged: current, 144–53, 160–62; projected, 168–69
Social Security Act: constitutionality of, 139; coverage of, 135–36, 144; "equity" versus "adequacy" in, 136–37, 211 n. 26; establishes age criteria, 149; financial cost considerations of, 133; growth of, 144; impact of, on the aged's economic status, 144, 149–50; impact of, on family relations, 152; impact of, on nursing homes and almshouses, 151; initial reception of, 138–39; 1939 amendments to, 136–37; old-age assistance provisions of, 134–35, 146, 210 n. 20; old-age insurance provisions of, 135–39, 144; other references concerning, 210 n. 12; passage of, 131–38; philosophical bases of, 132–33, 136–37; significance of, 2, 141
—Supplementary Security Income program, 146
—Title VIII, 136
Social Security Administration, 157, 160
Social Security Board: created, 134; initial actions of, 137, 139–40
South Carolina, 135
Spanish-speaking elderly, 160
Squier, Lee Welling, 85–86, 227
State government, responsibility of, for the aged: current, 147; early, 83, 121; and movement for old-age assistance measures, 122–23, 128; official records concerning, 225–26
Steinach, Eugene, 119
Suicide and the aged, 47, 197 n. 34
"Superannuate," 22, 50, 191 n. 50
Supernatural and the aged, 35–36, 194 n. 24. See also Death and dying
Supplementary Security Income program, 146

Technology: actual impact of, on the aged, 68–69, 104–5; presumed impact of, on the aged, 48, 114–15
Television and the aged, 163
Tennessee, 135
Theories of aging: current, 153–57; disengagement, 216 n. 56; early medical, 41–47, 119–20; social science, 114–17
Thomas, Robert B., 19
Thorndike, Edward L., 111
Townsend, Frances E., 129, 132, 138
Transcendentalism, 193 n. 8
Tuke, William, 42

"Uncle Sam," 25. See also Wilson, Samuel
Unemployment in old age, 128–29, 161
Union of American Biological Sciences, 141
Unions: early twentieth century activities of, 122; nineteenth-century efforts of, 82; pension programs of, disrupted by the Depression, 129; pressure on, for private pensions, 148; support Social Security movement, 130; view of retirement of, 137
United Auto Workers, 148
United Mine Workers of America, 122
Urbanization: actual nineteenth-century demographic impact of, 63–66; actual twentieth-century demographic impact of, 65, 94; effect of, on the aged's occupational status, 104; overall impact of, 166; presumed effect of, on the aged's well-being, 114
U.S. Bureau of Labor Statistics, 115, 157, 226
U.S. Chamber of Commerce, 134–35
U.S. Department of Agriculture, 157
U.S. Naval Home, 84
U.S. Soldiers Home, 84
U.S. Supreme Court: recent decisions by, 163; ruling of, on Railroad Retirement Act, 133; ruling of, on Social Security Act, 139

Values affecting the aged, 161–62, 164, 170–71
Van Rensselaer, Cortlandt, 17
Veneration of the aged, 18, 190 n. 30
Vermont, 134
Veterans benefits, 83–85, 124
Virchow, Rudolph, 42
Virginia, 135
Voronoff, Serge, 119
Voyage of Life, 26, 35

Wagner, Robert, 131
Ward, Lester Frank, 130
"War on Poverty": conceived, 145; escalates expectations, 158–59; unfulfilled, 151
Webster, Daniel, 30
Webster, Noah, 18, 22, 31, 50
"Welfare Mess," 158
Westinghouse, 121
White House Conferences on Aging, 144–45, 147

Whittier, John Greenleaf, as oral historian, 24, 30
Widowhood: and farming, 98; and poverty, 29; and Social Security, 136. *See also* Women, aged
Willich, Anthony, 13
Wilson, Charles, 148
Wilson, Samuel, 25. *See also* "Uncle Sam"
Wisconsin, 122
Witte, Edwin, 134, 139
Women, aged: as grandmothers, 23, 50–51; hints for, on staying young, 52, 199 n. 62; occupational status of, 66–73, 96–102, 115; and poverty, 29, 151; and sex, 47; and Social Security, 160. *See also* Aged, differences among, by sex

Youth and old age: attitudinal differences between, perceived, 111, 193 n. 8; difference in historical conception of, as stages of life, 1; Emerson on, 36–37; industry's perspective on, 50–51, 115; occupational differences between, 68, 70–71; and "progress," 51–52; reciprocal relationship between, 17–18; relative value of, 31–32, 52–53

THE JOHNS HOPKINS UNIVERSITY PRESS

This book was composed in Times Roman Quadritek text and display type by Brushwood Graphics from a design by Alan Carter. It was printed on 50-lb. Publishers Eggshell Wove and bound in Roxite pyroxylin-impregnated cloth by the Maple Press Company.

Library of Congress Cataloging in Publication Data

Achenbaum, W. Andrew
    Old age in the new land.

    Bibliography: p. 219
    Includes index.
    1. Aged—United States—History. 2. Aged—
United States—Public opinion. 3. Public opinion
—United States. I. Title.
HQ1064.U5A26   301.43'5'0973   77–28666
ISBN O–8018–2107–X